# First World War
## and Army of Occupation
# War Diary
## France, Belgium and Germany

48 DIVISION
145 Infantry Brigade
Oxfordshire and Buckinghamshire Light Infantry
1st Battalion
30 March 1915 - 31 October 1917

WO95/2763/2

The Naval & Military Press Ltd
www.nmarchive.com
**Published in association with The National Archives**

Published by

The Naval & Military Press Ltd

Unit 10 Ridgewood Industrial Park,
Uckfield, East Sussex,
TN22 5QE England
Tel: +44 (0) 1825 749494

www.naval-military-press.com
www.nmarchive.com

*This diary has been reprinted in facsimile from the original. Any imperfections are inevitably reproduced and the quality may fall short of modern type and cartographic standards.*

**© Crown Copyright**
**Images reproduced by permission of The National Archives, London, England, 2015.**

# Contents

| Document type | Place/Title | Date From | Date To |
|---|---|---|---|
| Heading | WO95/2763/2 1st Bucks Battalion Oxfordshire & Buckinghamshire Light Infantry | | |
| Heading | 48th Division 145th Infy Bde 1st Bucks Bn. Oxf & Bucks Lt Infy Apr 1915-1917 Oct | | |
| Heading | 145th Inf. Bde. 48th Div. Battn. Disembarked Boulogne From England 30.3.15 1st Bucks. Battn. The Oxford & Bucks. Light Inf. March (30 & 31.3.15) 1915 1 Mar 19 | | |
| War Diary | Chelmsford | 30/03/1915 | 30/03/1915 |
| War Diary | Osterhove near Boulogne | 31/03/1915 | 31/03/1915 |
| Heading | 145th Inf. Bde. 48th Div. 1st Bucks. Battn. The Oxford & Bucks. Light Inf. April 1915 | | |
| Heading | War Diary of Bucks Battn Oxf Bucks Lt. Infty. From 1 April 1915-30 April 1915 | | |
| War Diary | Tergenhem | 01/04/1915 | 04/04/1915 |
| War Diary | Meteren | 05/04/1915 | 07/04/1915 |
| War Diary | Le Bizet | 08/04/1915 | 12/04/1915 |
| War Diary | 13/4 Miles W of Steelwerck | 13/04/1915 | 15/04/1915 |
| War Diary | Ploegsteert | 15/04/1915 | 22/04/1915 |
| War Diary | Ploegsteert Wood | 23/04/1915 | 23/04/1915 |
| War Diary | Romarin | 24/04/1915 | 26/04/1915 |
| War Diary | Ploegsteert Wood | 27/04/1915 | 30/04/1915 |
| Heading | 145th Inf. Bde. 48th Div. 1st Bucks. Battn. The Oxford & Bucks. Light Inf. May 1915 | | |
| War Diary | Ploegsteert Wood | 01/05/1915 | 01/05/1915 |
| War Diary | Romarin | 02/05/1915 | 05/05/1915 |
| War Diary | Ploegsteert Wood | 06/05/1915 | 10/05/1915 |
| War Diary | Romarin | 11/05/1915 | 16/05/1915 |
| War Diary | Ploegsteert Wood | 16/05/1915 | 18/05/1915 |
| War Diary | Romarin | 19/05/1915 | 22/05/1915 |
| War Diary | Ploegsteert Wood | 23/05/1915 | 26/05/1915 |
| War Diary | Romarin | 27/05/1915 | 30/05/1915 |
| War Diary | Ploegsteert Wood | 31/05/1915 | 31/05/1915 |
| Heading | 145th Inf. Bde. 48th Div. 1st Bucks. Battn. The Oxford & Bucks. Light Inf. June 1915 | | |
| War Diary | Ploegsteert Wood | 01/06/1915 | 03/06/1915 |
| War Diary | Romarin | 04/06/1915 | 07/06/1915 |
| War Diary | Ploegsteert Wood | 07/06/1915 | 11/06/1915 |
| War Diary | Billets Petit Pont | 12/06/1915 | 15/06/1915 |
| War Diary | Douve Trenches | 16/06/1915 | 19/06/1915 |
| War Diary | Romarin | 20/06/1915 | 24/06/1915 |
| War Diary | Bailleul | 25/06/1915 | 25/06/1915 |
| War Diary | Vieux Berquin | 26/06/1915 | 26/06/1915 |
| War Diary | Busnettes | 27/06/1915 | 27/06/1915 |
| War Diary | Allouagne | 28/06/1915 | 30/06/1915 |
| Heading | 145th Inf. Bde. 48th Div. 1st Bucks. Battn. The Oxford & Bucks. Light Inf. July 1915 | | |
| War Diary | Allouagne | 01/07/1915 | 12/07/1915 |
| War Diary | Houchin | 13/07/1915 | 16/07/1915 |
| War Diary | Lieres | 16/07/1915 | 18/07/1915 |
| War Diary | Marieux | 18/07/1915 | 20/07/1915 |

| | | | |
|---|---|---|---|
| War Diary | Coigneux | 21/07/1915 | 21/07/1915 |
| War Diary | Bayencourt & Sailly | 22/07/1915 | 24/07/1915 |
| War Diary | Hebuterne | 24/07/1915 | 31/07/1915 |
| Heading | 145th Inf. Bde. 48th Div. 1st Bucks. Battn. The Oxford & Bucks. Light Inf. August 1915 | | |
| War Diary | Hebuterne | 01/08/1915 | 13/08/1915 |
| War Diary | Sailly | 14/08/1915 | 21/08/1915 |
| War Diary | Hebuterne | 22/08/1915 | 31/08/1915 |
| Heading | 145th Inf. Bde. 48th Div. 1st Bucks. Battn. The Oxford & Bucks. Light Inf. September 1915 | | |
| War Diary | Hebuterne | 01/09/1915 | 05/09/1915 |
| War Diary | Bus | 06/09/1915 | 06/09/1915 |
| War Diary | Couin | 07/09/1915 | 17/09/1915 |
| War Diary | Hebuterne | 17/09/1915 | 29/09/1915 |
| War Diary | Couin | 29/09/1915 | 30/09/1915 |
| Heading | 145th Inf. Bde. 48th Div. 1st Bucks. Battn. The Oxford & Bucks. Light Inf. October 1915 | | |
| War Diary | Couin | 01/10/1915 | 10/10/1915 |
| War Diary | Hebuterne | 11/10/1915 | 19/10/1915 |
| War Diary | Couin | 20/10/1915 | 26/10/1915 |
| War Diary | Hebuterne | 27/10/1915 | 31/10/1915 |
| Heading | 145th Inf. Bde. 48th Div. 1st Bucks. Battn. The Oxford & Bucks. Light Inf. November 1915 | | |
| War Diary | Hebuterne | 01/11/1915 | 04/11/1915 |
| War Diary | Couin | 05/11/1915 | 30/11/1915 |
| Heading | 145th Inf. Bde. 48th Div. 1st Bucks. Battn. The Oxford & Bucks. Light Inf. December 1915 | | |
| War Diary | Hebuterne | 01/12/1915 | 06/12/1915 |
| War Diary | Couin | 07/12/1915 | 14/12/1915 |
| War Diary | Hebuterne | 15/12/1915 | 22/12/1915 |
| War Diary | Couin | 23/12/1915 | 27/12/1915 |
| War Diary | Hebuterne | 28/12/1915 | 31/12/1915 |
| Heading | 145th Brigade. 48th Division. 1st Buckinghamshire Battalion (Oxf & Bucks L.I.) January 1916 | | |
| War Diary | Hebuterne | 01/01/1916 | 03/01/1916 |
| War Diary | Couin | 04/01/1916 | 20/01/1916 |
| War Diary | Hebuterne | 21/01/1916 | 26/01/1916 |
| War Diary | Couin | 27/01/1916 | 31/01/1916 |
| Heading | 145th Brigade. 48th Division. 1st Buckinghamshire Battalion (Oxf & Bucks L.I.) February 1916 | | |
| War Diary | Couin | 01/02/1916 | 01/02/1916 |
| War Diary | Hebuterne | 02/02/1916 | 15/02/1916 |
| War Diary | Courcelles | 16/02/1916 | 19/02/1916 |
| War Diary | Hebuterne | 20/02/1916 | 27/02/1916 |
| War Diary | Courcelles | 28/02/1916 | 29/02/1916 |
| Heading | 145th Brigade. 48th Division. 1st Buckinghamshire Battalion (Oxf. & Bucks. L.I.) March 1916 | | |
| War Diary | Courcelles | 01/03/1916 | 02/03/1916 |
| War Diary | Hebuterne | 03/03/1916 | 10/03/1916 |
| War Diary | Sailly | 11/03/1916 | 14/03/1916 |
| War Diary | Hebuterne Ft K17/5-K23/6 | 15/03/1916 | 22/03/1916 |
| War Diary | Sailly | 23/03/1916 | 26/03/1916 |
| War Diary | Hebuterne Ft K 10/5-K 15/1 | 27/03/1916 | 31/03/1916 |
| Heading | 145th Brigade. 48th Division. 1st Buckinghamshire Battalion (Oxf. & Bucks. L.I.) April 1916 | | |
| War Diary | Hebuterne | 01/04/1916 | 02/04/1916 |

| War Diary | Bayencourt | 03/04/1916 | 08/04/1916 |
| War Diary | Hebuterne | 09/04/1916 | 16/04/1916 |
| War Diary | Bayencourt | 17/04/1916 | 21/04/1916 |
| War Diary | Hebuterne | 22/04/1916 | 25/04/1916 |
| War Diary | Coigneux | 26/04/1916 | 30/04/1916 |
| Heading | 145th Brigade. 48th Division. 1st Buckinghamshire Battalion (Oxf. & Bucks L.I.) May 1916 | | |
| War Diary | Coigneux | 01/05/1916 | 02/05/1916 |
| War Diary | Hebuterne | 03/05/1916 | 04/05/1916 |
| War Diary | Coigneux | 05/05/1916 | 10/05/1916 |
| War Diary | Hebuterne | 11/05/1916 | 16/05/1916 |
| War Diary | Couin | 17/05/1916 | 18/05/1916 |
| War Diary | Beauval | 19/05/1916 | 31/05/1916 |
| Heading | 145th Brigade. 48th Division. 1st Buckinghamshire Battalion (Oxf. & Bucks. L.I.) June 1916 | | |
| War Diary | Neuville | 01/06/1916 | 03/06/1916 |
| War Diary | Agenvillers | 04/06/1916 | 09/06/1916 |
| War Diary | Occoches | 10/06/1916 | 10/06/1916 |
| War Diary | Couin | 11/06/1916 | 11/06/1916 |
| War Diary | Sailly | 12/06/1916 | 15/06/1916 |
| War Diary | Hebuterne | 16/06/1916 | 21/06/1916 |
| War Diary | Couin | 22/06/1916 | 30/06/1916 |
| Heading | 145th Inf. Bde. 48th Div. 1st Buckingham Battn. (The Oxfordshire & Buckinghamshire Light Infantry). July 1916 | | |
| Miscellaneous | From:- Officer Commanding 1/Bucks Battalion. | 31/07/1916 | 31/07/1916 |
| War Diary | Couin | 01/07/1916 | 01/07/1916 |
| War Diary | Mailly-Mallet | 02/07/1916 | 03/07/1916 |
| War Diary | Couin | 04/07/1916 | 05/07/1916 |
| War Diary | Coigneux | 06/07/1916 | 07/07/1916 |
| War Diary | Hebuterne | 08/07/1916 | 12/07/1916 |
| War Diary | Coigneux | 13/07/1916 | 14/07/1916 |
| War Diary | Senlis | 15/07/1916 | 18/07/1916 |
| War Diary | Bouzincourt | 18/07/1916 | 19/07/1916 |
| War Diary | Albert | 20/07/1916 | 26/07/1916 |
| War Diary | Arqueves | 27/07/1916 | 28/07/1916 |
| War Diary | Beauval | 29/07/1916 | 29/07/1916 |
| War Diary | Domleger | 30/07/1916 | 31/07/1916 |
| Heading | Brigade Operation Orders Nos. 100 & 101 | | |
| Operation(al) Order(s) | 145th Infantry Brigade Order No. 100 | 20/07/1916 | 20/07/1916 |
| Miscellaneous | 145 Inf Bde. No. 101 | 22/07/1916 | 22/07/1916 |
| Heading | 145th Brigade. 48th Division. 1st Battalion Buckinghamshire Regiment August 1916 | | |
| Miscellaneous | From Officer Commanding 1/Bucks Battalion. | 31/08/1916 | 31/08/1916 |
| War Diary | Domleger | 01/08/1916 | 09/08/1916 |
| War Diary | Beauval | 10/08/1916 | 10/08/1916 |
| War Diary | Varennes | 11/08/1916 | 11/08/1916 |
| War Diary | Bouzincourt | 12/08/1916 | 13/08/1916 |
| War Diary | Usna/Redoubt | 14/08/1916 | 14/08/1916 |
| War Diary | Trenches N.W. of Pozieres | 14/08/1916 | 16/08/1916 |
| War Diary | Bouzincourt Albert Line | 17/08/1916 | 18/08/1916 |
| War Diary | Usna Redoubt | 19/08/1916 | 19/08/1916 |
| War Diary | Bouzincourt | 20/08/1916 | 21/08/1916 |
| War Diary | Ovillers Post | 22/08/1916 | 23/08/1916 |
| War Diary | Battn in Trenches. (O.G.I. Pt. 81.R.31 D to pt 03.X.8.A) | 23/08/1916 | 23/08/1916 |

| | | | |
|---|---|---|---|
| War Diary | Battn in Trenches. | 23/08/1916 | 25/08/1916 |
| War Diary | Usna Redoubt | 26/08/1916 | 28/08/1916 |
| War Diary | Senlis Cross Road | 29/08/1916 | 29/08/1916 |
| War Diary | Bus | 30/08/1916 | 31/08/1916 |
| Miscellaneous | OC Organs. O.C. Bucks | 23/08/1916 | 23/08/1916 |
| Map | Map B. Portion of Trench Map. Ovillers. | | |
| Heading | 145th Brigade 48th Division. 1st Buckinghamshire Battalion (Oxf. & Bucks. L.I.) September 1916 | | |
| War Diary | Bus | 01/09/1916 | 05/09/1916 |
| War Diary | Trenches Opposite N end of Beaumont Hamel. | 06/09/1916 | 08/09/1916 |
| War Diary | Mailly-Maillet | 09/09/1916 | 10/09/1916 |
| War Diary | Bois De Warnimont | 11/09/1916 | 11/09/1916 |
| War Diary | Beauval | 12/09/1916 | 18/09/1916 |
| War Diary | Berneuil | 19/09/1916 | 29/09/1916 |
| War Diary | Coullemont | 30/09/1916 | 30/09/1916 |
| Heading | 145th Brigade. 48th Division. 1st Buckinghamshire Battalion (Oxf. & Bucks. L.I.) October 1916 | | |
| War Diary | Coullemont | 01/10/1916 | 01/10/1916 |
| War Diary | St. Amand. | 02/10/1916 | 05/10/1916 |
| War Diary | Trenches at Hebuterne | 06/10/1916 | 07/10/1916 |
| War Diary | Souastre | 08/10/1916 | 08/10/1916 |
| War Diary | Henu | 09/10/1916 | 09/10/1916 |
| War Diary | Warlencourt | 10/10/1916 | 19/10/1916 |
| War Diary | Warluzel | 20/10/1916 | 22/10/1916 |
| War Diary | Beauval | 23/10/1916 | 23/10/1916 |
| War Diary | Talmas | 24/10/1916 | 24/10/1916 |
| War Diary | Lahoussoye | 25/10/1916 | 31/10/1916 |
| Heading | 145th Brigade. 48th Division. 1st Buckinghamshire Battalion (Oxf. & Bucks. L.I.) December 1916 | | |
| War Diary | Shelter Wood Camp (North) | 01/12/1916 | 03/12/1916 |
| War Diary | Trenches N of Le Sars | 04/12/1916 | 07/12/1916 |
| War Diary | Scots Redoubt Camp South | 08/12/1916 | 12/12/1916 |
| War Diary | Middle Wood Camp | 13/12/1916 | 14/12/1916 |
| War Diary | B Camp Becourt | 15/12/1916 | 28/12/1916 |
| War Diary | Bresle | 29/12/1916 | 31/12/1916 |
| Heading | 145th Brigade. 48th Division. 1st Buckinghamshire Battalion (Oxf. & Bucks. L.I.) November 1916 | | |
| War Diary | Millencourt | 01/11/1916 | 02/11/1916 |
| War Diary | Martin Puich | 03/11/1916 | 05/11/1916 |
| War Diary | 26th Avenue | 06/11/1916 | 06/11/1916 |
| War Diary | Front line trenches at Le Sars | 07/11/1916 | 08/11/1916 |
| War Diary | 26th Avenue | 09/11/1916 | 10/11/1916 |
| War Diary | Acid Drop Camp | 11/11/1916 | 15/11/1916 |
| War Diary | Trenches N of Le Sars | 16/11/1916 | 17/11/1916 |
| War Diary | Martin Puich 70th Trench 26th Avenue | 18/11/1916 | 20/11/1916 |
| War Diary | Trenches N of Le Sars. | 21/11/1916 | 23/11/1916 |
| War Diary | Scotts Redoubt Huts | 24/11/1916 | 26/11/1916 |
| War Diary | Middle Wood Camp | 27/11/1916 | 30/11/1916 |
| Map | Le Sars To Loupart Wood And Le Barque | | |
| Heading | War Diary of the 1/Bucks Bn Rgt from Jan 1st 1917 to Jan 31st 1917 Vol 23 | | |
| War Diary | Bresle | 01/01/1917 | 09/01/1917 |
| War Diary | Neuville Au-Bois & Forceville Con-Vimeu) | 10/01/1917 | 19/01/1917 |
| War Diary | Neuville & Forceville | 20/01/1917 | 29/01/1917 |
| War Diary | Hamel | 30/01/1917 | 31/01/1917 |

| Type | Description | Start | End |
|---|---|---|---|
| Heading | War Diary Of 1st Bucks Battalion. From February 1st 1917 to February 28th 1917 Vol 24 | | |
| War Diary | Hamel (Camp. 8). | 01/02/1917 | 02/02/1917 |
| War Diary | Camp 56 Cappy | 03/02/1917 | 05/02/1917 |
| War Diary | Support Trenches | 06/02/1917 | 09/02/1917 |
| War Diary | Bn in Bde Reserve in TR. Sophie near Herbecourt | 10/02/1917 | 13/02/1917 |
| War Diary | Trenches N.E. of Barleux. | 14/02/1917 | 17/02/1917 |
| War Diary | Camp 56 Cappy | 18/02/1917 | 28/02/1917 |
| Heading | War Diary Of 1/Bucks Battalion. From 1st March 1917 to 31st March 1917 Vol 25 | | |
| War Diary | Trenches | 01/03/1917 | 01/03/1917 |
| War Diary | Tr. Sofie (H25L) | 02/03/1917 | 06/03/1917 |
| War Diary | Sofie Tr | 07/03/1917 | 07/03/1917 |
| War Diary | Trenches | 08/03/1917 | 11/03/1917 |
| War Diary | Support 2 Coys Flaucourt 2 Coys Desiree Valley | 12/03/1917 | 13/03/1917 |
| War Diary | Camp 56 (Cappy-Eclusier Rd) | 14/03/1917 | 20/03/1917 |
| War Diary | Peronne | 21/03/1917 | 21/03/1917 |
| War Diary | Doingt | 22/03/1917 | 26/03/1917 |
| War Diary | Tincourt | 27/03/1917 | 27/03/1917 |
| War Diary | Hamel | 28/03/1917 | 29/03/1917 |
| War Diary | Cartigny | 30/03/1917 | 31/03/1917 |
| Miscellaneous | 1/Bucks Battalion | 03/03/1917 | 03/03/1917 |
| Miscellaneous | O.C. Companies | 07/03/1917 | 07/03/1917 |
| Miscellaneous | 1/Bucks Battalion. | 20/03/1917 | 20/03/1917 |
| Map | 1st Bucks Battn. Outpost Dispositions. | | |
| Map | 1st Bucks. Battn. Outpost Dispositions. March 22nd 1917 | | |
| War Diary | Cartigny | 01/04/1917 | 03/04/1917 |
| War Diary | Longavesnes. | 04/04/1917 | 05/04/1917 |
| War Diary | Villers Faucon | 05/04/1917 | 05/04/1917 |
| War Diary | Outposts. Lempire (F15a) to Malassise Farm (F2D) | 05/04/1917 | 07/04/1917 |
| War Diary | Marquaix | 08/04/1917 | 13/04/1917 |
| War Diary | E 29 b 64. | 14/04/1917 | 15/04/1917 |
| War Diary | Outposts Malassise Farm. (excel) to X Tracks F17c 28. (inch) | 16/04/1917 | 16/04/1917 |
| War Diary | Outposts X Tracks F4d 99 Tombois Farm. F 17 b 88 | 17/04/1917 | 17/04/1917 |
| War Diary | E 29 b 64 | 18/04/1917 | 19/04/1917 |
| War Diary | Villers Faucon | 20/04/1917 | 25/04/1917 |
| War Diary | Bn HQ A Coy Lempire | 26/04/1917 | 26/04/1917 |
| War Diary | B Coy C Coy D Coy Camp E 18 D 20 | 26/04/1917 | 26/04/1917 |
| War Diary | Outposts F 11 b 16-Tombois-F18a 8095 | 27/04/1917 | 28/04/1917 |
| War Diary | Bn HQ D Coy Lempire | 29/04/1917 | 29/04/1917 |
| War Diary | B Coy C Coy D Coy Camp E 29 b 64 | 29/04/1917 | 29/04/1917 |
| War Diary | Dumps | 29/04/1917 | 29/04/1917 |
| War Diary | Hamel | 30/04/1917 | 30/04/1917 |
| War Diary | Mons En Chaussee & Estrees Encroussee. | 30/04/1917 | 30/04/1917 |
| Miscellaneous | O.C. Companies. Quartermaster. Transport Officer. | 04/04/1917 | 04/04/1917 |
| Heading | WO/95 2763 | | |
| Map | Map D | | |
| Heading | WO95/2763 | | |
| Map | | | |
| Miscellaneous | 1/Bucks Battalion. | 13/04/1917 | 13/04/1917 |
| Miscellaneous | 1/Bucks Battalion. | 16/04/1917 | 16/04/1917 |
| Miscellaneous | O.C. Companies | 16/04/1917 | 16/04/1917 |
| Miscellaneous | 1/Bucks Battalion. | 25/04/1917 | 25/04/1917 |

| | | | |
|---|---|---|---|
| Heading | War Diary of 1/1st Buckinghamshire Battalion of the oxfordshire Buckinghamshire Light Infantry From May 1st 1917 to May 31st 1917 Vol 27 | | |
| War Diary | Mons En Chausee and Estrees En Chausee | 01/05/1917 | 11/05/1917 |
| War Diary | Mons En Chausee and Estrees En Chausee and Flamicourt. | 11/05/1917 | 11/05/1917 |
| War Diary | Flamicourt and Maurepas | 12/05/1917 | 12/05/1917 |
| War Diary | Le Transloy | 13/05/1917 | 14/05/1917 |
| War Diary | Outpost Line | 14/05/1917 | 18/05/1917 |
| War Diary | Reserve Line | 19/05/1917 | 24/05/1917 |
| War Diary | Reserve Line and Outpost Line | 24/05/1917 | 24/05/1917 |
| War Diary | Outpost Line | 24/05/1917 | 28/05/1917 |
| War Diary | Outpost Line & Reserve | 29/05/1917 | 29/05/1917 |
| War Diary | Reserve | 30/05/1917 | 31/05/1917 |
| Miscellaneous | 1/Bucks Battalion. | 14/05/1917 | 14/05/1917 |
| Miscellaneous | 1/Bucks Battalion. | 26/05/1917 | 26/05/1917 |
| Heading | War Diary of 1/1st Bucks Battn June 1st to June 30th 1917 Vol 28 | | |
| War Diary | In Reserve | 01/06/1917 | 03/06/1917 |
| War Diary | In Reserve and Outpost Line | 03/06/1917 | 03/06/1917 |
| War Diary | Outpost Line | 03/06/1917 | 06/06/1917 |
| War Diary | Outpost Line K 26 Central to K 14c 39 (57c NE) | 07/06/1917 | 07/06/1917 |
| War Diary | Outpost Line K 26 Central to K 14c 39 | 08/06/1917 | 09/06/1917 |
| War Diary | 2 Coy Reserve Line 2 Coy & BNHQ Beaumetz | 10/06/1917 | 11/06/1917 |
| War Diary | 2 Coys Reserve Line 2 Coys & Beaumetz Bn HQ | 12/06/1917 | 14/06/1917 |
| War Diary | 2 Coy Reserve Line 2 Coy Beaumetz and Battn HQ and Outpost Line K26 Central to K 14c 3.9 | 15/06/1917 | 18/06/1917 |
| War Diary | Outpost Line K26 Central to K 14c 3.9 | 19/06/1917 | 21/06/1917 |
| War Diary | Battn in Reserve | 22/06/1917 | 26/06/1917 |
| War Diary | Battn in Reserve and Outpost Line K26 Central to K14c 39 | 27/06/1917 | 27/06/1917 |
| War Diary | Outpost Line K26 Central to K14c 3.9 | 28/06/1917 | 30/06/1917 |
| Miscellaneous | Appendix A | | |
| Miscellaneous | 1/Bucks Battalion. No. 1 | 07/06/1917 | 07/06/1917 |
| Miscellaneous | 1/Bucks Battalion. No. 2 | 08/06/1917 | 08/06/1917 |
| Miscellaneous | 1/Bucks Battalion. No. 3 | 14/06/1917 | 14/06/1917 |
| Miscellaneous | 1/Bucks Battalion. No. 4 | 19/06/1917 | 19/06/1917 |
| Miscellaneous | 1/Bucks Battalion. No. 5 | 20/06/1917 | 20/06/1917 |
| Miscellaneous | 1/Bucks Battalion. No. 6 | 27/06/1917 | 27/06/1917 |
| Miscellaneous | 1/Bucks Battalion. No. 7 | 29/06/1917 | 29/06/1917 |
| Miscellaneous | Appendix B | | |
| Miscellaneous | P.C.-Platoon Commander, L.G.-Lewis Gun. | 04/06/1917 | 04/06/1917 |
| Miscellaneous | To all Recipients of 1/Bucks Battn. O.O. No. 22 | 07/06/1917 | 07/06/1917 |
| Miscellaneous | 1/Bucks Battalion. | 09/06/1917 | 09/06/1917 |
| Heading | War Diary of 1/1st Bucks Bn of the Oxfordshire & Buckinghamshire Light Infty From 1st July 1917 to 31st July 1917 Vol 29 | | |
| War Diary | Forward Reserve | 01/07/1917 | 02/07/1917 |
| War Diary | Forward Reserve & at Velu | 03/07/1917 | 03/07/1917 |
| War Diary | Velu and Bihucourt | 04/07/1917 | 04/07/1917 |
| War Diary | Bihucourt and Bailleulval | 05/07/1917 | 05/07/1917 |
| War Diary | Bailleulval | 06/07/1917 | 21/07/1917 |
| War Diary | Bailleulval and Houtkerque | 22/07/1917 | 22/07/1917 |
| War Diary | Houtkerque | 23/07/1917 | 30/07/1917 |
| War Diary | Houtkerque and St. Jan Ter Biezen | 30/07/1917 | 30/07/1917 |
| War Diary | St. Jan Ter Biezen | 31/07/1917 | 31/07/1917 |

| | | | |
|---|---|---|---|
| Map | No. 1. | | |
| Heading | Appendix "A" to War Diary of 1/1st Bucks Bn of the Oxfordshire & Buckinghamshire L.J. From 1st July 1917 to 31st July 1917 Vol | | |
| Miscellaneous | 1/Bucks Battalion. Warning Order. | 03/07/1917 | 03/07/1917 |
| Miscellaneous | Appendix A | | |
| Miscellaneous | 1/Bucks Battalion. | 02/07/1917 | 02/07/1917 |
| Miscellaneous | 1/Bucks Battalion. | 03/07/1917 | 03/07/1917 |
| Miscellaneous | 1/Bucks Battalion. | 04/07/1917 | 04/07/1917 |
| Heading | War Diary. of. 1/1st Bucks Battalion of Oxford Bucks L.I. From 1st August to 31st August 1917 Vol 30 | | |
| War Diary | St Jan Ter Biezen | 01/08/1917 | 04/08/1917 |
| War Diary | Dambre Camp (B 27 d) | 04/08/1917 | 05/08/1917 |
| War Diary | Dambre Camp (B27d) and in Line | 05/08/1917 | 07/08/1917 |
| War Diary | In The Line St Julien & Line of Steenbeek | 07/08/1917 | 08/08/1917 |
| War Diary | Dambre Camp (B 27 d) | 09/08/1917 | 16/08/1917 |
| War Diary | In The Line. (Just N.E of St Julien) a 4 C 12c 96-C12a 62-C12a 44 | 17/08/1917 | 18/08/1917 |
| War Diary | Dambre Camp. B 27d (Map-Belgium Sheet 28 NW 1/20000) | 19/08/1917 | 19/08/1917 |
| War Diary | Dambre Camp | 19/08/1917 | 21/08/1917 |
| War Diary | Dambre Camp B 27d 1/20,000. Map Belgium Sheet 28 NN | 22/08/1917 | 27/08/1917 |
| War Diary | In The Line Support Positions Su Dispositions | 28/08/1917 | 28/08/1917 |
| War Diary | Reigursburg Camp. (H6d) | 29/08/1917 | 29/08/1917 |
| War Diary | On Move | 30/08/1917 | 31/08/1917 |
| Heading | War Diary 1/1 Bucks Bn, Oxf. & Bucks Lt Infty September 1917 Vol 31 | | |
| War Diary | Road Camp St Jan Ter Biezen | 01/09/1917 | 15/09/1917 |
| War Diary | Road Camp St Jan Ter Beizen | 13/09/1917 | 15/09/1917 |
| War Diary | St Jan Ter Beizen-Licques | 16/09/1917 | 16/09/1917 |
| War Diary | Licques | 17/09/1917 | 18/09/1917 |
| War Diary | St Jan Ter Beizen to Licques | 16/09/1917 | 16/09/1917 |
| War Diary | Licques | 19/09/1917 | 27/09/1917 |
| War Diary | Canal Bank | 28/09/1917 | 30/09/1917 |
| Heading | War Diary Of 1/1st Bucks Bn, Oxfd & Bucks L.I From 1st Oct to 31st Oct 1917 Vol 32 | | |
| War Diary | Line V 25c 96 to D1d 47 Map (Poelcapelle 1/10,000 See Appx B) | 01/10/1917 | 01/10/1917 |
| War Diary | The Line V 25c 96 to D1d 47 | 01/10/1917 | 02/10/1917 |
| War Diary | The Line V25c 96 to D1d 47 (NE of St Julien) | 03/10/1917 | 03/10/1917 |
| War Diary | Front Line to Reigursburg Camp | 04/10/1917 | 04/10/1917 |
| War Diary | Reigursburg Camp to Canal Bank | 05/10/1917 | 05/10/1917 |
| War Diary | Canal Bank | 06/10/1917 | 07/10/1917 |
| War Diary | The Line V26a 63 to D2b 45 | 07/10/1917 | 08/10/1917 |
| War Diary | Divl Reserve | 08/10/1917 | 10/10/1917 |
| War Diary | Dambre Camp (B27c) | 11/10/1917 | 12/10/1917 |
| War Diary | Road Camp St Jan Ter Beizen | 13/10/1917 | 14/10/1917 |
| War Diary | Maisnil-Bouche | 15/10/1917 | 17/10/1917 |
| War Diary | Villers-Au-Bois | 18/10/1917 | 31/10/1917 |
| Heading | Appendix "B" to War Diary Of 1/1st Bucks Bn, Oxfd & Bucks L.I From 1st Oct to 31st Oct 1917 | | |
| Heading | Appendix-A and B Nil. | | |

WO95/2763/2

1st Bucks Battalion Oxfordshire
+ Buckinghamshire Light Infantry

48TH DIVISION
145TH INFY BDE

1ST BUCKS BN, OXF & BUCKS LT INFY

APR 1915-MAR 1919

1917 OCT

145th Inf.Bde.
48th Div.

Battn. disembarked
Boulogne from
England 30.3.15.

1st BUCKS. BATTN. THE OXFORD & BUCKS. LIGHT INF.

M A R C H
(30 & 31.3.15)

1 9 1 5

Mar '19

Army Form C. 2118.

1/1 BUCKS BN
OXF & BUCKS LT INFTY

# WAR DIARY
or
# INTELLIGENCE SUMMARY.
(Erase heading not required.)

Instructions regarding War Diaries and Intelligence Summaries are contained in F. S. Regs., Part II. and the Staff Manual respectively. Title pages will be prepared in manuscript.

| Place | Date | Hour | Summary of Events and Information | Remarks and references to Appendices |
|---|---|---|---|---|
| CHELMSFORD | 30.3.15 | 5 pm | entrained by ½ Battalion & 5.30 pm, arrived FOLKESTONE 8.30pm, left 9.30pm on Steamer "INVICTA", arrived BOULOGNE 10.40 pm. marched 10.45 pm crossed to rest Camp OSTERHOVE. Strength 28 Officers 916 other ranks (including 1 R.C. Chaplain) | apps |
| OSTERHOVE near BOULOGNE | 31.3.15 | | Rest-Camp. — left parade 3.40pm, march to PONT DE BRIQUES station entrain 5.45 pm on same train as transport & M.G. section coming from HAVRE, arrive CASSEL 10.15 pm march to WILLES in farms near TERGENHEM, arriving 2. am 1.4.15 (Strength (3) Officers & 1002 other ranks — including 1 R.C. Chaplain & batman — Billets in farms barns, straw plentiful, average 3 farms per Company. Interpreter joined Bn on the train at PONT DE BRIQUES. — | apps |

appointmt.talk.RAJ

145th Inf.Bde.
48th Div.

**1st BUCKS. BATTN. THE OXFORD & BUCKS. LIGHT INF.**

A P R I L

1 9 1 5

# CONFIDENTIAL

WAR DIARY

of

BUCKS BATTN. OXF & BUCKS LT. INFTY.

from 1 April 1915 — 30 April 1915.

Army Form C. 2118.

1/BUCKS BN
OXF & BUCKS LT INFTY

# WAR DIARY
or
# INTELLIGENCE SUMMARY.
(Erase heading not required.)

Instructions regarding War Diaries and Intelligence Summaries are contained in F. S. Regs., Part II. and the Staff Manual respectively. Title pages will be prepared in manuscript.

| Place | Date | Hour | Summary of Events and Information | Remarks and references to Appendices |
|---|---|---|---|---|
| | APRIL | | | |
| TERGENHEM | 1. | | Bn in billets in farms | |
| " | 2 | | Brigade inspected by Gen. Sir H. Smith Dorrien 11 am at STEENVOORDE | Appx |
| " | 3 | | Companies at training close to billets - 5 men sick, sent to hospital | Appx |
| " | 4. | | Bn moved by road to billets via CAESTRE - FLETRE - METEREN. Ref Mob. 1/100,000 HAZEBROUCK Sheet 5.A. | |
| | | | to billets in farms about 6000 yards S.S.E of METEREN | |
| | | | Strength 31 off[icers] 997 other ranks | Appx |
| METEREN | 5 | | Bn in billets. Coys at training | Appx |
| " | 6 | | — " — | Appx |
| " | 7 | | Bn marched 2.30 p.m. via BAILLEUL - NIEPPE - ARMENTIERES - billets | Appx |
| LE BIZET | | | in LE BIZET (FRANCE) for attachment to 12th Bde, arriving 7 p.m. | |
| | 8. | | Bn under instruction of 12th Bde. A Coy into trenches at night with Lancashire | |
| | | | Fusiliers. C Coy with Essex Regt - D Coy + B Coy instructed during day by | |
| | | | 1/Monmouth Regt in billets - billets + trench digging. D Coy instructors in billets by | |
| | | | Kings Own Regt in billets by R.E. in rear trenches - D Coy 1 man wounded | |
| | | | afterwards died of wounds | Appx |
| | 9. | | A + C Coys in trenches. Mine exploded in TOUQUET by R.E. in | Appx |

# WAR DIARY
## or
## INTELLIGENCE SUMMARY.

Army Form C. 2118.

BUCKS BATTN. OXF. & BUCKS LT. INFTY

(Erase heading not required.)

| Place | Date | Hour | Summary of Events and Information | Remarks and references to Appendices |
|---|---|---|---|---|
| LE BIZET | | | Front of Lanes Fus Braches at 8.30 am afternoon bombardment by our guns for 20 minutes. No infantry attack. After explosion both explosion & guns shelled German communications from FREHLINGEN. Shelling reported successful. B & D Coys and Regt H.Q. in reserve in rear line of trenches. 2 men wounded. | |
| | 10. | | B & D Coy into trenches at night in relief of A & C Coys. | Appx |
| | 11. | | B & B Coy in trenches. A & C Coy under instruction in billets during the day. A & C Coy relieve B & D Coy at night. | Appx |
| | 12. | | A & C Coy in trenches. B & D under instruction in billets. A & C Coys relieve trenches between 6 pm & 10 pm. | Appx |
| | | | Bn moved gave marching via ARMENTIERES - NIEPPE - STEELWERCK - | |
| 1½ miles W of STEELWERCK | 13. | | billets in farms north of nord STEELWERCK - LEVERRIER, arriving 1 pm. Appx Bn H.Q at farm (ref. map 36.B Series 1/40000) A.14.c.S.W. | Appx |
| | 14. | | 2 Officers per Coy + 2 N.Co's per Bn instructed in bomb throwing under arrangements of 4th Divs - Officers + N.Co's instructed in bomb throwing | Appx |
| | 15. | | Bn moved, marching 8.30 am via LA CRECHE - TRABOT - PLOEGSTEERT | |

Army Form C. 2118.

# WAR DIARY
or
# INTELLIGENCE SUMMARY.   BUCKS BATTN. OXF. & BUCKS L.T. INFTY

(Erase heading not required.)

Instructions regarding War Diaries and Intelligence Summaries are contained in F. S. Regs., Part II. and the Staff Manual respectively. Title pages will be prepared in manuscript.

| Place | Date | Hour | Summary of Events and Information | Remarks and references to Appendices |
|---|---|---|---|---|
| | April | | | |
| PLOEGSTEERT | 15 | | to relieve Somersets Lt 2/Lt. in reserve. A Coy at 1675 Farm, B Coy TOUQUET BERTHE, C & D Coys in HUNTERSTOWN. Bn H.Q. in PLOEGSTEERT. A & B Coys in reserve to 4 Royal Berks, C & D Coys in reserve to 5/Glosters | appx |
| " | 16 | | Coys employed by day & night on working parties, behind ½ in trench line near R[egt?] | appx |
| | 17 | | ditto. A & B Coys moved with C to PLOEGSTEERT village | appx |
| | 18 | | ditto | appx |
| | 19 | | B Coy employed during day on working party. Took over trenches from 5/Glosters Regt ST YVES SECTION of centre sector. D.A.C Coys in | appx |
| | 20 | | front B in support. Bn trenches running from point U. 15.4.9, west just in road, U.21.6.5.8 to road north to point U.15.a.8. | appx |
| | | | front & road in jas in front V.15. a.8. | |
| | 20 | | Bn in trenches - situation normal | appx |
| | 21 | | " " 2/Lt Williamson slightly wounded in trenches in left hand whilst observing with field glasses. 1 man wounded. | appx |
| | 22 | | | appx |

Army Form C. 2118.

# WAR DIARY
## or
## INTELLIGENCE SUMMARY.

BUCKS BATTN. OXF. & BUCKS LT. INFTY.

(Erase heading not required.)

Instructions regarding War Diaries and Intelligence Summaries are contained in F.S. Regs., Part II. and the Staff Manual respectively. Title pages will be prepared in manuscript.

| Place | Date | Hour | Summary of Events and Information | Remarks and references to Appendices |
|---|---|---|---|---|
| PLOEGSTEERT WOOD | 23 | | Bn in trenches 5th relieved by 5/Glosters about 8 p.m. 1 man killed in trenches (D Coy) & 1 Sgt wounded (afterwards died) in wood near MOATED FARM. Bn marched by platoons to billets in ROMARIN in Divisional Reserve | |
| ROMARIN | 24 | | Bn resting. One Coy (A) all had baths in NIEPPE | appx |
| | 25 | | " " (B) " " " " | appx |
| | 26 | | " " " " " " " " | appx in work |
| PLOEGSTEERT WOOD | 27 | 8/pm | Bn into trenches in relief of 5/Glosters. 1 man wounded in relieving - snipers annoying | |
| | 28 | | Bn in trenches - All very quiet by day, good deal of sniping by night - 1 man (L.C. Holt A Coy) killed early morning. Whole weekly hand grenades | |
| | 29 | | Bn in trenches. Exceptionally quiet, hits by day & night | appx |
| | 30 | | " " All quiet in morning from 1.30 p.m. - 2.15 p.m. enemy shelled wood about SOMERSET Ho with 6" H.E. incendiary shells, 67 shells falling within a radius of about 70 yards. at 3 p.m. platoon of D Coy in THREE HUNS & HOLL'S BURNT FARMS were shelled with shrapnel. 2 men wounded. One man killed two wounded in new MOATED FARM left | |

1577 Wt.W10791/1773 500,000 1/15 D.D.&L. A.D.S.S./Forms/C. 2118.

**Army Form C. 2118.**

# WAR DIARY
## or
## INTELLIGENCE SUMMARY.
*(Erase heading not required.)*

BUCKS BATTN. O.+ B. BUCKS LT INFTY

Instructions regarding War Diaries and Intelligence Summaries are contained in F.S. Regs., Part II. and the Staff Manual respectively. Title pages will be prepared in manuscript.

| Place | Date | Hour | Summary of Events and Information | Remarks and references to Appendices |
|---|---|---|---|---|
| | | | by C Coy. Working party arranged for night to strengthen parados an observeth the front inspected. | ypus [signature] |

145th Inf. Bde.
48th Div.

1st BUCKS. BATTN. THE OXFORD & BUCKS. LIGHT INF.

M A Y

1 9 1 5

Army Form C. 2118.

1st Buckinghamshire

# WAR DIARY
## or
## INTELLIGENCE SUMMARY.
(Erase heading not required.)

| Place | Date | Hour | Summary of Events and Information | Remarks and references to Appendices |
|---|---|---|---|---|
| PLOEGSTEERT WOOD | 1.5.15 | | Bn in trenches. Quiet day - 1 man killed cas. morning in hour breastwork (C Coy) - Relieved by 5/ Glosters 8.30 p.m. Bn marched back by platoons to Willes in ROMARIN | |
| ROMARIN | 2.5.15 | | Bn in Willes - Divisional Reserve | |
| | 3 | | " " . 2 Coys on fatigue 6 p.m - 3 a.m in trenches of Warwick Brigade | |
| | 4 | | " " . | |
| | 5 | | " " . Marched to trenches by platoons, took over from 5/ Glosters 9 p.m - Sniping more lively than usual | |
| PLOEGSTEERT WOOD | 6. | | Quiet morning, rifle grenades used on both sides, two landed behind A Coy fire trench 4.15 p.m wounding Capt Reynolds, Bowyer, Lce Corp Green & 6 others ranks - 3 shells close to Bn Hd.Q. at 5 p.m. No man killed | |
| | 7 | | early morning (D Coy) in trench - Quiet up till 12.15 p.m. Enemy shelled support trenches behind centre Coy (A Coy) with little to little working along to our including left Coy trenches (C Coy), about 16 shells, no casualties - | |

Army Form C. 2118.

# WAR DIARY
or
# INTELLIGENCE SUMMARY.
(Erase heading not required.)

Instructions regarding War Diaries and Intelligence Summaries are contained in F. S. Regs., Part II. and the Staff Manual respectively. Title pages will be prepared in manuscript.

| Place | Date | Hour | Summary of Events and Information | Remarks and references to Appendices |
|---|---|---|---|---|
| PLOEGSTEERT WOOD | 8 | | Quiet day. | |
| | 9 | | Demonstration by division with gun rifle fire also trench mortars & rifle grenades - throughout the day with intermittent bursts of fast M.G. enemy. Enemy shelled PLOEGSTEERT throughout the day with HE & our left trench with shrapnel in afternoon - no damage. | |
| | 10 | | Total casualties during day 1 killed & 4 wounded by rifle bullets & rifle grenades. | appx |
| | | | Quiet day, relieved by 5/Cheshires at 9 p.m. Major Killed Div Reserve | appx |
| ROMARIN | 11 | | | appx |
| | 12 | | | appx |
| | 13 | | Relieved 3/Cheshires in trenches 9 p.m. Right | appx |
| | 14 | | Quiet day | appx |
| | 15 | | | appx |
| | 16 | | Demonstration - 9 a.m. Lewis guns fire by 1 & 2 Coys on roads in rear of enemy's trenches. 11 a.m. Artillery bombarded enemy's trench facing left Coy, that Coy opening with rapid fire | appx |

Army Form C. 2118.

# WAR DIARY
## or
## INTELLIGENCE SUMMARY.
(Erase heading not required.)

Instructions regarding War Diaries and Intelligence Summaries are contained in F. S. Regs., Part II. and the Staff Manual respectively. Title pages will be prepared in manuscript.

| Place | Date | Hour | Summary of Events and Information | Remarks and references to Appendices |
|---|---|---|---|---|
| PLOEGSTEERT WOOD | 16 | | In enemys trenches, 1.45 pm. Rifle grenade fire by enemy Coy. 4.15 pm - Trench mortar fired by right Coy hit with grenades on both sides of it, 3 bombs fired two taking effect in enemys trench - 6.15 pm - Long range fire on roads in rear. Little reply from enemy except at 4.45 pm when they sent about 20 rifle grenades back. Casualties during the day, 1 killed, 4 wounded | Appx |
| " | 17 | | Quiet day, no hostile artillery fire at all - | Appx |
| " | 18 | | Very quiet, enemys shelled PLOEGSTEERT Village - relieved about 8 pm by 5/Glosters. Running runt of day, Cenihas v. Wps. | Appx |
| ROMARIN | 19 | | Bn in billet, resting - | Appx |
| " | 20 | | — " — | Appx |
| " | 21 | | — " — | Appx |
| " | 22 | | — " — Relieved 5/Glosters in trenches 8 pm. 2 men wounded during relief. | Appx |
| PLOEGSTEERT WOOD | 23 | | Artillery bombardment at 3.30am. of BIRDCAGE - Enemy rifles with few stick shells. Our wires and into PLOEGSTEERT. | Appx |

Army Form C. 2118.

# WAR DIARY
## or
## INTELLIGENCE SUMMARY.
(Erase heading not required.)

| Place | Date | Hour | Summary of Events and Information | Remarks and references to Appendices |
|---|---|---|---|---|
| PLOEGSTEERT WOOD | 23. (cont) | | Intermittent shelling on both sides all day. Bn H.Q 2 hrs wind 900 yards back along the STRAND | |
| | 24 | | Quiet day | |
| | 25 | | Quiet day. Enemy transport heard at 9 p.m. behind lines & shelled by our guns | |
| | 26 | | Quiet day - relieved by 3/Gloucesters at 7 p.m. reached billets in ROMARIN by 9.45 p.m | |
| ROMARIN | 27 | | Bun. resting in billets | |
| | 28 | | " " " | |
| | 29 | | " " " | |
| | 30 | | " " ", relieved 3/Gloucesters 6.30 p.m. in trenches - Ploegsteert Wood | |
| PLOEGSTEERT WOOD | 31. | | Ridgway killed by hand grenade during bomb throwing practice at 3.30 p.m. Quiet day. Snipers been busy. Machine guns & enemy battery more active during night. | |

1577  Wt. W10791/1773  500,000  1/15  D. D. & L.  A.D.S.S./Forms/C. 2118.

145th Inf.Bde.
48th Div.

1st BUCKS. BATTN. THE OXFORD & BUCKS. LIGHT INF.

J U N E

1 9 1 5

# WAR DIARY
## or
## INTELLIGENCE SUMMARY.

BUCKS BATTN. OXF. & BUCKS LT. INFTY.

Army Form C. 2118.

| Place | Date | Hour | Summary of Events and Information | Remarks and references to Appendices |
|---|---|---|---|---|
| PLOEGSTEERT WOOD | June 1 | | Bn in trenches. 1 Coy 1/Scottish Rifles attached for instruction, 1 Platoon to Coy HQ, to D Coy, 1 Platoon to A Coy, 2 Platoons to B Coy. Quiet day. Sniping more lively. Enemy fired right & during night — at 10.30 p.m. Bombarded. Enemy working party with 4 machine guns ought to have drawn enemy rifle fire & aid it again — did considerable damage. Enemy filled PLOEGSTEERT village in afternoon. Postman wounded by shrapnel & 2/Lieut Humpden and 5 men wounded in D Coy. 2 p.m. rifle grenades. Others rifle bullets— | Appx ypres |
| | 2. | | Quiet day. | |
| | 3. | | Quiet day — relieved by 5/Glosters at 7 pm Bn in billets resting | nyns |
| ROMARIN | 4. | | | |
| | 5. | | | |
| | 6. | | Received orders 12.15 am to stand by. Mass known at 10 minute notice, when move in front of 4/OBLI. Trenches closed to be selected. | Appx |

# WAR DIARY or INTELLIGENCE SUMMARY.

Army Form C. 2118.

BUCKS BATTN. OXF. & BUCKS LT. INFTY.

(Erase heading not required.)

| Place | Date | Hour | Summary of Events and Information | Remarks and references to Appendices |
|---|---|---|---|---|
| ROMARIN PLOEGSTEERT WOOD | 8. | | Bn in Wk. — Relieve 5/Glosters at 7 p.m. in trenches — Bn in trenches 32 – 35 incl. Took over 32 from 4/Oxfords — Coys D Coy N° 32. S.32 & S.33 — A Coy 33. & 34. B Coy. 35. S.36. C Coy 2 platoons HUNTERS AVENUE, 2 platoons extending line breastworks — Quiet day, occasional shelling by enemy about and behind retaliatory line — (1 man killed trench 36) | Appx Appx |
| " | 9 | 7 am | enemy exploded small mine South of BIRDCAGE outside our trenches doing no damage. At same time shewing fire with M.G.s, Trench mortars & guns — Quiet day afterwards — heavy rain started 5.30 am & prevented all observation of mine explosion, who made all telephone communication with Coys bad — | Appx |
| | 10. | | Quiet day — | |
| | 11 | | Quiet day — relieved by 6/Warwicks at 5.30 p.m. Bn went to billet about PETIT PONT, Bn HQ W° COURT DREVE Farm A Coy at the HUNTING LODGE, B & D Coys at LA PETITE MUNQUE Farm | Appx |

Army Form C. 2118.

# WAR DIARY
## or
## INTELLIGENCE SUMMARY.

BUCKS BATTN. OXF. & BUCKS LT. INFTY.

(Erase heading not required.)

| Place | Date | Hour | Summary of Events and Information | Remarks and references to Appendices |
|---|---|---|---|---|
| Wulsh PETIT POINT | 12 | | Bn resting in Billets. Brigade Reserve | Appx |
| | 13 | | " | Appx |
| | 14 | | 2.15 am – Enemy exploded mine in front of BIRDCAGE section, & bombarded with shells. Ordered to Stand to 2.45 am till 3.35 am – Quiet afterwards – 3 Coys 9/Essex Regt attached for instruction | Appx |
| | 15. | | Resting in Billets where 57 Glosters at 9 pm in trenches 64-73 (incl) between MESSINES PLOEGSTEERT and road MESSINES – WULVERGHEM – Bn HQ at LA PLUS DOUVE FARM on Ruis DOUVE. 4 Coys in front line ABCD left to right | Appx |
| DOUVE Trenches | 16. | | Quiet day | Appx |
| | 17 | | " | 2/Lt Brown with patrol from Trent 72 but enemy patrol one or more, but could not catch any} Appx |
| | 18 | | | Patrol from T.72, found 2 w/h, a cart horse hooves left by German patrol showing items to the Barricade there were handles to grenades lying 3/Corbes retali. ordi. Wks war in trenches at the turn Appx |

# WAR DIARY
## or
## INTELLIGENCE SUMMARY.
(Erase heading not required.)

Army Form C. 2118.

BUCKS BATTN. OXF. & BUCKS LT. INFTY.

| Place | Date | Hour | Summary of Events and Information | Remarks and references to Appendices |
|---|---|---|---|---|
| DOUVE | 19 | | Quiet day. Relieved by 4/Glosters at 9 p.m. Bn marched back to billets at ROMARIN arriving 1 am | Appx |
| Trenches | | | | |
| ROMARIN | 20 | | Bn in billets. | Appx |
| | 21 | | " | Appx |
| | 22 | | " | Appx |
| | 23 | | Bn inspected 7 am by Major Gen R Fanshawe | Appx |
| | 24 | | " Moved billets 9 hrs to BAILLEUL, billeted in the town. Area D | Appx |
| BAILLEUL | 25 | | Bn marched 9.15 a.m. to billets at VIEUX BERQUIM, billetg HQ in village, Coys in farms N.W. edge | Appx |
| VIEUX BERQUIN | 26 | | Bn marched 9.10 p.m. via MERVILLE – ROBECQ – BUSNETTES arriving 2.50 am. bivouced in orchards in the village – | Appx |
| BUSNETTES | 27 | | Bn marched 6.40 pm – to billet at ALLOUAGNE | Appx |
| ALLOUAGNE | 28 | | Bn in billets, resting | Appx |
| " | 29 | | Bn in billets. Platoon masking by Coys | Appx |
| " | 30 | | " Coys training in wood LE MARAQUET | Appx |

[signature]

145th Inf.Bde.
48th Div.

1st BUCKS. BATTN. THE OXFORD & BUCKS. LIGHT INF.

J U L Y

1 9 1 5

145th Inf.Bde.
48th Div.

1st BUCKS. BATTN. THE OXFORD & BUCKS. LIGHT INF.

J U L Y

1 9 1 5

**WAR DIARY**
or
**INTELLIGENCE SUMMARY.**
(Erase heading not required.)

Army Form C. 2118.

Instructions regarding War Diaries and Intelligence Summaries are contained in F. S. Regs., Part II. and the Staff Manual respectively. Title pages will be prepared in manuscript.

| Place | Date | Hour | Summary of Events and Information | Remarks and references to Appendices |
|---|---|---|---|---|
| ALLOUAGNE | JULY | | | |
| | 1 | | Bn in Billets – Coy training | appx |
| | 2 | | " " " " | appx |
| | 3 | | " " " " | appx |
| | 4 | | " " " " | appx |
| | 5 | | " " " " | appx |
| | 6 | | " " " " | appx |
| | 7 | | " " " " | appx |
| | 8 | | Bn lined road LILLERS – CHOCQUES to see Kitchener | appx B |
| | 9 | | Practice attack by night by Bde, 2/Bucks + 4/Oxford repg in trenches, Bucks and 5/Glosters putting attack by daylight. appx | appx |
| | 10 | | | appx D |
| | 11 | | | |
| | 12 | | Bn marched (6.30pm) to vicinity of NOEUX LES MINES – Bn in bivouac (10.30pm) ½ mile east of HOUCHIN & about ¾ mile W of NOEUX LES MINES | |
| HOUCHIN | 13 | | Bn in bivouac | appx |
| | 14 | | " – A+B Coys working parties on 2nd line trenches 8 pm | appx |
| | | 11.30am | " " " " " | appx |
| | 15 | 11 pm | " – all Coys C & D | appx B |

# WAR DIARY
## or
## INTELLIGENCE SUMMARY.

*(Erase heading not required.)*

Army Form C. 2118.

| Place | Date | Hour | Summary of Events and Information | Remarks and references to Appendices |
|---|---|---|---|---|
| LIERES | 16 | | At B Coy working parties 11.30am — 4pm | |
| | 17 | | Bn. marched 9.30pm via MARLES LES MINES — South edge of ALLOUAGNE — Billets in LIERES and LESPESSES — Very wet - march raining — almost all the time - arr 3.15am — | Appx |
| " | 17 | | Bn. in billets. B Coy in LESPESSES remainder in LIERES - | Appx |
| | 18 | | Bn. moved by train from BERGUETTE (6.57pm) to DOULLENS (arr 14.25pm) MARIEUX (arr. 4.45am), behind French line. | Appx Appx |
| MARIEUX | 19 | | Bn. in bivouac - | Appx |
| | 20 | | " | Appx |
| | 21 | | Bn. marched 8.30pm to bivouac at COIGNEUX. | Appx |
| COIGNEUX | 21 | | " | Appx |
| | 22 | | Bn. march 8.15 pm. Bn HQ MG Sect B & C Coy to billets BAYENCOURT | Appx |
| BAYENCOURT & SAILLY | 23 | | C & D Coys under Major Hawking at SAILLY " | Appx |
| " SAILLY | 24 | | Relieved 5/Glosters 9pm in trenches N.E. of HEBUTERNE. | Appx |

**Army Form C. 2118.**

# WAR DIARY
or
## INTELLIGENCE SUMMARY.

(Erase heading not required.)

Instructions regarding War Diaries and Intelligence Summaries are contained in F. S. Regs., Part II and the Staff Manual respectively. Title pages will be prepared in manuscript.

| Place | Date | Hour | Summary of Events and Information | Remarks and references to Appendices |
|---|---|---|---|---|
| HEBUTERNE | 25th | | B Coy on right, trenches Bataille, Jena, Morand & Macdonald | appx |
| " | 26 | | C " centre " Davonst, Lefebvre, Legin, Murat, Mahet & Marceau | appx |
| " | 27 | | D " left " Lannes, Ney, Barat | appx |
| " | 28 | | A " Reserve Coy in village of HEBUTERNE | appx |
| | | | Bn in trenches, quiet day – 2 German Soldiers  of B Coy 11pm in } appx | |
| | | | front of BATAILLE trench | appx |
| | | | " " | appx |
| | | | " " | appx |
| | | | " relieved by 5th GLOSTERS at 9 pm Bn moved | appx |
| | 29 | | to billets in village of HEBUTERNE – | appx |
| | 30 | | Bn in billets | appx |
| | 31 | | " " " | appx |

M/M Mottish Lieut Col
Comdr 1/4 Gloster R
1/4 R. Sh

145th Inf.Bde.
48th Div.

1st BUCKS. BATTN. THE OXFORD & BUCKS. LIGHT INF.

A U G U S T

1915

Army Form C. 2118.

WAR DIARY
or
INTELLIGENCE SUMMARY.
(Erase heading not required.)

Instructions regarding War Diaries and Intelligence Summaries are contained in F. S. Regs., Part II. and the Staff Manual respectively. Title pages will be prepared in manuscript.

| Place | Date | Hour | Summary of Events and Information | Remarks and references to Appendices |
|---|---|---|---|---|
| HEBUTERNE | AUG 1 | | Pte in killed – working parties on HEBUTERNE defences | appx |
| | 2 | " | | appx |
| | 3 | " | | appx |
| | 4 | " | | appx |
| | 5 | " | Took over trenches from 5/Gloster – C Coy MORAND - MARBOT/MARCEAU (incl) – A Coy MARCEAU – BARAT. B & D Coy in local reserve in WULU North and NorthEast outskirts of HEBUTERNE | appx |
| | 6 | | Quiet day except for occasional shelling – | appx |
| | 7 | | " " " – Patrol C Coy under | |
| | | | Cpl Markham found 2 dead germans & recovered rifle, cado & sundry other trophies – Later sent out Bn Bbe. – | appx |
| | 8 | " | Capt. Reid took out patrol to reconnoitre a | |
| | 9 | | house reported to be being entrenched by enemy and found no signs of any works | appx |

Army Form C. 2118.

# WAR DIARY
## INTELLIGENCE SUMMARY.
(Erase heading not required.)

Instructions regarding War Diaries and Intelligence Summaries are contained in F. S. Regs, Part II. and the Staff Manual respectively. Title pages will be prepared in manuscript.

19

| Place | Date | Hour | Summary of Events and Information | Remarks and references to Appendices |
|---|---|---|---|---|
| HEBUTERNE | 9 | | quiet day — A & C Coys relieved by D & B Coys respectively | Appx |
| | 10 | | " | |
| | 11 | | " | |
| | 12 | | very little shelling | |
| | 13 | | Bulk of coys by 1/5 Gloucesters and moved to billets in SAILLY (9 p.m). | D |
| SAILLY | 14 | Sunday | Rest | B |
| | 15 | | " | |
| | 16 | | working parties on trench LARREY. | |
| | 17 | | " | |
| | 18 | | ditto | also on bursts making at Authie |
| | 19 | | ditto | ditto |
| | 20 | | " took over trenches from 5/ Gloucesters | |
| | 21 | | " B & D Coys in Support C & A Coy in day. Colt. Reid with patrol of 16 officers | |
| HEBUTERNE | 22 | at 9 pm. intermittent shelling all day. reconnoitred enemy's wire in front of Left Coy — | Appx |

1577 Wt. W10791/1773 500,000 1/15 D. D. & L. A.D.S.S./Forms/C. 2118.

Army Form C. 2118.

# WAR DIARY
## or
## INTELLIGENCE SUMMARY.
*(Erase heading not required.)*

Instructions regarding War Diaries and Intelligence Summaries are contained in F.S. Regs., Part II. and the Staff Manual respectively. Title pages will be prepared in manuscript.

| Place | Date | Hour | Summary of Events and Information | Remarks and references to Appendices |
|---|---|---|---|---|
| HEBUTERNE | 23 | | Shelling on North Side all day, little rifle fire | Sgd |
| | 24 | | Quiet day | Sgd |
| | 25 | | " " B & D Coy relieved C & A Coy in trenches 7.30 pm | Sgd |
| | | | B & D Coy demonstratin 11 pm - 12 mn | |
| | | | Brigade M.G.S. took over trenches MORAN GODIN STERN and 4/R Warks | Sgd |
| | | | A Coy & B Batta.s from 4/R Warks | |
| | 26 | | Quiet day BnHQ 1 plat 11/R Warwick arrived 8.15 pm per | |
| | 27 | | " " attached for instruction — A Coy int for | |
| | | | trenches — B Coy & D Coys strong extended to their | |
| | | | right — D Coy trenches BARAT — MURAT — B Coy | |
| | | | "—" SECUR — BATAILLE | |
| | | | A Coy 11/R Warwick attached to B & C Coy — Coy HQ at 2 | |
| | 28 | | platoon to B, 2 platoon to C, Coy HQ 3 platoon D Coy | |
| | | | 11/R Warwick to D & A Coy, Coy HQ & 1/P.t.  1 pl & 1 pl spd | |
| | 29 | | A & C Coys relieved platoons of 11/R Warwick in trenches and in Keep Reserve | |
| | | | D & B Coy at 9.30 by Chinny round Reinforcement 1 Cbo 116 R.D. arrived 11/Warwick | |
| | | | in trenches on complete platoon West | |
| | 30 | | Shelling & rifle fire all day. | |

Army Form C. 2118.

# WAR DIARY
## or
## INTELLIGENCE SUMMARY.
(Erase heading not required.)

| Place | Date | Hour | Summary of Events and Information | Remarks and references to Appendices |
|---|---|---|---|---|
| HEBUTERNE | Aug 31. | | Shelling intermittent all day - 11/Warwick attached platoon change over - | appx |

A/W Bartlett Capt A/Adj

145th Inf.Bde.
48th Div.

1st BUCKS. BATTN. THE OXFORD & BUCKS. LIGHT INF.

S E P T E M B E R

1 9 1 5

Army Form C. 2118.

# WAR DIARY
## or
## INTELLIGENCE SUMMARY.
(Erase heading not required.)

1/ BUCKS BATTN. OXF. & BUCKS LT. INFTY.

Instructions regarding War Diaries and Intelligence Summaries are contained in F. S. Regs., Part II. and the Staff Manual respectively. Title pages will be prepared in manuscript.

| Place | Date | Hour | Summary of Events and Information | Remarks and references to Appendices |
|---|---|---|---|---|
| | Sept | | | |
| HEBUTERNE | 1 | | Bn in trenches HEBUTERNE — quiet day | Appdx |
| | 2 | | " " " A Coy & ½ D Coy 1/Warwicks take over & portion | appdx |
| | 3 | | intermittent shells abts of line on complete units — | appdx |
| | 4 | | " " " " " " | appdx |
| | 5 | | relieved 1.30pm – 3pm — relieved at 6pm by 6/Gloster – Bn to | appdx |
| BUS | 6 | | billets at BUS | appdx |
| | 7 | | Bn in billets | appdx |
| COUIN | 8 | | Bn moved 11am — to billets at COUIN — 2 Coys working parties | appdx |
| | 9 | | Bn in billets — 2 Coys working parties. 1 Coy trainining | appdx |
| | 10 | | " " | appdx |
| | 11 | | " " | appdx |
| | 12 | | " " | appdx |
| | 13 | | Bn Route march — ST LEGER – AUTHIE – LOUVENCOURT. recd by L. Gen Snow on the | appdx |
| " | 14 | | march at LOUVENCOURT. G.O.C. Div ordered practice attack on B.U.S., marched back there direct to billets | appdx |

# WAR DIARY or INTELLIGENCE SUMMARY

Army Form C. 2118.

1/ BUCKS BATTN. OXF. & BUCKS LT. INFTY.

| Place | Date | Hour | Summary of Events and Information | Remarks and references to Appendices |
|---|---|---|---|---|
| COUIN | Sept 14 | | Bn in billets – 2 Coys working parties | Appx |
| " | 15 | | " | Appx |
| " | 16 | | " | Appx |
| " | 17 | | " Relieve 6/Gloster in trenches, at 5 p.m. – K Sector – A Coy left Sub sector, C Coy Right Subsector – D Coy Sublnt FONQUEVILLERS Road – B Coy in KEEP. 2 Coys 13/Manchesters attached, one Coy in complete Coy in place of C Coy – one Coy in KEEP | Appx |
| HEBUTERNE | 18 | | 13/Manchesters left at 2 p.m. – quiet day | Appx |
| " | 19 | | quiet day | Appx |
| " | 20 | | " | Appx |
| " | 21 | | Our guns shelled enemy dumps at 3.0 a.m. and 8.45 p.m. in reply immediately but enemy shelled HEBUTERNE at 8 p.m. | Appx |
| " | 22 | | guns shelled enemy enemy trenches & village, no reply, except few at 3 and 5 p.m. further | Appx |
| " | 23 | | guns shelled enemy's trenches and ran in front and twice wire at pt 862 – no reply | Appx |

# WAR DIARY
## INTELLIGENCE SUMMARY.

(Erase heading not required.)

1/BUCKS BATTN. OXF. & BUCKS LT. INFTY.

Army Form C. 2118.

| Place | Date | Hour | Summary of Events and Information | Remarks and references to Appendices |
|---|---|---|---|---|
| | Sept | | | |
| HEBUTERNE | 24 | | In trenches - Guns shelled enemy trenches 2.30 p.m & 5.30 p.m - No reply | apps |
| " | 25 | | " " " " " 2 p.m and intermittently | apps |
| " | 26 | | " " guns shelled enemy line intermittently, no reply | apps |
| " | 27 | | " " Quiet day - Enemy shelled into orchard intermittently | apps |
| " | 28 | | " " " | apps |
| | 29 | | Relieved by 6/GLOSTERS at 1 p.m - Bn to billets at COUIN in Bn! Reserve - | app |
| COUIN | 30. | | Bn in billets | apps |

ORDERLY ROOM
No.......
2 - OCT 1915
1/BUCKS. BATTN.
OXF. & BUCKS. LT. INFTY

W Whitton Capt & Adjt
1/Bucks Bn

145th Inf.Bde.
48th Div.

1st BUCKS. BATTN. THE OXFORD & BUCKS. LIGHT INF.

OCTOBER

1915

**Army Form C. 2118.**

# WAR DIARY for OCTOBER 1915

## or INTELLIGENCE SUMMARY.

(Erase heading not required.)

1/1 BUCKS BATTN. OXF & BUCKS L.T. INFTY.

Instructions regarding War Diaries and Intelligence Summaries are contained in F.S. Regs., Part II. and the Staff Manual respectively. Title pages will be prepared in manuscript.

| Place | Date | Hour | Summary of Events and Information | Remarks and references to Appendices |
|---|---|---|---|---|
| | OCT | | | |
| COUIN | 1 | | Bn in billets - Coy training - working parties | Appx |
| " | 2 | | " | |
| " | 3 | | " | Appx |
| " | 4 | | " | |
| " | 5 | | " | |
| " | 6 | | " | |
| " | 7 | | Bn outmarch ST LEGER - AUTHIE - LOUVENCOURT - BUS - ST LEGER | Appx |
| " | 8 | | - COUIN | Appx |
| " | 9 | | Coy training - working parties | Appx |
| " | 10 | | " " | Appx |
| | | | Church parade - Chateau grounds | Appx |
| HEBUTERNE | 11 | | Relieved 6/GLOSTERS in trenches 1.30 pm - B Coy 10/R Irish Rfls attached for instruction | Appx |
| " | 12 | | Bn in trenches. Quiet day - at 4 pm. our guns shelled enemys trenches and GOMMECOURT WOOD after we had fired for 10 minutes to draw enemy with rifle fire - 16 French aeroplanes went over towards ACHIET to drop bombs at 3.55 pm | Appx |

1577 Wt.W10791/1773 500,000 1/15 D.D. & L. A.D.S.S./Forms/C. 2118.

Army Form C. 2118.

# WAR DIARY
or
## INTELLIGENCE SUMMARY.
(Erase heading not required.)

BUCKS BATTN. OXF. & BUCKS LT. INFTY.

Instructions regarding War Diaries and Intelligence Summaries are contained in F.S. Regs., Part II. and the Staff Manual respectively. Title pages will be prepared in manuscript.

26

| Place | Date | Hour | Summary of Events and Information | Remarks and references to Appendices |
|---|---|---|---|---|
| HEBUTERNE | OCT 13 | | Bn in trenches - quiet day - Enemy Machine Guns traversed HEBUTERNE always harassing from inside GOMMECOURT WOOD, mostly firing high. | apps |
| " | 14 | | Quiet day - foggy until 7.30 am - | apps |
| " | 15 | | Fog lasted till 12 noon, found very hopeful for wiring parties in the morning. Germans doing the same, but we had to push our work before opening fire on them. Cy 10/R Irish Rifles completed their individual instruction at 5 pm. A & C Coy relieved D & B Coys. apps | |
| " | 16 | | Quiet day - B Coy 10/R.I.R. into trenches on completion Coy at 8.30 pm, taking over inner half of both Coy lines - | apps |
| " | 17 | | Quiet day 11 Coy 10/R.I.R. left trenches at 10 am | apps |
| " | 18 | | 2.30 pm enemy shelled in front of our right Coy and front trenches of BERKS and OXFORDS very heavily 5.9" & 8" for ½ – ¾ hour, also trench mortar field gun at into GOMMECOURT WOOD - No damage to us - | apps |
| | 19 | | Relieved by 6/GLOSTERS at 1 pm - Bn to billet COUIN | apps |

1577  Wt.W10791/1773  500,000  1/15  D. D. & L.   A.D.S.S./Forms/C. 2118.

# WAR DIARY
## or
## INTELLIGENCE SUMMARY.

*(Erase heading not required.)*

BUCKS BATTN. OXF. & BUCKS LT. INFTY.

Army Form C. 2118.

| Place | Date | Hour | Summary of Events and Information | Remarks and references to Appendices |
|---|---|---|---|---|
| COUIN | Oct 20 | | Bn in billets - | |
| | 21 | | " " Bn sending parties each march - working parties - | signed |
| | 22 | | " " | signed |
| | 23 | | " " | signed |
| | 24 | | " " | signed |
| | 25 | | " " | signed |
| | 26 | | " " | signed |
| HEBUTERNE | 27 | | Bn relieved 6/GLOSTERS at 12.30 p.m. A & B Coys in trenches C & D Support. B Coy 10/R Irwickells finishing communication trench for attack - 2 platoons to each A & B. Coy HQ to A Coy - rain when not B Coy - | signed |
| | 28 | | Bn in trenches - Quiet day - rain all day - | signed April |
| | 29 | | — Bombardment of enemy's trenches by our guns, field and 5.1 m Howitzer at 3.10 p.m. - little reply from enemy - several direct hits noticed by our guns | signed |
| | 30 | | — Quiet day - | signed |

Army Form C. 2118.

# WAR DIARY
## or
## INTELLIGENCE SUMMARY.

(Erase heading not required.)

BUCKS BATTN. OXF. & BUCKS LT. INF TY)

Instructions regarding War Diaries and Intelligence
Summaries are contained in F. S. Regs., Part II.
and the Staff Manual respectively. Title pages
will be prepared in manuscript.

| Place | Date | Hour | Summary of Events and Information | Remarks and references to Appendices |
|---|---|---|---|---|
| | Oct- | | | |
| HEBUTERNE | 31 | | Men in trenches - quiet day with shells & snipers bring afraid | |

A/Lt Col H H Cope R.N.D.
1/Bucks 15

145th Inf.Bde.
48th Div.

1st BUCKS. BATTN. THE OXFORD & BUCKS. LIGHT INF.

N O V E M B E R

1 9 1 5

# Army Form C. 2118.

## WAR DIARY
## or
## INTELLIGENCE SUMMARY.
*(Erase heading not required.)*

| Place | Date | Hour | Summary of Events and Information | Remarks and references to Appendices |
|---|---|---|---|---|
| HEBUTERNE | Nov 1 | | Bn in trenches. B Coy 10/ Inniskillings took over section of trench a Complete Coy. Very wet night. Trenches fell in in places. | |
| " | 2 | | B Coy 10/ Inniskillings left. Trenches 10.30 p.m. quiet day – wet day – All men very nearly Weather dry. | appx |
| " | 3 | | Very chilly – hot – many – no casualties. Trenches still slipping in bits. Kept clear with Coats now work – | appx |
| " | 4 | | Weather improved – Relieved by 6/G Glosters at 1 p.m. – Slight shelling by field guns during relief, one Slight Casualties. | appx |
| | | | Bn to billets in COUIN – | |
| COUIN | 5 | | Bn in billets | |
| " | 6 | | " " working parties – | appx |
| " | 7 | | " " " | appx |
| " | 8 | | " " " | appx |

Army Form C. 2118.

# WAR DIARY
## or
## INTELLIGENCE SUMMARY.
(Erase heading not required.)

| Place | Date | Hour | Summary of Events and Information | Remarks and references to Appendices |
|---|---|---|---|---|
| | Nov | | | |
| COUIN | 9 | | Bn in billets. Working parties. | RLh |
| " | 10 | | Route march. M°Kegan & Arthur Manchesters = Arthur Conner. Very wet | RLh |
| " | 11 | | Working Parties | RLh |
| " | 12 | | Returned 6 Gloucesters in Trenches - 130 p.m. - Trenches in bad state | RLh |
| " | 13 | | Bn in trenches working on collapsed trenches | RLh |
| " | 14 | | Quiet day. All men working party active | RLh |
| " | 15 | | — Our machine gun | RLh |
| " | 16 | | — Very misty. Our team used rifles on gun target | RLh |
| " | 17 | | — B coy R.I.R took over left sector from D coy. Display of new Red rockets by Germans in enemy trenches. | RLh |
| " | 17 | | — Considerable enemy artillery activity. Chiefly on own trenches | RLh |
| " | 18 | | — Several duds reported | RLh |
| " | 19 | | — Quiet day | RLh |
| " | 20 | | — Relieved by 8 Gloucesters in afternoon, at 1p.m. B coy R.I.R took over left sector. | RLh |

Army Form C. 2118.

# WAR DIARY
## or
## INTELLIGENCE SUMMARY.

(Erase heading not required.)

Instructions regarding War Diaries and Intelligence Summaries are contained in F. S. Regs., Part II. and the Staff Manual respectively. Title pages will be prepared in manuscript.

| Place | Date | Hour | Summary of Events and Information | Remarks and references to Appendices |
|---|---|---|---|---|
| COUIN | 21 | | Bn in billets - Church parade for 2 coys | R.L. |
| " | 22 | | " " - Working parties 2 coys | R.L. |
| " | 23 | | " " - Route march | R.L. |
| " | 24 | | " " - Working parties ST LEGER - BUS - COUIN | R.L. |
| " | 25 | | " " - Working parties 2 coys 475 men | R.L. |
| " | 26 | | " " 1 coy 75 men | R.L. |
| " | 27 | | " " 2 coys | R.L. |
| " | 28 | | Bn relieved 1/Gloucesters in trenches at 10.30am A.B & B coys in front line C & D coys in support.  B coy 20/Manchester arrived in evening for attachment to Bn - 2 platoons to each of A & B coys. (1 platoon in front line, 1 in KEEP) - | |
| | | | Coy H.Qrs to B coy | R.L. |
| " | 29 | | Bn in Trenches - Very quiet day. Rain in evening lasting till 3 am | R.L. |
| " | 30 | | " " Trenches in bad condition after rain - | Bn Hd |

R.L.W. Hd Ranks Batt

145th Inf.Bde.
48th Div.

### 1st BUCKS. BATTN. THE OXFORD & BUCKS. LIGHT INF.

### DECEMBER

### 1915

Army Form C. 2118.

# WAR DIARY
## or
## INTELLIGENCE SUMMARY.
(Erase heading not required.)

Instructions regarding War Diaries and Intelligence Summaries are contained in F.S. Regs, Part II. and the Staff Manual respectively. Title pages will be prepared in manuscript.

1 Bucks Batt

| Place | Date | Hour | Summary of Events and Information | Remarks and references to Appendices |
|---|---|---|---|---|
| HEBUTERNE | Dec 1 | | Bn in trenches. Quiet day. More rain. Trenches getting more in ruins. | RLh |
| " | 2 | | Good deal of shelling all morning on both sides. The Germans sent 4 explosive shells into the KEEP & many little hullus. | RLh |
| " | 3 | | Some shelling - more rain. | RLh |
| " | 4 | | Quiet day. 9/Lt Going took out 1 man on patrol to enemy's wire, getting useful information as to distance apart of sentries. | RLh |
| " | 5 | | 2/Manchesters left trenches. | RLh |
| " | 6 | | Relieved by 6/Gloucesters about 3 pm. | RLh |
| COUIN | 7 | | Bn in Billets. Coys at disposal of OC Coys. | RLh |
| " | 8 | | 2 Coys x 75 men working party. Coysfire. | RLh |
| " | 9 | | 2 Coys + half working parties | RLh |
| " | 10 | | Working parties cancelled. Very wet. | RLh |
| " | 11 | | More rain. Working parties started late. 2 cors x half | RLh |
| " | 12 | | Route March through Fonquevillers. | RLh |
| " | 13 | | 75 men working party. 2 Coys practised wire cutting. | RLh |
| " | 14 | | Relieved 6/Gloucesters in trenches. At Bcoy in front line | RLh |

1577 Wt. W10791/1773 500,000 1/15 D.D. & L. A.D.S.S./Forms/C. 2118.

Army Form C. 2118.

# WAR DIARY
## or
## INTELLIGENCE SUMMARY.
(Erase heading not required.)

Instructions regarding War Diaries and Intelligence Summaries are contained in F. S. Regs., Part II. and the Staff Manual respectively. Title pages will be prepared in manuscript.

1 Bn [Bucks Bn?]

| Place | Date | Hour | Summary of Events and Information | Remarks and references to Appendices |
|---|---|---|---|---|
| HEBUTERNE | 15 | | Bn in Trenches. 4/Royal Berks on our right & Warwicks on our left. Pretty quiet day. Enemy sent over 4 MINNENWERFER SHELLS close to BARM[?] | P/h. |
| " | 16 | | Patrols sent out during morning under cover of mist, brought in some German bombs found in what was believed to be a dummy post. MINNENWERFER very active in afternoon. Considerable damage to trenches. One casualty — shell shock | P/h. |
| " | 17 | | Own guns, field, heavy & howitzer bombarded enemy's trench at 1 pm. Observation difficult owing to mist. GERMAN MINNENWERFER put 5 torpedoes into our left coys trenches during day. | P/h. |
| " | 18 | | Weather thick - C. coy sent out patrol during morning under mist, there seen during night in front of front line. I casualty wounded. Very little artillery activity - B. coy sent out patrol on evening to Z Hedge & found it occupied & were fired on - no casualties | P/h. |
| " | 19 | | Very clear. Good deal of shelling by both sides - Aeroplanes active on both sides - Two air fights taking place, in which German planes driven back each time. | P/h. |
| " | 20 | | Two MINNIES fell in left coys lines. Very good reprisals on own part. | P/h. |

Army Form C. 2118.

1 Bucks Batt.

# WAR DIARY
## or
## INTELLIGENCE SUMMARY.
(Erase heading not required.)

| Place | Date | Hour | Summary of Events and Information | Remarks and references to Appendices |
|---|---|---|---|---|
| HEBUTERNE | — | | Patrol of 2 officers & 24 NCO's & men sent out to occupy 2 hedges under Capt Coombes. One MG Taken. | |
| " | — | | At 8 pm 3 parties of Germans were seen about 20 yards away. He opened fire with MG & rifle for 4 men were seen to fall. Germans retired. Casualties 1 Rfn & 1/1st Liverpools. | Rfn |
| " | 21 | | Own heavies & howitzers bombarded enemys works round CEMETERY in K3D at 2 pm - very Act. | |
| " | — | | Relieved by 6th Gloucesters about 2 pm. Bn marched to billets via Couturey path & JENA. | Rfn |
| Couin | 22 | | Bn in billets - | |
| " | 23 | | — Working parties | (T) (T) (T) (T) |
| " | 24 | | — Xmas day, no working parties | |
| " | 25 | | — 300 men working parties | |
| " | 26 | | — 300 men working parties | |
| " | 27 | | — | |
| HEBUTERNE | 28 | | moves to HEBUTERNE, took over trenches from 6th Gloucesters. Some "humming" at 2 pm | (T) (T) |
| " | 29 | | In trenches Artillery active on both sides. | (T) (T) |
| " | 30 | | — Artillery quick. 1 humming only at 2.30 pm. | |
| " | 31 | | — Bombardment by our guns between 12 & 1.30 pm including 20 rounds from 8.2 and 10 from 9.2 Howitzers. Enemy did fire for first time. | |

[signature] Lt Col
1/Bucks Bn

145th Brigade.

48th Division.

------

1st BUCKINGHAMSHIRE BATTALION

(Oxs & Bucks L.I.)

JANUARY 1 9 1 6

Army Form C. 2118.

# WAR DIARY
## INTELLIGENCE SUMMARY.

1/Bucks Battⁿ
Oxf & Bucks L.I. 2/147

(Erase heading not required.)

| Place | Date | Hour | Summary of Events and Information | Remarks and references to Appendices |
|---|---|---|---|---|
| HEBUTERNE | Jan 1ˢᵗ | | Bn in trenches. Artillery quiet. | P.L.N. |
| " | 2ⁿᵈ | | " " " | P.L.N. |
| " | 3ʳᵈ | | Relieved by 6ᵗʰ GLOSTERS. Back to billets in COUIN. | P.L.N. |
| COUIN | 4ᵗʰ | | Bn in billets. Coys at disposal of OC coys. | P.L.N. |
| " | 5ᵗʰ | | 2 Offrs & 200 men trenching parties | P.L.N. |
| " | 6ᵗʰ | | 5 " 250 " " | P.L.N. |
| " | 7 | | 6 " 300 " " | P.L.N. |
| " | 8 | | Coys at disposal of OC coys | P.L.N. |
| " | 9 | | Relieved 6/GLOSTERS in trenches. | P.L.N. |
| " | 10 | | Bn in trenches. Quiet day. A & B coys in trenches. | P.L.N. |
| " | 11 | | " " 4ᵗʰ Royal Berks on right. Lancashires on left | P.L.N. |
| " | 12 | | Intermittent shelling on both sides - no casualties | P.L.N. |
| " | 13 | | Quiet day | P.L.N. |
| " | " | | Artillery (Divl. Corps & Army Groups) bombarded German works from 10.30 am to 12.30 pm. No reply by enemy | P.L.N. |
| " | 14 | | Quiet day. | P.L.N. |
| " | 15 | | Relieved by 6/GLOSTERS. Back to billets in COUIN. | P.L.N. |

# WAR DIARY or INTELLIGENCE SUMMARY.

Army Form C. 2118.

(Erase heading not required.)

| Place | Date | Hour | Summary of Events and Information | Remarks and references to Appendices |
|---|---|---|---|---|
| COUIN | 16th | am | Batt in billets – Church parade. 30 men per Coy. | Ph. |
| " | 17 | " | Coys at disposal O.C. Coys for training | Ph. |
| " | 18 | " | — | Ph. |
| " | Jan 19th | 7 pm | Found 300 men for working parties. | Ph. |
| " | Jan 20th | 9 pm | Coys at disposal of O.C. Coys for training | E.W. |
| HÉBUTERNE | 21st | 10 p.m. | Battalion took over new Section of trenches relieving 1/7 WORCESTERS in 6 section viz. from K23 b23 to K17 c.2.4½. 2nd SEAFORTHS of 4th Division right, 5th GLOSTERS on left. Dispositions. 8 posts of 1 N.C.O. y 6 men in Front Line. 1 Platoon K23 a.2.2. – 1 Platoon K22 b.88. 2 Platoons y Coy Hd Qrs K22 b.03. K22 d.25 – 1 Section at K22 c.43. – 1 Section K22 b.21. 2 Platoons & Coy Hd Qrs K22 a 38. E.W. Battalion Hd Qrs K22 A 3.0. Remainder of Battalion in HÉBUTERNE Village. (Ref. TRENCH MAP Sheet 57D 3 and 4 (Parts of ). | |
| " | 22nd | 8 pm | Trenches very muddy. Right Company and front line of left Company relieved over land at night. | E.W. |
| " | 23rd | 9 pm | Quiet day. Machine Guns of enemy active after dusk. | E.W. |
| " | 24th | 10 pm | Situation normal. Work on clearing trenches progressed | E.W. |
| " | 25th | 10.30 pm | " " | Sutton Fusiliers relieved 2nd SEAFORTHS on our right. E.W. |
| " | 26th | 9 pm | " " | 2/Lt R.B. FURLEY killed. E.W. |

Army Form C. 2118.

# WAR DIARY
## or
## INTELLIGENCE SUMMARY.
(Erase heading not required.)

Instructions regarding War Diaries and Intelligence Summaries are contained in F. S. Regs., Part II. and the Staff Manual respectively. Title pages will be prepared in manuscript.

| Place | Date | Hour | Summary of Events and Information | Remarks and references to Appendices |
|---|---|---|---|---|
| COUIN | Jan. 27th | 10pm | Battalion relieved by 1/7th WORCESTERS in trenches. MAJOR L.C. HAWKINS assumed command at night vice LtCol. C.P. DOIG. D.S.O. injured by fall from horse on way back to billets. | EMW. |
| " | 28th | 9 p.m. | Battalion in billets. Companies at disposal of O.C. Companies. | EMW. |
| " | 29th | 8.30 p.m. | " " — Provided working parties of 300 men. | EMW. |
| " | 30th | 8.45 p.m. | " " — Companies at disposal of O.C. Companies | EMW. |
| " | 31st | 9 p.m. | " " — Provided working party of 100 men. | EMW. |

Le Knott
Major
Comdg 1/Bucks Battn

145th Brigade.

48th Division.

--------

1st BUCKINGHAMSHIRE BATTALION

(Oxs & Bucks L.I.)

FEBRUARY 1 9 1 6

Army Form C. 2118.

# WAR DIARY /Buckinghamshire Battn., Oxford & Bucks L.I./
## or
## INTELLIGENCE SUMMARY.
(Erase heading not required.)

| Place | Date | Hour | Summary of Events and Information | Remarks and references to Appendices |
|---|---|---|---|---|
| COUIN | Feb. 1st | 8 p.m. | Battalion in billets. Found working party of 100. Battalion Training for remainder. | E.W. |
| HÉBUTERNE | " 2nd | 9 p.m. | Took over trenches from 1/7th WORCESTERS. Front line trenches from R.23.b.2.3 to K.17.c.24. DUBLIN FUSILIERS on right. 1/5th GLOSTERS on left. (Ref. TRENCH MAP SHEET 57.D N.E. 3 and 4 (Parts of) 1st Ed'n) | E.W. |
| " | " 3rd | 8.30 p.m. | Battalion in trenches - Quiet day. Transport moved from COUIN to LOUVENCOURT. | E.W. |
| " | " 4th | 9.30 p.m. | " . Quiet day. | E.W. |
| " | " 5th | 8.30 p.m. | " . Rather more Artillery activity than usual | P.K.h. |
| " | " 6th | 9 p.m. | " . Quiet day | P.K.h. |
| " | " 7th | 7.30 p.m. | " . " | P.K.h. |
| " | " 8th | 8 p.m. | " . Enemy artillery v. active all day. Shooting has good. & many direct hits on our trenches being made. Between 10 A.M - 12 noon shells were coming into section at rate of 1 per 45 seconds. 3 casualties in R.E. working party. | P.K.h. |
| " | " 9th | 8.30 p.m. | " . Artillery activity on part of enemy continued. Shells falling again through out the day in this section. Shooting again good. Our reply v. feeble. | P.K.h. |
| " | " 10th | 8 p.m. | " . Enemy's artillery not so active as 2 previous days. Relieved by 1/5 VERRINGERY with 6 in & 8 in. - V. Good shooting - 10 casualties. 7 killed, 1 wounded, 2 shell shock. Killed. | P.K.h. |

CAPT. J.W. BACKHOUSE. A.D.S.S./Forms/C. 2118.

**Army Form C. 2118.**

# WAR DIARY
## or
## INTELLIGENCE SUMMARY.
*(Erase heading not required.)*

Instructions regarding War Diaries and Intelligence Summaries are contained in F. S. Regs., Part II. and the Staff Manual respectively. Title pages will be prepared in manuscript.

| Place | Date | Hour | Summary of Events and Information | Remarks and references to Appendices |
|---|---|---|---|---|
| HEBUTERNE | Feb 11th | 7.20pm | Battalion in trenches. Enemy artillery much the same as yesterday. Wet. | RLh |
| " | 12th | 8 pm | Rather less shelling by enemy. | RLh |
| " | 13th | 7.45pm | As yesterday | RLh |
| " | 14th | 10 pm | Bombardment of enemy's trenches & banks by our guns in morning. Change in dispositions. 2 Coys of 5/GLOSTERS took over front line this evening. OC Bucks in command till tomorrow when we move to divisional reserve in COURCELLES or SAILLY. | RLh |
| " | 15th | 10 pm | Battalion in Billets. 2 Coys (C+D) in SAILLY - 2 Coys (A+B) in COURCELLES. HQ COURCELLES. | RLh RLh |
| COURCELLES | 16th | 7.30pm | All Coys resting. | RLh |
| " | 17th | 7 pm | — | RLh |
| " | 18th | 8 am | — | RLh |
| " | 19 | 6 am | Relieved 5/GLOSTERS in G section. Scouts in front line. A.B.C. Coys in reserve. A+B coys in fire B days. B+D relieve in the night every 24 hours. | RLh |
| | | | At 6pm enemy opened heavy bombardment on trenches about 400 yards to our right in 12th Bde lines. Lasted about half an hour. All quiet after 8 pm. | RLh |
| HEBUTERNE | 20 | 7 pm | Bn in Trenches. Quiet day. Our aeroplanes v. active. v. little hostile shelling. | RLh |

Army Form C. 2118.

# WAR DIARY
## or
## INTELLIGENCE SUMMARY.

(Erase heading not required.)

Instructions regarding War Diaries and Intelligence Summaries are contained in F. S. Regs., Part II. and the Staff Manual respectively. Title pages will be prepared in manuscript.

| Place | Date | Hour | Summary of Events and Information | Remarks and references to Appendices |
|---|---|---|---|---|
| HEBUTERNE | 21st | 8 pm | Bn in Trenches. Quiet day. | Plh. |
| " | 22nd | 9 pm | do — Our artillery bombarded GOMMECOURT at 11.30pm | Plh. |
| " | 23rd | 9 pm | do | Plh. |
| " | 24th | 10 pm | do Heavy fall of snow. | Plh. |
| " | 25th | 9 pm | do | Plh. |
| " | 26th | 4 pm | do. Knee deep. Trenches wet. | Plh. |
| " | 27 | 10 pm | Relieved by 4/Royal Berks. A & B coys moved to SAILLY & C & D coys to COURCELLES — B Last coy (D) arrived in billets 10 pm | Plh. Plh. |
| COURCELLES | 28 | 9 am | All coys resting | Plh. |
| " | 29 | — | do | Plh. |

On Service
1-3-16.

Lieutenant Major,
Comdg. 1/ ...... Battalion.

145th Brigade.

48th Division.

----------------

1st BUCKINGHAMSHIRE BATTALION

(Oxf. & Bucks. L.I.)

MARCH 1916

# WAR DIARY or INTELLIGENCE SUMMARY.

Army Form C. 2118.

1/Bucks Battn, Oxford & Bucks L.I.

| Place | Date | Hour | Summary of Events and Information | Remarks and references to Appendices |
|---|---|---|---|---|
| COURCELLES | March 1st | | Battalion in billets. All coys resting. | P/h |
| | 2nd | | Relieved 5th Glosters in trenches. Relief complete by noon. 4 Oxfords on left, 4th Royal Berks on right. | |
| | | | Trenches in bad condition owing to rain & frost. A, B & C Coys in front line. | P/h |
| HEBUTERNE | 3rd | | Bn in trenches. Reliefs in rotation from the right. | P/h |
| do | 4th | | Quiet day. Some snow – very cold. | P/h |
| do | 5th | | " | P/h |
| do | 6th | | Enemy artillery slightly active, but no damages done. | P/h |
| do | 7th | | Quiet day | P/h |
| do | | | do – Capt Combs took out patrol of 2/Lt & Co's & men to 16 | |
| | | | POPLARS after dark. Bombed enemy, who were found working in CHEMIN CREUX. Germans suffered at least 12 casualties. Our casualties 3 very slightly wounded. All at duty. [names list] | P/h |
| do | 8th | | Quiet day. | P/h |
| do | 9th | | do | |
| do | 10th | | Relieved by 4/Royal Berks. Relief complete by noon. Bn in billets in SAILLY. | P/h |

# WAR DIARY
## or
## INTELLIGENCE SUMMARY.

Army Form C. 2118.

(Erase heading not required.)

| Place | Date | Hour | Summary of Events and Information | Remarks and references to Appendices |
|---|---|---|---|---|
| SAILLY | Mch 11th | | Bn in billets. All Cos resting | PLh |
| do | " 12th | | do | PLh |
| do | " 13th | | do | PLh |
| do | " 14th | | Relieved 5/GLOSTERS in "G" Sections 4th Royal BERKS on left. 4/GLOSTERS on right | PLh |
| | | | Enemy Trench Artillery rather more active | PLh |
| AFDUTERNE AT K17/5 – K25/6 | " 15th | | Bn in trenches. Artillery rather active on both sides. | PLh |
| do | " 16th | | " " Quiet day. | PLh |
| do | " 17th | | " " do | PLh |
| do | " 18th | | " " do | PLh |
| do | " 19th | | 6.0.42 AM Enemy opened a violent bombardment of our right Coys Trenches & left Batt 3/144 Bde. The bombardment continued till 7.30 AM. Trenches suffered most – DOMINIQUE – CLISSOLD & FT K23/7. Gas was distinctly smelt at 3 am. This developed into quite a cloud. Colour white & smelt strong acidic. No attack developed though our Artillery & machine guns fire. At 4 pm all was quiet. Our casualties 13. All wounded. Snipers & coy. | PLh |
| do | " 20th | | Artillery a little more active than usual on both sides. | PLh |

Page 3.

**WAR DIARY**
or
**INTELLIGENCE SUMMARY.**

Army Form C. 2118.

(Erase heading not required.)

Instructions regarding War Diaries and Intelligence Summaries are contained in F. S. Regs., Part II. and the Staff Manual respectively. Title pages will be prepared in manuscript.

| Place | Date | Hour | Summary of Events and Information | Remarks and references to Appendices |
|---|---|---|---|---|
| HEBUTERNE FT K17/5 – K23/6 | Oct 20th | | Bn in trenches. Quiet day. | RLb. |
| do | " 22nd | | Relieved by 1/4 Royal Berks. Batt in billets in SAILLY. A good deal of artillery activity during night. 5/Glosters from J section & marines from left Bde attempting raids on enemy trenches. Enemy wire being found too strong. | RLb. |
| SAILLY | " 23rd | | Bn in billets. All boys resting. | RLb. |
| | " 24th | | do | RLb. |
| | " 25th | | do | RLb. |
| | " 26th | | Relieved 5/Gloster Regt in J section – 4/Oxfords on left – 4/R Berks on right | RLb. |
| | " 27th | | Bn in trenches. Quiet day. 4 officers Rt Msgr inspected 13th York & Lancs Regt attached to Batt. 30th RLb. Final Fanshawe Cup. Result 7/Worcesters 2 pts Bucks n/a RLb. Inspections by CO. | RLb. |
| HEBUTERNE FT N16/1 | " 28th | | – Rather more shelling in morning. 8 casualties in FT 10/4 from a S.9 shell. 3 killed 5 wounded. | RLb. |
| | " 29th | | Artillery quiet on both sides. Machine gun active. | RLb. |
| | " 30th | | do | RLb. |
| | " 31st | | do | RLb. |

L. Hawes
Comdg 1/Bucks Major
1/4/16

145th Brigade.

48th Division.

------

1st BUCKINGHAMSHIRE BATTALION

(Oxf. & Bucks. L.I.)

APRIL 1916

Army Form C. 2118.

# WAR DIARY
## or
## INTELLIGENCE SUMMARY.
(Erase heading not required.)

Instructions regarding War Diaries and Intelligence Summaries are contained in F. S. Regs., Part II. and the Staff Manual respectively. Title pages will be prepared in manuscript.

| Place | Date | Hour | Summary of Events and Information | Remarks and references to Appendices |
|---|---|---|---|---|
| HEBUTERNE | April 1st | | Bn in trenches. J section - 1/4 OXFORDS on k/r - 1/5 GLOSTER REGT on right. A patrol under CAPT COMBS went out at 8 p.m., & the following are extracts from the 3rd Corps Summaries. Dated 3rd April. "A patrol of 2 officers & 25 O.R. advanced during the night of 1/2nd April in the direction of 16 POPLARS, with the intention of intercepting or capturing an enemy patrol. The enemy apparently becoming early aware of this patrol sent out a strong party of 50 men to oppose them. Our patrol after putting up a good fight, retired safely behind our lines. Our casualties were 4 killed & 2 wounded all of which were brought in. Casualties to the enemy are unknown, though a few of the bomber's rifle grenades must have seen to burst well amongst them." Dated 4th April "with reference to the Patrol report in yesterday's summary, attention is drawn to the fact that the enemy were robbed of any possible identification by the calmness & resource shown by the patrol in getting back the killed & wounded to our own trenches. The behaviour of all ranks was excellent. Although it is difficult to distinguish one man's services from another, Sergt L.J. BALDWIN, Lce Corpl GOLDSWAIN and Lce Corpl JENNINGS are deserving of special notice. Although Sergt BALDWIN was wounded, not only did he assist in carrying back one of the dead men, but came | |

# WAR DIARY or INTELLIGENCE SUMMARY.

Army Form C. 2118.

(Erase heading not required.)

| Place | Date | Hour | Summary of Events and Information | Remarks and references to Appendices |
|---|---|---|---|---|
| HEBUTERNE | April | 1st | "back again to assist the covering party when the enemy were almost on top of them." "During the first arrival of the grenades which were thrown amongst the enemy caused considerable havoc, loud cries & groans were heard." The GOC 48th Div & the GOC 145 Bde. congratulated the Battalion on the work of this patrol. | P.L.h. |
| do | " | 2nd | Bn relieved by 1/5 GLOSTERS, who took over from FT K9/1/5 to FT K10/3 & by 4 OXFORDS who took over from FT K10/3 to FT K4/1 (both incl). Battalion marched to billets in BAYENCOURT, reaching there about 1.30 p.m | P.L.h. |
| BAYENCOURT | " | 3rd | Bn in billets. All coys resting. | P.L.h. |
| do | " | 4th | —— Coys training under coy arrangements. | P.L.h. |
| do | " | 5th | —— Inspection by CO of last two drafts. | P.L.h. |
| do | " | 6th | —— Battalion parade. CO congratulated men on patrol work | P.L.h. |
| do | " | 7th | —— Coy training. | P.L.h. |
| do | " | 8th | Relieved 4/OXFORDS in K SECTION, taking over FT K9/1 to FT K10/3 (incl). Relief complete by 11am. Detachmt 5/SUSSEX on left, 6/ROYAL BERKS on right. | P.L.h. |
| HEBUTERNE | " | 9th | Bn in trenches. Quiet day. Enemy artillery & machine guns active during day. A covering party & consolidation party N/a large digging party remained out all night while an advanced tunnel in front of J section was dug. This was successfully carried out. Bn's casualties 1 Pte/4 OR | P.L.h. |

1577   Wt. W10791/1773   500,000   1/15   D. D. & L.   A.D.S.S./Forms/C. 2118.

# WAR DIARY or INTELLIGENCE SUMMARY

Army Form C. 2118.

Instructions regarding War Diaries and Intelligence Summaries are contained in F. S. Regs., Part II. and the Staff Manual respectively. Title pages will be prepared in manuscript.

(Erase heading not required.)

| Place | Date | Hour | Summary of Events and Information | Remarks and references to Appendices |
|---|---|---|---|---|
| HEBUTERNE | April 10th | | Bn. in Trenches - Enemy artillery fairly active - Twenty drops fired on our right - shelled heavily in evening, but no damage done owing to bad shooting. | R.J.h. |
| do | " 11th | | Quiet day. | R.J.h. |
| do | " 12th | | do | R.J.h. |
| | | | Enemy minenwerfer very active on our left - trenches during evening. | |
| do | " 13th | | Relieved the company of 3/ROYAL SUSSEX on our left - Just before relief commenced at 6.30 p.m., enemy opened with minenwerfer on those trenches. Good shooting. Good deal of damage done to trenches. Sussex had about 6 casualties. | R.J.h. |
| do | " 14th | | Quiet day. Enemy bombarded new trench at 11.30 p.m. & again at 12.30 A.M. | |
| | | | 2.30 A.M. - 3/GLOSTERS who had taken over from 4/R. BERKS had severalcasualties. | R.J.h. |
| do | " 15th | | Minenwerfer very active on our left-trenches about 6.30 p.m. Some damage done to trenches. 1 casualty. | |
| | | | The following rewards for gallantry in the field were awarded by the Commander-in-Chief. CAPT. H.V. COMBS - Military Cross. No. 18155 Sgt. BALDWIN W.J. - D.C.M. No. 2582 L/Cpl P. JENNINGS - Military Medal. No. 2217 L/Cpl T.W. VINCENT - Military Medal. | R.J.h. |

# WAR DIARY
## or
## INTELLIGENCE SUMMARY

Army Form C. 2118

(Erase heading not required.)

| Place | Date | Hour | Summary of Events and Information | Remarks and references to Appendices |
|---|---|---|---|---|
| HEBUTERNE | April | 16th | Relieved by 1/4 OXFORDS. Relief complete by 11 A.M. Batt in billets in BAYENCOURT by 1.30 pm. | P.L.h. |
| BAYENCOURT | " | 17th | Bn in billets. All coys resting. | P.L.h. |
| do | " | 18th | Training postponed owing to v. bad weather. Lectures etc. | P.L.h. |
| do | " | 19th | Very wet again. Lectures etc. | P.L.h. |
| do | " | 20th | Coy training. | P.L.h. |
| do | " | 21st | Relieved 7th WORCESTERS in G section. R17C33 to K23D34. 4th Royal BERKS on left, 1/5th WEST YORKS on right. Trenches on right in bad condition. Three coys in front line. | P.L.h. |
| HEBUTERNE | " | 22nd | Bn in trenches. 1 post of right coy (B) bombed by enemy just before daylight. Several bombs fell among post causing us 6 casualties. Post being isolated, impossible to withdraw casualties before dark & then with difficulty. 2 killed, 3 wounded. Some shelling on both sides during night. | P.L.h. |
| do | " | 23rd | Great difficulty in getting killed & wounded down to Dressing Station, on account of distance to bring stretchers. Quiet day, one casualty in C coy | P.L.h. |
| do | " | 24th | Artillery active on both sides. | P.L.h. |
| do | " | 25th | Relieved by 7th WORCESTERS in evening. Batt in billets in COIGNEUX by 12.30 pm. | P.L.h. |

# WAR DIARY or INTELLIGENCE SUMMARY

Army Form C. 2118

| Place | Date | Hour | Summary of Events and Information | Remarks and references to Appendices |
|---|---|---|---|---|
| COIGNEUX | April 26th | | Battn in Billets - All Coys resting. | P/b |
| do | 27th | | Coys training. | P/b |
| do | 28th | | Battn doing field work, with 4/Royal Berks, under Brigade. | P/b |
| do | 29th | | Coy training. Musketry, rapid turning etc Batts. | P/b |
| do | 30th | | Battn paraded for Church at Doctype. Coy in at 10.30am | P/b |

Li Rason Lt Col
Comdg 1/Bucks Battn

145th Brigade.

48th Division.

-----

1st BUCKINGHAMSHIRE BATTALION

(Oxf. & Bucks L.I.)

M A Y   1 9 1 6.

# WAR DIARY or INTELLIGENCE SUMMARY

**Army Form C. 2118**

1/Bucks BATTN.

| Place | Date | Hour | Summary of Events and Information | Remarks and references to Appendices |
|---|---|---|---|---|
| COIGNEUX | May | 1st | Battn in billets. – Regtl tour under BDE. CO, 2nd in command, Adjutant, all Coy commanders, debris line officer attended. Rendezvous S.7965 at 10 a.m. Orders received in evening to take over line. | R.L.h. |
| " | do | 2nd | " " " | R.L.h. |
| HEBUTERNE | do | 3rd | Relieved 5/GLOSTERS in K section. Relief complete by 12.30 p.m – 5/4GLOSTERS on right, 4/WARWICKS on left. Manoeuvres for actions during afternoon. No damage. | R.L.h. |
| " | do | 4th | Battn in trenches. Enemy artillery active during day. | R.L.h. |
| " | do | " | 1 German pte gave himself up at 3.45 a.m, surrendering in PT K10/9. Identity disc marked as follows. BRUNO BARBE. ISERNHAGEN HANNOVER. 13.3.95. ERS-BATL 2. GARDE RES R. 5K NR 1108. | |
| COIGNEUX | do | 5th | Relieved by 3rd Londons & 8th MIDDLESEX in evening. Reached billets in COIGNEUX 10.30 p.m | R.L.h. |
| " | do | 6th | Battalion in billets. – Coys resting & firing, grouping practice | R.L.h. |
| " | do | 7th | " – Companies training | R.L.h. |
| " | do | 8th | " – " " | R.L.h. |
| " | do | 9th | " – Abt 450 men on tactical practice. Chiefly touring cables. | R.L.h. |
| " | do | 10th | " – " " " | R.L.h. |
| " | do | " | " – Relieved 5/GLOSTERS in H section. – Trenches FT K11/9 to FT K17/2 both inclusive. Relief complete by 10.30 p.m – 1st LONDONS on left; 4/ROYAL BERKS on right; A.T.C coys in trout line. B in support billets. D in reserve in SAILLY. | R.L.h. |
| HEBUTERNE | do | 11th | Battalion in Trenches. – Quiet day. | R.L.h. |

# WAR DIARY
## or
## INTELLIGENCE SUMMARY

(Erase heading not required.)

Army Form C. 2118

1/Bucks Batth.

| Place | Date | Hour | Summary of Events and Information | Remarks and references to Appendices |
|---|---|---|---|---|
| HEBUTERNE | May | 12" | Bn in Trenches. Quiet day. Considerable amount of shelling during evening, causing us 4 casualties. Chiefly directed on west trench, dug-outs, mouth. | P.h. |
| do | " | 13" | Enemy's artillery very active all day. Many 5.9's fell on trenches on our left, occupied by 4th LONDONS. Coy relief. | P.h. |
| do | " | 14" | Enemy artillery active. | — |
| do | " | 15" | Quiet day. At 12.30 Am the night 15/16" enemy opened heavy bombardment of our trenches, & trenches of Batts on our right & left. Bombardment lasted till 1.30 Am, when it died down considerably. No enemy entered our trenches. All quiet by 2.30 AM. Our casualties 1 killed, 14 wounded. | P.h. |
| do | " | 16" | Bn relieved by 8th GLOSTER BATT. Marched to bivouacs at COUIN, arriving about 7.30 pm | P.h. P.h. |
| COUIN | " | 17" | Bn in bivouacs. All Coys resting. | P.h. |
| do | " | 18" | Battn paraded at 7.30 Am for march to billets in BEAUVAL. Very hot march. 27 or fell out. Marched as a bde. Reached BEAUVAL about 11 AM. Billets fair. | P.h. |

Lt Knowns v/Col

# WAR DIARY
## or
## INTELLIGENCE SUMMARY
(Erase heading not required.)

1/BUCKS BATTN.    Army Form C. 2118

Instructions regarding War Diaries and Intelligence Summaries are contained in F. S. Regs., Part II. and the Staff Manual respectively. Title Pages will be prepared in manuscript.

| Place | Date | Hour | Summary of Events and Information | Remarks and references to Appendices |
|---|---|---|---|---|
| BEAUVAL | 19th May | | Battn in billets. All hours resting | R.H.W. |
| do | 20th | " | Coy training. Baths at GEZAINCOURT. New shortcuttees issued | R.H.W. |
| do | 21st | " | do    do | R.H.W. |
| do | 22nd | " | do    do | R.H.W. |
| do | 23rd | " | do    do | R.H.W. |
| do | 24th | " | do. Musketry & Drill | R.H.W. |
| | | | Battn Route march - moved off 7am - Returned 10am | |
| | | | Route - x roads in M9a - M9d - BEAUQUESNE - (Pt 101 | |
| | | | H23c) - Pt 91, G16 b d. | R.H.W. |
| do | 25th | " | Coy training. Musketry & drill | |
| do | 26th | " | do | I.C.H. |
| do | 27th | " | Bde Route march - moved off 7am. Returned 11am. | |
| | | | Route - CANDAS - MONTRELET - BONNEVILLE - VALERCUX | |
| do | 28th | " | Bde Church Parade at 10am. | I.C.H. |
| do | 29th | " | Coy training - musketry. Instruction Trench mortar demolition | I.C.H. |
| | | | by 145/1 & 145/2. T.M. Battn'lo | I.C.H. |

Ker Hearty Lt Col

# WAR DIARY
## or
## INTELLIGENCE SUMMARY

*(Erase heading not required.)*

1/BUCKS BATTN. Army Form C. 2118

| Place | Date | Hour | Summary of Events and Information | Remarks and references to Appendices |
|---|---|---|---|---|
| BEAUVAL | MAY 30 | | Battn in billets. Coy training, musketry. | WSA |
| " | 31 | | Bde marched to ST RIQUIER training area. Bucks Bn billeted in NEUVILLE. Route - CANDAS - FIENVILLERS - BAUMETZ - COULONVILLERS - about 18 miles - three men fell out, one being through injury. Lieut—— | WSA |

145th Brigade.
48th Division.

------

1st BUCKINGHAMSHIRE BATTALION

(Oxf.& Bucks.L.I.)

JUNE 1916

Army Form C. 2118

# WAR DIARY /Bucks Batt<br>Oxf & Bks. Light Infty<br>INTELLIGENCE SUMMARY

(Erase heading not required.)

Instructions regarding War Diaries and Intelligence Summaries are contained in F.S. Regs., Part II. and the Staff Manual respectively. Title Pages will be prepared in manuscript.

| Place | Date | Hour | Summary of Events and Information | Remarks and references to Appendices |
|---|---|---|---|---|
| NEUVILLE | JUNE 1. | | Batn in billets – marched to ONEUX + on to training area. Bn exercised in attack under supervision of the Brigadier. – | W38. |
| " | 2. | | Batn in billets – March to ST RIQUIER for field training – finished close to MILLENCOURT. Lieut Col L.C. HAWKINS damaged his shoulder owing to a fall from his horse. MAJOR L.L.C. REYNOLDS assumed command | W39. |
| " | 3. | | Batn in billets. March across country to YVRENCH for field training. | W39. |
| AGENVILLERS | 4. | | Batn marched to AGENVILLERS. | W39. |
| " | 5. | | Field training under supervision of the Brigadier with the 1/4 OXFORD & BUCKS L.I. | W39. |
| " | 6. | | Brigade night operations. Finished with an attack on BOIS GRAMBUS close to YVRENCH. | do |
| " | 7. | | Batn resting. | PKW |
| " | 8. | | Field training 14.5th 9/144th Brigades under supervision of General FANSHAWE. | PKW |
| " | 9. | | Attack practice do do | PKW |
| | | | Started from PENDANT COPSE just N. B. ONEUX + attacked the high ground between AGENVILLERS + GAPENNES. | PKW |
| OCCOCHES. | 10. | | The Brigade marched eastwards thro AUXI-LE-CHATEAU + FROHEN LE GRAND – distance 20 miles – | PKW |
| COUIN | 11. | | The Bucks Bn was billeted in OCCOCHES. The Brigade continued its eastward march assembling at OCCOCHES + passing HEM DOULLENS – ORVILLE – THIEVRES – AUTHIE – Bucks Bn in halts at COUIN distance about 15 miles – | PKW |
| SAILLY | 12. | | Bucks Bn moved to bivouacs close to the DEER West of SAILLY. Employed on working parties – | PKW |

16.8<br>3 sheet

# WAR DIARY or INTELLIGENCE SUMMARY

Army Form C. 2118

| Place | Date | Hour | Summary of Events and Information | Remarks and references to Appendices |
|---|---|---|---|---|
| SAILLY | JUNE 13. | | Batt in bivouacs - day the Batt. working by day & half by night. | R/w |
| " | 14. | | do. | R/w |
| " | 15. | | do. | R/w |
| HEBUTERNE | 16. | | Batt. relieved the 1/4 OXFORD & BUCKS L.I. in Trenches - G section - 1/4 Royal Berks on left. 12p. YORK & LANCS on right. A party of B coy. being posted by 2/Lieut Rollestone to cover a training party in front of K23/2, was met by enemy patrol with Bombs & rifle shots, were exchanged in which encounter we had 1 officer & 3 men wounded & 1 missing. | R/w |
| " | 17 | | Batt. in trenches. Quiet day. Great aeroplane activity on both sides. Large parties at work on our trenches throughout day & night. | R/w |
| " | 18 | | Quiet day. Aeroplanes again active. | R/w |
| " | 19 | | Enemy artillery fairly active. 2 casualties. | R/w |
| " | 20 | | Quiet day. | R/w |
| " | 21. | | Some shelling on both sides during day. | R/w |
| COUIN | 22 | | Batt relieved in trenches by 1/5 Royal WARWICKS. moved to huts in COUIN PARK. | R/w |
| " | 23. | | do. | |
| " | 24. | " | ⎫ | |
| " | 25. | " | ⎬ Companies engaged in musketry, bayonet fighting & bombing practice. | |
| " | 26. | " | ⎭ | R/w |

Army Form C. 2118.

# WAR DIARY
## or
## INTELLIGENCE SUMMARY
*(Erase heading not required.)*

Instructions regarding War Diaries and Intelligence Summaries are contained in F. S. Regs., Part II. and the Staff Manual respectively. Title Pages will be prepared in manuscript.

| Place | Date JUNE | Hour | Summary of Events and Information | Remarks and references to Appendices |
|---|---|---|---|---|
| COVIN | 27 | | Batln in trenches | |
| " | 28 | | ⎫ | |
| " | 29 | | ⎬ Coys engaged in musketry, bombing practice, wire breaking, bayonet fighting, manoeuvres etc | Photos. |
| " | 30 | | ⎭ | |
| | On Service 30/6/16 | | | L. F. C. Reynolds Major Comdg 1/ Roscho Fusrs. |

2449 Wt. W14957/M90 750,000 1/16 J.B.C. & A. Forms/C.2118/12.

145th Inf.Bde.
48th Div.

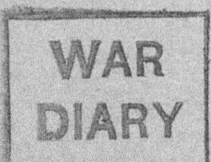

1st BUCKINGHAM BATTN. (THE OXFORDSHIRE &
BUCKINGHAMSHIRE LIGHT INFANTRY).

J U L Y

1 9 1 6

Attached:

Brigade O.Os. Nos.
100 & 101.

From: Officer Commanding
      1/ BUCKS BATTALION.

To:   Headquarters,
      145TH INFANTRY BRIGADE.
------------------------------------------------

     Herewith War Diary for the month of July, 1916.
Please acknowledge receipt.

                                    *V.L.C Reynolds*
                                    Lieut. Colonel,
                              Comdg. 1/ BUCKS BATTALION.
31/7/16.

# WAR DIARY
## or
## INTELLIGENCE SUMMARY

*(Erase heading not required.)*

1st BUCKS BATTN.

| Place | Date | Hour | Summary of Events and Information | Remarks and references to Appendices |
|---|---|---|---|---|
| | JULY | | | |
| COUIN. | 1. | 9am | 145th Infantry Brigade marched to MAILLY-MAILLET (via BERTRAN COURT & BEAUSSART) - bivouaced in plantations to the South West of this place. The 145th & 144th Inf. Bdes | 1/3/4 |
| MAILLY-MAILLET | 2. | | remained there all the day in Corps Reserve during the VIII Corps offensive. Batn.in bivouacs - Bucks Battn remained here in divisional Reserve to a proposed offensive of the 8th, 144th & 145th Inf. Bdes on July 3rd - such offensive was subsequently cancelled owing to a change in the situation. | 2/3/4 |
| MAILLY-MAILLET | 3. | | Batn in bivouacs. At 6 p.m. the 145th Inf Bde left MAILLY MAILLET - Bucks BATTN marched to huts in COUIN CHATEAU Park. | 3/3/4 |
| COUIN. | 4. | | Batn in huts. Companies engaged in bayonet fighting. | 4/3/4 |
| COUIN. | 5. | | Batn in huts - At 10.15 am Bucks Battn marched to bivouacs between COIGNEUX and SAILLY AU BOIS. | 5/3/4 |
| COIGNEUX. | 6. | | Batn in bivouacs - Company training. | 6/3/4 |
| do. | 7. | | do. | 7/3/4 |
| HEBUTERNE | 8. | | Bucks BATTN relieved 1/4 OXF & BUCKS L.I. in Q section - 1/4th R BERKS on left, 1/4th GLOUCESTERS on right. | 8/3/4 |
| do. | 9. | | Batn in trenches. Trenches very wet + in many places flooded owing to continuous heavy - hostile artillery quiet. | 9/3/4 |
| do. | 10. | | Batn in trenches - B on 14 O drained - a new trench connecting the supports in front of H section with the 1st barricade on the HEBUTERNE - SERRE road was dug ; 'A' Coy | 10/3/4 |

# WAR DIARY
## INTELLIGENCE SUMMARY

1st BUCKS BATT'N

(Erase heading not required.)

Instructions regarding War Diaries and Intelligence Summaries are contained in F. S. Regs, Part II. and the Staff Manual respectively. Title Pages will be prepared in manuscript.

| Place | Date | Hour | Summary of Events and Information | Remarks and references to Appendices |
|---|---|---|---|---|
| | JULY. | | | |
| HEAUTERNE | 11. | | 1st BUCKS BN provided a covering party of 2 platoons. | |
| | | | Batt'n in trenches. A quiet day. On endeavour was made to put out a wire in front of the new trench dug the previous evening; 'B' Coy 1st BUCKS BN provided a covering party of 2 platoons. Work was hindered by hostile machine gun fire. | J.A.M. |
| HEAUTERNE | 12. | | Batt'n in trenches. The Batt'n was relieved early in the morning by 1/4 OXFORD & BUCKS L.I. — moved to bivouacs close to the BUS — BAYENCOURT & SAILLY — COIGNEUX cross roads. | J.A.M. |
| COIGNEUX. | 13. | | Batt'n in bivouacs. Company training — The bivouacs were shelled during the night — were temporarily vacated. | J.A.M. |
| COIGNEUX | 14. | | Batt'n in bivouacs. Bivouacs handed over to the 11th Bn MIDDLESEX REGT & the 1/4 ....'s BN moved in motor lorries to BUZINCOURT, marching thence to billets at SENLIS. | J.A.M. |
| SENLIS. | 15. | | Batt'n in billets. | J.A.M. |
| SENLIS. | 16. | | do | |
| SENLIS | 17. | | do . At 7pm the Bn marched through ALBERT. | |
| | 18. | | Bn in W.30. A South of the ALBERT – BAPAUME road. A reconnaissance in force of 6 points in the enemy front line was carried out. Batt'n HQ were established at X.9.D.5b,72. A & D Companies, under the command of CAPT. E.V. BIRCHALL, carried out the operation + attacked in the sickel shaped trench running through X.9.B — X.3.D.C. B+C Companies supplied carrying parties. At 1a.m. 18th inst. our platoons 2 of 'A', B, C, B.& R19D5p left our trenches + attacked point X.3.D.9.7 + secured this objective at 2a.m., barricades were at once erected + the party commenced consolidating | OVILLERS 57.D.S.E.4 Scales 2.B. 1/10,000 — The map is attached as Appendix called "A.A.A" |

2449  Wt. W14957/Mgo 750,000 1/16  J.B.C. & A.  Forms/C.2118/12.

# INTELLIGENCE SUMMARY

1st BUCKS BATTN.

Instructions regarding War Diaries and Intelligence Summaries are contained in F.S. Regs., Part II. and the Staff Manual respectively. Title Pages will be prepared in manuscript.

(Erase heading not required.)

| Place | Date | Hour | Summary of Events and Information | Remarks and references to Appendices |
|---|---|---|---|---|
| | JULY. 18 (cont). | | Repeated enemy bombing attacks were driven off — The party was withdrawn owing to the other enterprises failing. On the 25th July 2nd Lt. R.C. RIGDEN was awaited an immediate grant of the Military Cross for his good work on this occasion. 2nd Lt. C. HALL and one platoon attacking from X.3.B.I.X were held up by machine gun fire & were ordered to withdraw. He was wounded severely in the head whilst bringing in casualties. 2nd Lt. R.C. NORWOOD with one platoon attacked from X.3.c.7.9 & was also held up by machine gun fire & was forced to halt. The Sergeant in charge was ordered to retire & a further attack was made for 2nd Lt. R.C. NORWOOD. As a result of the reconnaissance the position & strength of the German dispositions in this neighbourhood was established & the Battn. received the congratulations of the G.O.C. 48th Division. The Battn marched to billets in BOUZINCOURT about 3. a.m. | Casualties O.R. Killed 2 Wounded 34 Missing 18. WDA WDA |
| BOUZINCOURT. | | | The Battn. in billets — One Coy of the Battn. relieved 1 Coy. 1/5th R.WARWICKS. During the night 18/19 July 2nd Lt. R.E.M. YOUNG took out a patrol of 1 Sergeant & 12 men of B Coy. to reconnoitre the German wire on the Western Edge of POZIERES/low KP. | WDA |
| BOUZINCOURT | 19. | | ALBERT — BAPAUME road in a northerly direction. The Battn in billets — At 5 p.m. the Battn. relieved 1/4th R. ALBERT + GOR over (initials) in W. 30.a. from the 1/5th R. WARWICKS. | Appx 'A' WDA |

# INTELLIGENCE SUMMARY

## 1ST BUCKS BATTN.

| Place | Date | Hour | Summary of Events and Information | Remarks and references to Appendices |
|---|---|---|---|---|
| ALBERT | JULY 20. | | Further orders. During the night 20/21 July, the attack on the German front line in X.3. was resumed by the 48th Division. The objective of the Bucks Bn was points X.3.B.11 & points X.3.D.28 & trenches adjoining these points — the 1/5 GLOUCESTER Regt was attacking immediately to the left of the Bucks Bn — The Bucks Bn attacked in 4 waves, one behind the other, on a front of 2 companies, 'C' Coy on the right & 'A' Coy on the left. These companies were disposed in a line of columns of platoons, two platoons being in the front line of each company front. The fourth wave was supplied by 'B' Coy which supported both front line companies — followed close behind them. A tape was laid 175 yards from the German front line by the R.E. — the attacking companies assembled in the Sickel-shaped Trench (X.9.B. — X.3.D & C) & moved forwards up to the tape | map 'A'. 145 Inf Bde Order No. 151 attached |
| | 21. | | at 2.30 am. 'D' Company repaired the sickel-shaped trench after the attack. As 2.30 am the enemy watch sending up numerous white flares. After a few minutes red flares as a result of which machine guns opened fire. At 2.45 am an intense artillery barrage opened on the German front line & lifted at 2.47 am. The attack could not be pushed home owing to the large number of enemy machine guns | S.3.A |

# INTELLIGENCE SUMMARY

(Erase heading not required.)

1st BUCKS BATTN.

| Place | Date | Hour | Summary of Events and Information | Remarks and references to Appendices |
|---|---|---|---|---|
| | 22. | | ground, though one party of 1 Officer & 6 men succeeded in entering the German line on the extreme right of the attack. Casualties were heavy. Killed CAPT. L.W. CROUCH, 2nd Lt. E.G. ABREY, 2nd Lt. J.P. CHAPMAN, 2nd Lt. R.W. TRIMMER and 7 O.R. Wounded 2nd Lt. B.C. RIGDEN, 2nd Lt. H.C.E. MASON, 2nd Lt. H.V. SHEPHERD & 97 O.R. Missing CAPT. G.G. JACKSON & 42 O.R. About 9 a.m. the Battn. was withdrawn from the trenches & returned to bivouacs | J.3A. |
| ALBERT. | | | | |
| do. | 23. | | Battn. in bivouacs. At 10 p.m. the 1 Bucks Bn moved to trenches in X.13.B. on supports in an attack by the 1/5 GLOUCESTER REGT. Early in the morning the Bucks Bn were ordered to conform to the attack on the German front line & to attack at 6.30 a.m. 'D' Coy were on the right & proceeded up the eastern communication leading in a N.E. direction from X.8.B.68 to X.3.C.7.9. till they came to a bombing barricade about 150 yds from the German trench. 'B' Coy on the left went up the western communication direction from X.8.B.68 to X.3.C.7.9. Both Companies were ordered to get out of these trenches & extend inwards so as to get into touch each other & then met the German line | WDH 145 X/13 Bn order N° 101 attached. Map 'A' |

# INTELLIGENCE SUMMARY

*or*

(Erase heading not required.)

1ST BUCKS BATTN

| Place | Date | Hour | Summary of Events and Information | Remarks and references to Appendices |
|---|---|---|---|---|
| | July 23 (cont). | | 'D' Company moved out of the trench to their jumping off place amid a barrage of 15 cm shells in a very steady manner — they then collected & rushed the German front line before our own barrage had lifted — It was entirely due to this that they were enabled to carry out successfully what two other similar enterprises had failed to accomplish ; this was confirmed by a captured German officer who stated they were taken entirely by surprise & were waiting for the British barrage to lift. CAPT E.V.D. BIRCHALL who commanded 'D' Coy at the time was seriously wounded in the leg.<br><br>'A' Company under CAPT. N.S. ARD were drawn up in the S.W. end of the easternmost communication & as soon as 'D' Coy entered the trench CAPT ARD led his company up the communicator, pushed down the barricade & entered the German trench — Consolidation was immediately commenced & a bombing section quickly got in to touch with the 1/4 R. BERKS. REGT on the right.<br><br>'B' Company under CAPT O.V. VINEY went up the westernmost communicators | JVH |

2449  Wt. W14957/M90  750,000  1/16  J.B.C. & A.  Forms/C.2118/12.

# INTELLIGENCE SUMMARY

1st BUCKS BATTN.

| Place | Date | Hour | Summary of Events and Information | Remarks and references to Appendices |
|---|---|---|---|---|
| | JULY 23 (cont'd) | | but were seriously impeded & somewhat disorganised by our own barrage which caused them casualties & compelled them to withdraw a little. They were unable to take part in the attack, but one platoon & a Lewis gun managed to gain the German trench via the westernmost communicator. One platoon of 'C' Company was sent up to reinforce the left of the captured trench & the rest of this company had employees carrying up S.A.A. & bombs etc. About 150 Germans & 2 officers surrendered & 2 machine guns were captured. Frequent enemy bombing attacks were beaten off during the day. During the afternoon a bombing section reached Point 40 (X.3.A.) & advanced some 90 yards up the German trench but were driven back by rifle grenades & a heavy artillery barrage. In the evening 'C' Company took over the front line assisted by some 60 men from the other three companies. | S.A.A. |
| | 24. | | Between midnight & 1 a.m. (24 inst.) the Germans put a heavy barrage on the captured front line but the majority of the shells went over. The front line & communicators were intermittently shelled throughout the morning. At 12 noon the 1/5th GLOUCESTER REGT commenced relieving | |

# INTELLIGENCE SUMMARY

1st Bucks BATTN.

(Erase heading not required.)

| Place | Date | Hour | Summary of Events and Information | Remarks and references to Appendices |
|---|---|---|---|---|
| | JULY | | | |
| | 24 (cont). | | The BUCKS BN who returned to bivouacs near ALBERT. Casualties. Killed 8 O.R. wounded CAPT. E.V.D. BIRCHALL CAPT. O.V. VINEY LIEUT. E.N.C. WOOLERTON – 70 O.R. missing 8 O.R. | JAH |
| ALBERT | 25. | | Battn in bivouacs. The G.O.C. 145 Inf Bde reviewed the Battalion & congratulated it. | JAH |
| ALBERT | 26. | | Battn in bivouacs. At 7am the Battn left the bivouacs & marched to ARQUÈVES to billets – distance about 8 miles – Route via BOUZINCOURT, HEDAUVILLE, VARENNES. | JAH JAH |
| ARQUÈVES | 27. | | Battn in billets. | JAH |
| ARQUÈVES | 28. | | do – The 145 Inf Bde march to BEAUVAL via RAIN CHEVAL & BEAUQUESNE. The Battn in billets. | JAH |
| BEAUVAL | 29. | | Battn in billets – The 145 Inf Bde leaves BEAUVAL & marched via CANDAS, FIENVILLERS, BERNAVILLE to BEAUMETZ where the Bns split up, the Bucks BN moving to billets at DOMLÉGER. distance about 14 miles. | JAH |
| DOMLÉGER | 30. | | Battn in billets | JAH |
| DOMLÉGER | 31. | | do – Company training – Bombing & Lewis gun servis started | JAH |

V.K.C. Reynolds Lieut. Col.
Comdg 1/ Bucks Battn.

BRIGADE OPERATION ORDERS NOS. 100 & 101.

SECRET.                                                    Copy No. 4
              145th INFANTRY BRIGADE ORDER NO.100.
              ================================================

Ref. Map.                                                  20/7/16.
OVILLERS     1.
           ------
           10,000
57d.S.E.     1.
           ------
           20,000.

1. The Division will continue the attack tonight.

2. The 144th Bde will be west of point X.3.a.40
and 145th Bde will attack that point and also the
following further East X.3c.79.-X.3b.11-X3d28.

3. A smoke barrage will be established by Special
R.E. if wind is favourable.

4. The attack will be carried out behind a short
intense artillery barrage, the infantry entering
the hostile trenches almost in our own barrage
which will left at O.2.

5. The 1/5th GLOSTER REGT will attack points
X.3b.40 and X.3c.79. and trenches adjoining.
The 1/ BUCKS BN. will attack point X.3b.11 and
X.3d.28. and trenches adjoining these points.

6. The attack by each Battn. will be in four
lines one behind the other.

7. The O.C. of each Battn. will be at the Bde
Report Centre with officers at forward observation
points.    The positions of these points are to be
reported to Bde. H.Q. as soon as possible.

8. O.C. M.G.COY. will arrange for close direct
and also indirect fire on neighbouring points to
those being assaulted both in rear and on right
flank, also on any Germans who show in a counter
attack.

9. Attacking troops will go as light as possible but everyone must have bombs, water, food, ammunition also flares, artillery screens and pigeons will be taken forward. The Divisional white patch will be worn on the back.

10. The 1/4th R.BERKSHIRE REGT will evacuate the trench in X9.b. from POZIERES road to junction with 1/5th GLOSTER REGT, in order to leave it free for th 1/ BUCKS BN. This will be done by 1-30 a.m. tonight

11. The 1/4th OXFORD & BUCKS L.I. will move from BOUZINCOURT so as to arrive at the Bivouacs now occupied by 1/ BUCKS BN. at 1.a.m. but not before, tomorrow morning (21st)

12. Dressing Stations (1)X.14.B.3.1.(Nr BOISSELLES)
(2) BVILLERS.
(3) BAPAUME POST (near barrier on ALBERT-BOISSELLES Road at W.24.d.5.7,

13. Bde. H.Q. will be at OSMA REDOUBT.

14. Report Centre at X.14.a.5.6.

15. acknowledge

T.J.LEAHY. Captain,
Brigade Major.
145th Infantry Brigade.

SECRET.                                         Copy No 3.

145 Inf. Bde. No. 101.

1. 145 Inf. Bde. will attack tonight in conjunction with 144 Inf. Bde. – dividing line is the Railway in X.3.c. inclusive to 145 Inf. Bde.

2. 1/5 Gloucesters will attack O2 to 79 on their Right and the Railway on their left. They will capture Point 79 from West and Point 40 from East. 144 Inf. Bde. are attacking point 40 from North. 1/4 O&B & Bucks will advance left just East of point 28 Right on point 81. They will send flank parties to seize and occupy points 97 and 81. They will cross trench 28–81 and attack point 28 from East and North and point 11 from East sending a strong bombing stop up trench towards point 54.
Both Batts will join hands North of and in trench 79–11

3. Such points in the Railway bank North of point 11 as are necessary will also be captured

4. Every trench and post captured must be consolidated and a sufficient garrison left to hold it.

5. Stokes guns will fire on points 39 and 40 under instructions given separately.

6. M.G. Coy. will carry out special duties which have been given them.

7. Zero time has been notified to all concerned.

8. 1/Bucks and 1/4 Royal Berks will be prepared to continue or resume the operations under instructions already given and by order of this office.

9. Flares on O2 let off at 5 a.m., 8 a.m., 12 noon, 4 p.m., 8 p.m.

10. Reports to this office. Ot. Roy. Berks will endeavour to get information about the progress of operations on our Right through his RIGHT Coy.

with 1 Sect. 143. M.G. Coy attached

11. 7th Roy. Warwicks will move up tonight and will be responsible for holding La BOISSELLE and the 2nd and 3rd lines of Defence should the present Garrison move forward, in accordance with instructions given personally to O.C. 7th Roy Warwicks.

12. 1 Sect. R.E. is attached to each of the assaulting Battns and is at the disposal of Officers commanding.

Issued verbally to
C.O.s 2.20 pm.
copy (in writing) to follow.

W Brady Lt.Col.
Bcldsong. 145th Inf. Bde.

22/7/16.

145th Brigade.
48th Division.
-----------

1st BATTALION

BUCKINGHAMSHIRE REGIMENT

AUGUST 1 9 1 6

From Officer Commanding,
    1/ Bucks Battalion.

To   Headquarters,
        145th Infantry Brigade.
------------------------------------

    Herewith War Diary of the Battalion under my command for the month of August 1916,

    Please acknowledge receipt.

                                L.L.C Reynolds
                                Lieut. Colonel,
                                Comdg. 1/ Bucks Battn.

31.8.16.

Army Form C. 2118

# WAR DIARY
## or
## INTELLIGENCE SUMMARY
(Erase heading not required.)

1st BUCKS BATTN

Instructions regarding War Diaries and Intelligence Summaries are contained in F.S. Regs., Part II and the Staff Manual respectively. Title Pages will be prepared in manuscript.

| Place | Date | Hour | Summary of Events and Information | Remarks and references to Appendices |
|---|---|---|---|---|
| | 1916 August | | | |
| DOMLEGER | 1. | | Batt in billets – Company training : Bombing & Lewis gun courses commenced. | LBM – LBM – |
| do. | 2. | | do. | LBM. |
| do. | 3. | | do. | LBM. |
| do. | 4. | | do. | LBM. |
| do. | 5. | | Batt. went for a 10 mile route march in the morning. | LBM. |
| do. | 6. | | Company Training in acelest – | LBM. |
| do. | 7. | | Range Practice at AGENVILLE – | LBM. |
| do. | 8. | | do. | LBM. |
| do. | 9. | | At 8.30 am the 145 Inf Bde moved to BEAUVAL in FIENVILLERS & CANDAS – Bucks BN bro last billets in BEAUMETZ, BERNAVILLE. My dir & firing day for marching – Battn in billets in chief of march. 14 miles. – | |
| BEAUVAL | 10. | | At 5 am the 145 Inf Bde moved to VARENNES, Bucks BN leading – Battn in bivouac – | LBM – JBM – |
| VARENNES | 11. | | Battn in bivouac. At 7.45 am the 145 Inf Bde marched to BOUZINCOURT to hits. At 3pm the BUCKS BATTN was moved to Q bivouac in fields just East of the BOUZINCOURT – HEDAUVILLE road to avoid shelling. (Trench Map, FRANCE 57D S.E. – V.I.a.c. p.5). | JBM – |

Army Form C. 2118

# WAR DIARY
## or
## INTELLIGENCE SUMMARY

(Erase heading not required.)

1st BUCKS BATT'N

| Place | Date | Hour | Summary of Events and Information | Remarks and references to Appendices |
|---|---|---|---|---|
| BOUZINCOURT | 1916. AUGUST. 12. | | Batt'n in bivouacs — | |
| " | 13. | | do | |
| | | | At 6am the Bn marched from the bivouacs & took over a line of gun-pits to the west of the USNA REDOUBT about half way between ALBERT & OVILLERS LA BOISELLE — A & B companies bivouaced there; C & D moved up to OVILLERS LA BOISELLE but were subsequently withdrawn owing to lack of accomodation. | hap. OVILLERS 57D. S.E. 4 (scale 2/3). hereafter called "Map A" J.V.H |
| USNA REDOUBT | 14. | | Batt'n in gun-pits. At 3am 'C' & 'D' Coy's moved up to the Old German front line in X.8 c where placed under the orders of the O/C 1/4th R. BERKS, while 2 companies of that regiment were engaged in making a bomber-attack on 6th AVENUE which had been lost. | See map '15' attached J.V.H |
| TRENCHES N.W. of POZIERES. | | | At 12 noon the Bn moved up to the line & 5th Ave Trenches from the 1/4 OX BUCKS L.I. 'A' Coy took over 5th AVENUE. 'B' Coy 3rd AVENUE from pt. 11 eastwards & part of 8th STREET.; 2 platoons of 'C' Coy were placed in 3rd AVENUE close to Bn Hq (pt. 47); 2 platoons of 'C' Coy & whole of 'D' Coy were kept in reserve in OVILLERS until night when they were brought up into the line — Shortly after 10 p.m. 2 bombing parties & 1 platoon of 'C' Coy under 2nd Lt D FALLON worked up the right hand communication between 5th & 6th AVENUES in R.33.c. & eventually succeeded in gaining 6th AVENUE without opposition; they then worked outward & made S.W. of ? contact with the ANZACS on the right, and Lt J.F.ARNOTT with one platoon of 'D' Company was sent up about 10 p.m. down 2 bombing sections up the left hand communicat'n between 5th & 6th AVENUES & on reaching 6th AVENUE without opposition worked outwards. A bombing stop was erected at X.2.13.9.9 | See 145 M/30le order No 116 attached J.V.H 6th AVENUE was subsequently named "SKYLINE TRENCH" J.V.H |
| | 15. | | AVENUE was held from Form 81 (R 33 a) to pt 88 (X.2.3.) 'A' Coy at about 10 pm down 2 bombing sections up the left. By about 5 am. 6th. | J.V.H |

# WAR DIARY or INTELLIGENCE SUMMARY

1st BUCKS BATTN.

| Place | Date 1916 | Hour | Summary of Events and Information | Remarks and references to Appendices |
|---|---|---|---|---|
| TRENCHES N.W. of POZIERES. | August 15 | (cont) | At about 9 am 'A' Coy were sent back to their posn W. of the entrance to OVILLERS & 'C' & 'B' Coys took over the line. About 11.30 am the Germans opened heavy shell fire on the right of 5th AVENUE & about mid-day they started systematically flattening 6th AVENUE starting from the right & working down the trench. Very heavy shells were employed & trench mortars & a minenwerfer from the direction of MOUQUET FARM enfiladed the trench. M. heavies opened on the latter & momentarily eased the situation. Owing to the extremely heavy shelling, it was found necessary to withdraw from 6th AVENUE & hold the head of the right & left communications. This bombardment was kept up practically without cessation until about 10 p.m. — at about 8 pm 'B' Coy took over the front line & established a line of posts 100 yds outside 6th AVENUE; 'D' Coy & 2 platoons of 'C' were posted into 5th AVENUE & the other 2 platoons of 'C' were withdrawn into 5th AVENUE. | map '78' Lan |
| do | 16. | | At 12.30 am after 1/4 hr bombardment by our guns 'A' Coy under Capt. N.S.REID.D.S.O attempted a bombing attack on points 78, 59, 48 starting from pt 99. Shortage of bombs prevented the attack being successful. | Le 145 by Pile Notes No. 117 attached. W34. map 73. W34 Eng |

# WAR DIARY or INTELLIGENCE SUMMARY

(Erase heading not required.)

1st BUCKS BATTN

| Place | Date | Hour | Summary of Events and Information | Remarks and references to Appendices |
|---|---|---|---|---|
| | 1916 August | | | |
| | 16(cont). | | At about midnight the line of posts of 'B' Coy were withdrawn into the trench, as the bombardment of 6th AVENUE had by that time ceased. In the early hours of the morning a patrol was sent along 5th AVENUE as far as the POZIÈRES-THIEPVAL road; it then turned & came down the road towards POZIÈRES but failed to find any troops with whom to get into touch. Accordingly 2 platoons of 'B' Coy were withdrawn into 5th AVENUE & the other 2 platoons to held points Q.9.a.14. From 6am onwards the situation was quite quiet. At 11am the Battn was relieved by the 1/4th OX & BUCKS L.I. — The casualties as a result of these operations were severe — Officers Wounded LIEUT. F.D. EARL. CAPT. V.S.C. HEATHCOTE-HACKER. 2nd LT. D. FALLON. 2nd LT. F.C. DIXON. (7th BATTN. MANCHESTER REGT. relief 1st BUCKS BN) O.R. Killed 15. Wounded 159. Missing 23. | |
| BOUZINCOURT – ALBERT line | 17. | | On relief the Battn marched to the BOUZINCOURT-ALBERT line in W.21.a. | G.S.N. |
| do. | 18. | | Battn in bivouacs — | O.S.N. Instr. |
| | | | Battn in bivouacs — At 9.4 pm the Battn marched to the grounds west of the | |

# WAR DIARY or INTELLIGENCE SUMMARY

(Erase heading not required.)

**1st BUCKS BATTN**

| Place | Date August | Hour | Summary of Events and Information | Remarks and references to Appendices |
|---|---|---|---|---|
| USNA REDOUBT | 19. | | USNA REDOUBT & bivouaced in the open. At 8 am the Battn moved into the gunpits behind the USNA REDOUBT. A.1 leaving 's Battn HQ was in the USNA REDOUBT. At 3 pm the Battn was relieved by the 1/6 GLOSTERS & marched to BOUZINCOURT. A & B Coys were in huts, C & D in billets. | LBH — |
| BOUZINCOURT | 20. | | Battn in billets & huts — do. | LBH |
| | 21. | | At 4.30 pm the Battn marched to trenches at OVILLERS POST via AVELUY. About X.7.c.4 was placed at the disposal of the G.O.C 144 Inf Bde for offensive purposes. | LBH hop'd 'a' coy LBH. |
| OVILLERS POST | 22. | | Battn in Reserve trenches. | |
| do. | 23. | | do. At 9.15 am the Battn moved up into the line & took over trenches from the 1/6th GLOSTERS — The 1/4th OXFORD & BUCKS L.I were on the right & the 3rd Battn WORCESTERS for the left. At 3 pm 'A' & 'C' Coys of the 1st BUCKS BATTN attacked the enemy's front line at points 33, 31 & 79. 'A' Coy attacked the trench between points 33 & 31 (both inclusive), 'C' Coy from pt 31 to 79. A preliminary bombardment was carried out by our heavy guns & Stokes mortars & from 3 pm – 3.5 pm our field guns placed a barrage on the objective. The attacking companies advanced in two lines but were unable to attain their objective owing to a heavy barrage of hostile field guns & machine guns. A slight advance was made however toward point 31 along the trench 19 – 31. Most of the trench 27 – 79 was occupied, a bomb stop being erected about 70 yds west of point 79. Casualties were heavy — Killed. 2nd Lieut. E.H.G. BATES. 2nd Lieut. W.R. HEATH. O.R. 24. Wounded. 2nd Lieut H.M. BOWEN. 2nd Lieut H.M. BRETON (7th Bn MANCHESTER REGT attached 1st Bucks (BR)) O.R. missing O.R. 14. | LBH (17/1/Bde 25th Div)LBH hop 'B'. Lee 145th Inf Bde Orders Nos 123, attached Nos. |

2449 Wt. W14957/M90 750,000 1/16 J.B.C. & A. Forms/C.2118/12.

Instructions regarding War Diaries and Intelligence Summaries are contained in F.S. Regs., Part II. and the Staff Manual respectively. Title Pages will be prepared in manuscript.

# INTELLIGENCE SUMMARY
(Erase heading not required.)

1st BUCKS BATTN.

| Place | Date 1916 August | Hour | Summary of Events and Information | Remarks and references to Appendices |
|---|---|---|---|---|
| BATTN in Trenches. | 23. | | 'B' Coy 1/5 GLOSTERS moved into the Trenches in support to the 1st BUCKS BATTN. Repeated efforts were made to capture points 31 & 79 by bombing attacks but they could not be pushed home. During the night a new trench was commenced joining up the front steps in Trenches 27-79 & 79-76. The 1/4 OXF & BUCKS L.I. co-operating on the right. A patrol was sent out from Trench 19-81 to Wurstgate point 33. | App. 'B'. Instr. |
| do. | 24. | | In the early morning a German prisoner belonging to the 28th I.R. was taken about point 19. The day was fairly quiet. After the unsuccessful attack of the 7th Inf. Bde. in the LEIPZIG REDOUBT, German artillery shelled the front line from points 81-19-29-46 heavily with 15cm shells from 4.30 to 7.30 pm; Trench 24-46 was caught in enfilade & badly hit in places. The damage was made good during the night. Further attempts to gain points 31 & 79 by bombing attacks were made but were held up by enemy machine guns trained down the Trenches. A patrol left our lines & ascertained the enemy held points 31 & 79 in some strength. What a working party was at work in the trench between them. | do. W.D. |
| do. | 25. | | Our guns opened fire on this target & appeared to do (some) shooting. The enemy retook Trench 31-79 across the green at about 4.45 a.m. – our own guns opened fire on them & caused them about 20 casualties. At 7.am the Battn was relieved by the 1/5th GLOSTERS & returned to Ivor pits behind the USNA REDOUBT. | W.D. |
| USNA REDOUBT. | 26. | | Battn in Ivor pits. At 4 pm 'B' Coy moved up to the Trenches as a support to the 1/5 GLOSTERS. A working party of 2 officers & 100 men was provided at night. | W.D. W.Dch |

For the 1/4 Bn R. BERKS —

2449 Wt. W14957/Mgo 750,000 1/16 J.B.C. & A. Forms/C.2118/12.

# WAR DIARY
## or
## INTELLIGENCE SUMMARY

(Erase heading not required.)

1st BUCKS BATTN.

| Place | 1916 Date August | Hour | Summary of Events and Information | Remarks and references to Appendices |
|---|---|---|---|---|
| USNA REDOUBT | 27. | | Battn in dugouts – At 12.30 pm 'B' Coy relieved 'D' Coy in the trenches in support Coy to 1/5 GLOSTERS. 7pm Attack by the 1/5 GLOSTERS, 1/4 R. BERKS + one Platn of the 1/43rd M.G. Bde on German line – None the objectives of the two former regiments were attained | 1/3/4. |
| do. | 28. | | Battn in dugouts. At 6 am the Battn moved to bivouacs in fields just east of the BOUZINCOURT – HEDAUVILLE + SENLIS – ENGLEBELMER Cul MAIN | Trench maps. FRANCE 57.D. S.E. Edition 2.B. 1/20,000. V.12 c. 8.5. MAIN – 1/3/4. 2/3/4. 1/R/4. |
| SENLIS CASSA ROAD | 29. | | Battn in bivouacs – At 6.30 am the Battn marched to huts at BUS arriving there at 9.10 am Route via HEDAUVILLE, FORCEVILLE, BERTRANCOURT – later in the morning the 1/43 M.G. Bde moved to the same place. | |
| BUS. | 30. | | Battn in huts. | |
| BUS | 31. | | — do — Company training. + Lewis Gunn course started. | |

On Revine
31.8.16

N.K.C. Ryroft
Lieut. Colonel
Comdg. 1/Bucks Battn.

BM 157/8.

Runner/ OC onjnd.
OC Rukn.

Re msn. 156/S of today re heavy artillery:—

Heavies will stop firing on pt. 100ᵞ
WEST of PT X2A49 at 2.45 pm.
—(other heavy artillery will carry on as arranged)
as requested by OC Rukn.

23/8/18.

W. Sutherland Col.
Bdeby. 145 Inf Bde.

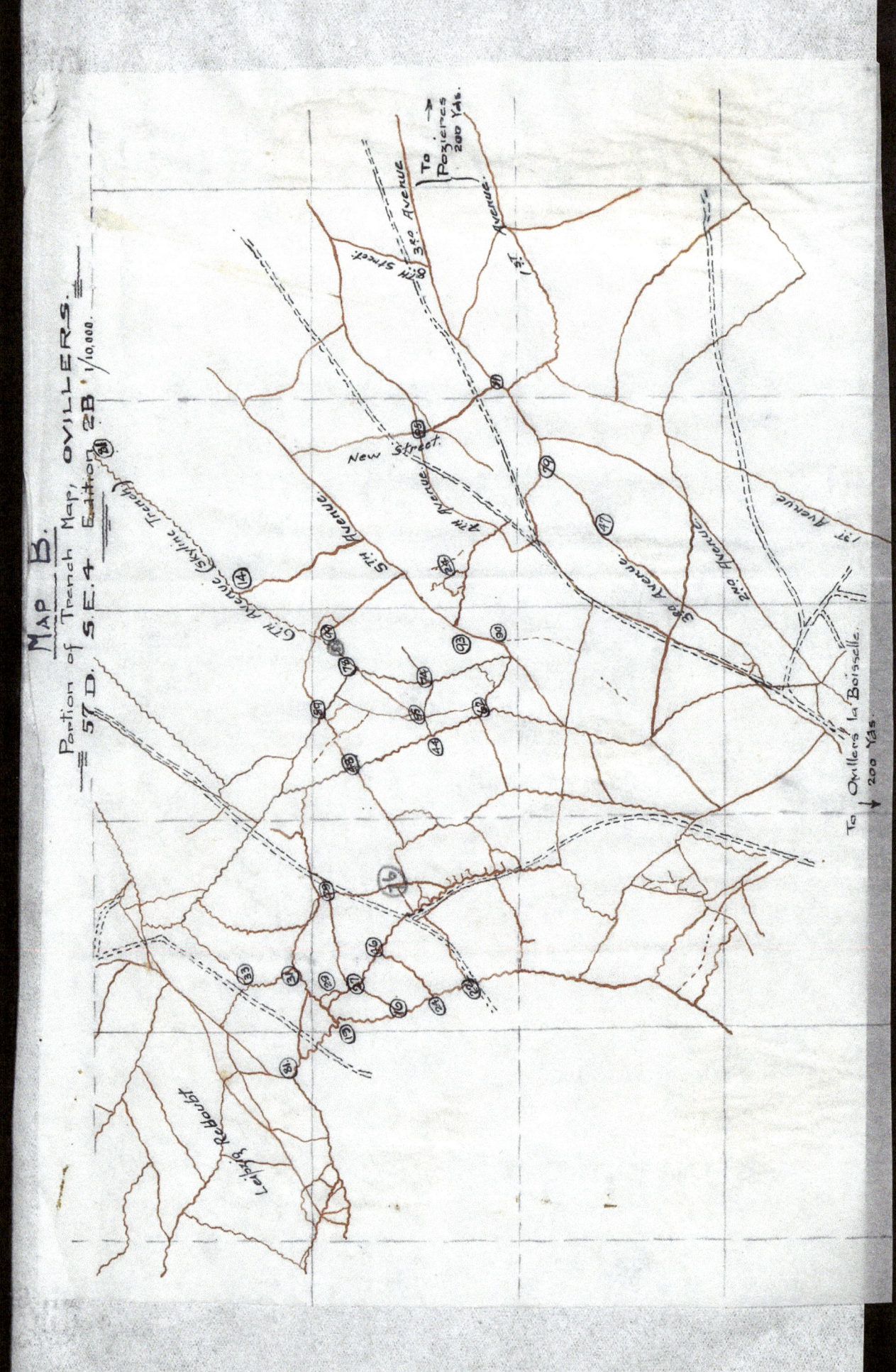

145th Brigade.
48th Division.
------

1st BUCKINGHAMSHIRE BATTALION

(Oxf. & Bucks.L.I.)

SEPTEMBER 1 9 1 6

# WAR DIARY
## or
## INTELLIGENCE SUMMARY

*(Erase heading not required.)*

Army Form C. 2118.

1st BUCKS BATT<sup>n</sup>.

| Place | Date 1916 SEPTEMBER. | Hour | Summary of Events and Information | Remarks and references to Appendices |
|---|---|---|---|---|
| BUS. | 1. | | Batt<sup>n</sup> in huts. Company training + Lewis Gun + Bombing training continued. | L/W. |
| do. | 2. | | — do — | L/W. |
| do. | 3. | | — do — At 9.30 am the Batt<sup>n</sup> was inspected by the G.O.C. 48<sup>th</sup> Division. | L/W. |
| do. | 4. | | — do — Company training was carried on as above. | L/W. |
| do. | 5. | | — do — At 12.30 p.m. the Batt<sup>n</sup> marched via BERTRANCOURT + BEAUSSART to MAILLY-MAILLET + took over the line between WATLING STREET + the NEW BEAUMONT ROAD (Q.4.) from the 1/8 WORCESTERS. Batt<sup>n</sup> H.Q. were in the WHITE CITY (Q.4.a.45.25). The 1/4 OXF + BUCKS L.I. were on the right + the 12<sup>TH</sup> R. FUSILIERS on the left. "A" + "B" took over the right + left of the line respectively. "C" was in support in the WHITE CITY + "D" in reserve in THE BOWERY. | Trench map FRANCE SHEET 57<sup>d</sup> S.E. Edition 2.B. 1/20,000. |
| Trenches opposite N and E of BEAUMONT-HAMEL. | 6. | | Batt<sup>n</sup> in trenches. THE BOWERY was shelled with 77 mm in the morning + NORTH STREET was blown in in places with 15 cm shells about 7 p.m. | L/W. |
| | 7. | | — do — From 2.20 am to about 3.15 am the enemy heavily shelled the front line with minenwerfer + the support lines + WHITE CITY with shells up to 15 cm calibre — No subsequent action took place — | L/W. |
| do. | 8. | | — do — In the course of the morning the Batt<sup>n</sup> was relieved by the 1/5 GLOSTERS + returned to billets in MAILLY-MAILLET. Batt<sup>n</sup> H.Q. was billetted N<sup>o</sup> 71. | L/W. |
| MAILLY-MAILLET. | 9. | | Batt<sup>n</sup> in billets. The Batt<sup>n</sup> supplied parties working parties throughout the day to work (inter alia) on 4<sup>TH</sup> + 5<sup>TH</sup> AVENUES. | L/W. |
| do. | 10. | | — do — Early in the morning the Batt<sup>n</sup> marched to huts in the BOIS DE WARNIMONT + huts was subsequently joined there by the 1/4 R. BERKS + 1/5 GLOSTERS. | L/W. |
| BOIS DE WARNIMONT. | 11. | | Batt<sup>n</sup> in huts. At 2 p.m. the 145<sup>th</sup> Inf Bde marched to billets on BEAUVAL Route via AUTHIE, MARIEUX, BEAUQUESNE + TERRAMESNIL. | L/W. |

# WAR DIARY
## or
## INTELLIGENCE SUMMARY

*(Erase heading not required.)*

Instructions regarding War Diaries and Intelligence Summaries are contained in F. S. Regs., Part II. and the Staff Manual respectively. Title Pages will be prepared in manuscript.

1st BUCKS BATTN.

Summary of Events and Information

| Place | Date 1916 SEPT. | Hour | Summary of Events and Information | Remarks and references to Appendices |
|---|---|---|---|---|
| BEAUVAL | 12. | | Battn in billets — Company training — Bombing & Lewis gun courses commenced. Training required 6 hours per day — | W.M. — |
| " | 13. | | — do — | L.W. |
| " | 14. | | — do — | L.W. |
| " | 15. | | — do — | W.M. |
| " | 16. | | Companies exercised in open order moving across country — Lewis as above continued | |
| " | 17. | | The 145th Inf Bde exercised in open order moving across country under BRIG- GEN. DONE. D.S.O. — Revolver range opened. Companies as disposed of O.C. Companies for interior economy. | W.M. — |
| " | 18. | | The 145th Inf Bde left BEAUVAL. 1st BUCKS BN was the leading Bn + left the starting point at 10am + marched to billets at BERNEUIL — Route via CANDAS + FIENVILLERS — | |
| BERNEUIL | 19. | | Company Training — Bomb & Lewis gun classes started — | W.M. — |
| " | 20. | | — do — Range practice | L.W. — |
| " | 21. | | commenced — Revolver training continued — | L.W. |
| " | 22. | | — do — | |
| " | 23. | | Inoculation — Remnant of Battn resumed in field training + range practice — | W.M. — |
| " | 24. | | field training — | W.G.M. — |
| " | 25. | | Coy as disposed of O.C. Coys for interior economy — Musketry — range practice — Company training — Musketry — Range practice — Va afternoon a Regimental tour was conducted over the ground between the ST. LEGER LES DOMART + BERNEUIL — | L.W. — L.W. — W.M. — |

2449 Wt. W14957/M90 750,000 1/16 J.B.C. & A. Forms/C.2118/12.

**WAR DIARY**
or
**INTELLIGENCE SUMMARY**

(Erase heading not required.)

Army Form C. 2118.

1st Bucks BATTN.

| Place | Date 1916. September | Hour | Summary of Events and Information | Remarks and references to Appendices |
|---|---|---|---|---|
| BERNEUIL | 26 | — | Battn in billets — At 9 am the Battn marched to ST. LEGER LES DOMART — starting from this place an attack on BERNEUIL was practised. | with — |
| " | 27 | — | do — The above programme was repeated. | with — |
| " | 28 | — | do — Company training — Bomb & Lewis gun courses continued — Range practice. | with — |
| " | 29 | — | do — At 8.30 am the Battn marched to CANDAS & there joined the 145 Inf Bde which moved via DOULLENS - GROUCHES - FROUCHES - LUCHEUX & were separated the 1st BUCKS BN marched to billets at COULLEMONT. Total distance about 20 miles — | with — |
| COULLEMONT | 30 | — | do — Company training + bomb & Lewis gun courses recommenced — | with — |

On Service
30-9-16

V.L.C. Reynolds
Lt Col
Cmg 1/Bucks Battn

145th Brigade.

48th Division.

-----

1st BUCKINGHAMSHIRE BATTALION

(Oxf. & Bucks.L.I.)

OCTOBER 1 9 1 6

# WAR DIARY
## or
## INTELLIGENCE SUMMARY

*(Erase heading not required.)*

Army Form C. 2118.

VOL 20
1st BUCKS BATTN

| Place | Date 1916 OCTOBER | Hour | Summary of Events and Information | Remarks and references to Appendices |
|---|---|---|---|---|
| COULLEMONT | 1. | | Battn in billets. At 11 am the Battn marched via GAUDIEMPRE to ST AMAND — Two companies were in billets & two in huts. | 1/8/H |
| ST. AMAND. | 2. | | Battn in billets & huts — Company training — Lewis gun & Bombing classes resumed. | 2/3H |
| do. | 3. | | do — Lectures in morning owing to heavy rain — Company training in the afternoon. | L.Sgt |
| do. | 4. | | Battn in huts — C & D Coys went into huts — Lectures — Company training in afternoon. | 1/9/H |
| do. | 5. | | At 9.30 am the Battn moved to SOUASTRE & had dinners there. At 2 pm the Battn marched via BAYENCOURT & SAILLY to BIVOUACS at HEBUTERNE. 'C' Coy on the right & 'A' on the left — The Battn front was between YUSSIF ST & YANKEE ST both inclusive. The Battn relieved the 1/5 R. WARWICKS in THAT area & on the right were the 7th Bn The Border Regiment & the 1/5 R. WARWICKS on the left. A very quiet day — The 17th Divisional Artillery had been cutting the enemy wire opposite the enemy wire opposite. The wire from K.4.d.3.4 to K.4.c.B.5 & found it very thick especially about K.4.d.1.6 — 2nd Lt McEWEN & 30.R. reconnoitred the wire between these points & was not damaged but no gaps were apparent — | →The Bn were in support of Sept 3rd in relieve of 1/5 R. Wcks in the HEBUTERNE READ. 1/7/H Trench Map HEBUTERNE 57d N.E. 3rd (Pulled) Edition 2D 1/7/H |
| Trenches at HEBUTERNE | 6. | | Battn in trenches — In the afternoon D Coy took over the right of the line & B Coy the left, C moved into support & 'A' into reserve — wire cutting by the 17 Divl. Artillery was continued & patrols examined the wire at night — With the exception of a few 77 mm shells the enemy guns were quiet. 2 Lt A. STORRS & 30.R. examined the wire between K.H.d.5.30 K.H.c.9.4 & found it still very thick especially about K.H.d.16. | 20.S. 3 sheet 1/7/H |

2449 Wt. W14957/Mgo 750,000 1/16 J.B.C. & A. Forms/C.2118/12.

# WAR DIARY
## INTELLIGENCE SUMMARY

**1st BUCKS BATTN.**

Army Form C. 2118.

| Place | Date 1916 OCTOBER | Hour | Summary of Events and Information | Remarks and references to Appendices |
|---|---|---|---|---|
| Trenches at HEBUTERNE | 7. | 2 AM | 2nd Lt F.G. VAUGHAN & 3 O.R. examined the wire in front of trench FIRM [K.H.49H & K.H.2.66] but were unable to approach nearer than 25 yds of the enemy wire owing to the presence of a working party who appeared to be wiring along the front to the reconnoitred. 'A' & 'C' Coys supplied R.E. working parties. Battn. in trenches. The 2nd Lt Terriss Artillery commenced cutting the wire in front of trench FIRM. At about 6 pm the 2nd front line 'A' & 'C' Coys returned in HEBUTERNE to supply R.E. working parties. 'B' Coy & 1/3rd Qroisters — 'D' Coys marched to huts in SOUASTRE. | 4/3 H — N/3 H. |
| SOUASTRE. | 8. | About 7.30 am 'B' & 'C' Companies arrived at SOUASTRE. At 10.15 am the Battn. marched to HENU to have standings — | 4/3 H — |
| HENU. | 9. | Battn. under canvas. At 2.15 pm the Bn marched via GAUDIEMPRE to WARLENCOURT & moved into huts vacated by the 1/5 GLOSTERS — | 1/3 H — |
| | | | | 2/3 H — |
| WARLENCOURT. | 10. | Battn. in huts. Company Training resumed. At 12 noon MAJOR CAMPBELL gave a lecture on bayonet fighting — | 1/3 H — |
| do. | 11. | — do — Company Training & practice in wire cutting — | |
| do. | 12. | — do — do. Bn practices attack on flagged trenches. | 2/3 H. |
| do. | 13. | — do — do. | N/3 H |
| do. | 14. | — do — do. | 3/3 H |
| do. | 15. | — do — Church service in morning | |
| do. | 16. | — do — Company training — | 1/3 H — |
| do. | 17. | — do — do. | 2/3 H — |
| do. | 18. | — do — In afternoon the Commanding Officer & Company Commanders attended a Staff Ride held by G.O. C 48th Division. | 4/3 H — |

Army Form C. 2118.

# WAR DIARY
# or
# INTELLIGENCE SUMMARY

*(Erase heading not required.)*

1st BUCKS BATTN

Instructions regarding War Diaries and Intelligence Summaries are contained in F.S. Regs., Part II. and the Staff Manual respectively. Title Pages will be prepared in manuscript.

| Place | Date 1916 OCTOBER | Hour | Summary of Events and Information | Remarks and references to Appendices |
|---|---|---|---|---|
| WARLENCOURT | 19. | | Battn in huts. — At 2 pm the Battn. marched via COUTURELLE & COULLEMONT to billets at WARLUZEL 3 1/4. OXFORD & BUCKS L.I. — 145th Inf Bde dig date. | 2/Bn. |
| WARLUZEL | 20. | | Battn in billets. Company Training | 1/3H. |
| do. | 21. | | do. — do. | 2/13H. — |
| do. | 22. | | do. — At 9.30 am the Battn. marched to HUMBERCOURT where it joined the 145th Inf Bde & marched via DOULLENS to billets at BEAUVAL. Distance 12 miles. | 2/Bn. |
| BEAUVAL | 23. | | do. — At 2.30 pm the 145th Inf Bde marched to billets at TALMAS. Distance 5 1/2 miles. | |
| TALMAS | 24. | | do. — At 7.40 am the Battn moved from TALMAS was the leading Battn in the Bde line of march — It rained intermittently all day — The 1 BUCKS 6xF & BUCKS L.I. marches to billets at LAHOUSSOYE, the rest of the Bde staying at BEHINCOURT. Route via RUBIEMPRE, MOLLIENS AU BOIS, MONTIGNY & BEHINCOURT. Distance 12 miles. | 3/3H. |
| LAHOUSSOYE | 25. | | — do — Companies engaged in physical drill, bayonet fighting &c. | 1/BH. |
| do. | 26. | | — do — — do — The C.O. Adjutant & Coy Cmdrs rode to FRICOURT & CONTALMAISON to inspect roads. | 1/BH. |
| do. | 27. | | — do — Companies occupied in physical drill, bayonet fighting & interior economy. | 2/BH. |
| do. | 28. | | — do — — do — | 2/BH. — 1/BH. |
| do. | 29. | | — do — Church Parade service | 2/BH. |
| do. | 30. | | — do — Company training | 1/BH. |
| do. | 31. | | — do — The Battn marched by platoons to MILLENCOURT to look over No. 2 CAMP. To be our the camp there. | 2/BH. |

G. Nervier
31-10-16

R.E.C. Rogershaw Lieut Colonel
Commanding 1/Bucks Battn

2449 Wt. W14957/M90 750,000 1/16 J.B.C. & A. Forms/C.2118/12.

145th Brigade.

48th Division.

1st BUCKINGHAMSHIRE BATTALION

(Oxf. & Bucks.L.I.)

DECEMBER 1 9 1 6

# WAR DIARY or INTELLIGENCE SUMMARY

(Erase heading not required.)

1st Bucks Bn. O+B. L.I.

Army Form C. 2118.

| Place | Date | Hour | Summary of Events and Information | Remarks and references to Appendices |
|---|---|---|---|---|
| SHELTER WOOD CAMP (NORTH) | 1st Sept 1916 | | Batt" under canvas. Companies supplies R.E. working parties. | /MW/ |
| " | 2nd Sept | | Batt" under canvas. Companies supplies R.E. working parties. | /MW/ |
| " | 3rd Sept | | " | |
| | | 3.15 p.m. | Batt" moved by platoon to Front line and relieved 1/5 Gloucester Regt in trenches N. of LE SARS. A Coy & D Coy took over Left and Right front positions respectively. C Coy and B Coy took over left and Right Support positions respectively. 51st Division on our left and 1st Lt Infty Bde on our right. | /MW/ |
| TRENCHES N. of LE SARS | 4th Sept | | Batt" in Trenches. Occasional shelling of Front line Coy H'Qrs and Left support Coy H'Qrs. Patrol consisting of Lt NEAVE + 3 O.R. left CHALK PIT at 1.15 am + returned 2.30 am. Enemy's trench position was seen partially in our front line. Enemy aeroplane flew up + down the front line fairly low + made occasional dives down on lines. They were fired on by our Lewis guns. | /MW/ |
| " | 5th Sept | 4 am | Batt" in trenches. Intermittent shelling of front line and front Coy H'Qrs. Left support Coy H'Qrs. Enemy patrol of about 20 men was fired on. No damage noted. | |
| | | 1.30 am | Patrol under LT KNIGHT G.R.E. + 3 O.R. left CHALK PIT at 1.30 am + returned at 2.30 am. No enemy patrols were seen. | |
| | | 6 p.m. | B Coy relieved D Coy in Right front position. C Coy relieved A Coy in Left front position. | /MW/ |

Army Form C. 2118.

# WAR DIARY
## or
## INTELLIGENCE SUMMARY
(Erase heading not required.)

1st Bucks Bn

| Place | Date | Hour | Summary of Events and Information | Remarks and references to Appendices |
|---|---|---|---|---|
| TRENCH ESQ[?] STRT N of LE SARS | 1916 6 | | Batt'n in trenches. Enemy artillery fairly quiet. Front line fired on by several hostile snipers during the morning | Nil? |
| " | 7 | | Batt'n in trenches. Enemy Artillery shelled left support and front line Coy HQrs intermittently during the day. | |
| | | 7pm | Batt'n relieved by 4th Royal Berkshire Reg't and moved by platoons to SCOTS REDOUBT CAMP SOUTH | Nil |
| SCOTS REDOUBT CAMP SOUTH | 8 | | Batt'n in NISSEN Huts. Improvements on the Camp were carried out. | Nil |
| " | 9 | | Batt'n in NISSEN HUTS. Companies supp'd to the R.E. working parties & improved Camp | Nil? |
| " | 10 | | do do | Nil? |
| " | 11 | | do do | Nil? |
| " | 12 | | do do | Nil? |
| | 13 | 2pm | Batt'n moved to MIDDLE WOOD CAMP, and relieved 1/5 Gloucester Reg't | Nil |
| MIDDLE WOOD CAMP | 13 | | Batt'n in bivouacs. C & D Coys in Sept and Right forward positions respectively, A & B Coys relieved C & D Coys in forward positions. Coys found R.E. working parties | Nil? |

Army Form C. 2118.

# WAR DIARY
## or
## INTELLIGENCE SUMMARY

*(Erase heading not required.)*

1st Buffs B⁴

Instructions regarding War Diaries and Intelligence Summaries are contained in F. S. Regs., Part II and the Staff Manual respectively. Title Pages will be prepared in manuscript.

| Place | Date | Hour | Summary of Events and Information | Remarks and references to Appendices |
|---|---|---|---|---|
| MIDDLE HUTS CAMP | 14th | 11.45am | Batt" moved by platoons to B. Camp Bécourt. | /nil |
| "B"Camp Bécourt | 15th | | Batt" in Nissen Huts. Companies found R.E. Working Parties & worked on Camp improvement | /nil |
| " | 16th | | do | /nil |
| " | 17th | | do | /nil |
| " | 18th | | do | /nil |
| " | 19th | | do | /nil |
| " | 20th | | do | /nil |
| " | 21st | | do | /nil |
| " | 22nd | | do | /nil |
| " | 23rd | | do | /nil |
| " | 24th | | do | /nil |
| " | 25th | | Christmas Day. Church service Reverend Hoskins | /nil |
| " | 26th | | Companies found R.E. Working parties & worked on Camp improvement | /nil |

2449 Wt. W14957/M90 750,000 1/16 J.B.C. & A. Forms/C.2118/12.

Army Form C. 2118.

# WAR DIARY
## or
## INTELLIGENCE SUMMARY

(Erase heading not required.)

1st Bucks 18/9

| Place | Date | Hour | Summary of Events and Information | Remarks and references to Appendices |
|---|---|---|---|---|
| BECOURT B'Camp | Nov 1916 27 | | Batt" in Niron Huts. Conferences carried out Training & found R.E. working parties | fps |
| " d° | 28 | 7.0 | Batt: moved by platoons to BRESLE and relieved 1/6 7" Br Northumbd Fusiliers (50th Division) in billets. | Nil |
| BRESLE | 29 | | Batt" in billets. Training carried out | Nil |
| " | 30 | | d° | Nil |
| " | 31 | | d° Church parades & inspections | Nil |

J.L.C. Reynolds
Lieut Colonel
Comdg 1/1 Bucks Battalion
31-12-16.

145th Brigade.

48th Division.

-----

1st BUCKINGHAMSHIRE BATTALION

(Oxf. & Bucks. L.I.)

NOVEMBER 1 9 1 6

CONFIDENTIAL

Army Form C. 2118.

WAR DIARY or INTELLIGENCE SUMMARY

(Erase heading not required.)

1ST BUCKS BATTN

JM 21

| Place | Date 1916 NOVR. | Hour | Summary of Events and Information | Remarks and references to Appendices |
|---|---|---|---|---|
| MILLENCOURT | 1. | | Battn in camp in tents. Companies employed in improvements to the camp. | LBW. |
| do. | 2. | | do. At 8am the Battn left MILLENCOURT + marched by platoons via ALBERT and MILLEN LA BOISELLE to CONTALMAISON where it halted + ate dinners. At 7.30 pm the Battn relieved the 13th Bn R Scots in the 'C' line at MARTINPUICH ; 'A' Coy occupied the FACTORY LINE 'B' Coy dugouts in the BAZENTIN ROAD + village, 'C' & 'D' Coy HAM TRENCH. Bn Hqr at M32.d.50. | LBW. JBW. |
| MARTINPUICH | 3. | | Battn in 'C' line – 'A' Coy supplied a salvage party of 100 men + the other companies found parties for road mending. | LBW. |
| do. | 4. | | Battn in 'C' line – 'C' Coy supplied a salvage party of 100 men ; the others road mending parties – The Battn supplied a carrying party of 200. O.R + officer at night – An observation post was started at the MILL, MARTINPUICH. | v LBW. |
| do. | 5. | | Battn in 'C' line. 'C' Coy supplied a salvage party of 100 men, the others road mending parties. At 5:30 pm the Battn relieved the 1/5 GLOSTERS in the support line (26TH AVENUE), one platoon of 'D' Coy being in DESTREMONT FARM. Battn Hq were in 26.AVENUE about M. 27.a.20.55". | Trench map, FRANCE Sheet 57c.S.W. Edition 4.A. |
| 26TH AVENUE | 6. | | Battn in support trenches – The enemy shelled LE SARS + DESTREMONT FARM intermittently throughout the day ; also O.9.1 + O.9.2 in M.15 a & c d. At 9.30 pm relieved the 1/4 OXFORD & BUCKS L.I. in the front line ; the 1/6th GLOSTERS were on our right + the 47th CANADIANS on our left – A + D Coy took over the left 9 night respectively of the front line (SCOTLAND TRENCH + CHALK TRENCH), + C + B Coy the left & right of the support (O.9.1 & O.9.2). Battn Hq were in 26.AVENUE about M.27.a.7.7. Casualties during relief were – killed 3 wounded 4 | 1/20,000. LBW (Hereafter called map "A") LBW map. A. ES 6 sheet map LBW. JBW |

**Army Form C. 2118.**

# WAR DIARY
## or
## INTELLIGENCE SUMMARY
*(Erase heading not required.)*

Instructions regarding War Diaries and Intelligence Summaries are contained in F. S. Regs., Part II. and the Staff Manual respectively. Title Pages will be prepared in manuscript.

1ST BUCKS BATT<sup>N</sup>.

| Place | Date 1916 Nov<sup>r</sup> | Hour | Summary of Events and Information | Remarks and references to Appendices |
|---|---|---|---|---|
| Front line trenches at LE SARS. | 7. | | During the night 2nd Lt S. WISEMAN took out a patrol of 2 O.R. & explored the DRY DITCH which he found to be obliterated by shell fire – (M.9.c.a.15.a) 2nd Lt J. TACK & 2 O.R. left our line about M.15.6.9.9 & explored the enemy wire in front of GALLWITZ TRENCH which was found to be abundant. | Map 'A' L/W |
| Batt<sup>n</sup> in trenches. | | | LE SARS & DESTREMONT FARM & O.G.1, O.G.2. shelled with 10.5 cm & 9.15 cm shells at intervals during the day. At 11:45 pm 2nd Lt J.D. TUCKER & 2 O.R. left the CHALK PIT (M.15.6.2.8) & worked eastward along GALLWITZ TRENCH, locating two enemy posts at about M.9.c.75.55 & M.9.d.15.60. 2nd Lt JOHNSTONE & 2 O.R. left SCOTLAND TRENCH & explored the small wood at M.10.c.9.5.15 – about M.10.c.6.7. On moving westward a party of about 30 of the enemy were discovered repairing their wire during the night & were put to flight. | Map 'B' L/W |
| do. | 8. | | Batt<sup>n</sup> in trenches. 5 men of the 64th R.I.R. were taken prisoners. The enemy appeared nervous & shelled LE SARS, DESTREMONT FARM, O.G.1 & 2 & MARTIN PUICH. At 5:30 pm the enemy sent up multitudinous coloured rockets & opened a barrage on SCOTLAND TRENCH but more especially on our trenches opposite the BUTTS DE WARLINCOURT. At 9:30 pm the Batt<sup>n</sup> was relieved by the 1/4 R BERKS & moved back into the support line. | L/W |
| 26th AVENUE. | 9. | | Batt<sup>n</sup> in support trenches. The enemy shelled 26th AVENUE during the day & in the afternoon scored a direct hit on Bn H.Q. at 5 pm he put a barrage between 26th AVENUE & DESTREMONT FARM & the front salients on the BAPAUME ROAD. Rations to the front line as usual. Casualties 4 OR killed, 20 OR wounded. | P.R.M. L/W |

Army Form C. 2118.

# WAR DIARY
## or
## INTELLIGENCE SUMMARY

*(Erase heading not required.)*

1st AVON'S BATTN.

Instructions regarding War Diaries and Intelligence Summaries are contained in F.S. Regs., Part II. and the Staff Manual respectively. Title Pages will be prepared in manuscript.

| Place | Date 1916 Nov. | Hour | Summary of Events and Information | Remarks and references to Appendices |
|---|---|---|---|---|
| 26TH AVENUE F. | 10. | | German aeroplanes were more active, one firing a machine gun into 26 AVENUE during the afternoon. | 1/34 |
| | | | Battn in support trenches. A quiet day + night. At 3.30 pm the Battn was relieved by one Company of the 1/8 R WARWICKS & moved back to ACID DROP CAMP prior to retire CONTALMAISON. | 1/34 |
| ACID DROP CAMP | 11. | | Battn in hats. Companies supplied working parties for R.E. + for work in the camp. | |
| do. | 12. | | do. The Battn supplied working parties for R.E. + for work in the camp. | 1/34. |
| do. | 13. | | do. | 1/34. |
| do. | 14. | | do. — CONTALMAISON was shelled | 1/34. |
| do. | 15. | | during the morning + in the evening with lachrymatory shells. In the evening the Battn relieved the 1/8 R. WARWICKS in trenches in the No. 60 L.E. SAPS on the left of the Division front. The 1/5 GLOSTERS are on the R, the CANADIANS on the less At 2 am a patrol of 3 O.R. under 2.Lt PIPERNO left our lines about M.15 B. 7.3 + proceeded in a N.12 direction through M.10.c.; when close to GALLWITZ TR they encountered a strong hostile patrol (about 15 men + witnesses on enemy post was located in the bank as M.15 a 4.8 by 2 Lt DEACON + a patrol of 3.O.R. ; 2nd DEACON was wounded. At 2 am 2.Lt BORE + 2.O.R left the CHALK PIT (M.15 B) + moved in a easterly direction — owing to enemy flares the patrol could not get nearer the german line than about M.15.a.6.8 — one enemy post was discovered at M.15 a. 8.0. 3.5". | 1/34. hap A. 1/34. 1/34 |

Army Form C. 2118.

# WAR DIARY
or
## INTELLIGENCE SUMMARY
(Erase heading not required.)

1ST BUCKS BATTN.

| Place | Date 1916 NOV. | Hour | Summary of Events and Information | Remarks and references to Appendices |
|---|---|---|---|---|
| TRENCHES N of LE SARS. | 16. | | Battn in Trenches - A quiet morning. In the afternoon the enemy fired salvoes of 15 cms & 77 m.m. into DESTREMONT FARM, LE SARS, GILBERT ALLEY. At 6 p.m. a hostile barrage was put on to our Trenches in front of FAUCOURT L'ABBAYE. At 1.45 am 2/LT R. HILLMAN & 3.O.R. left SCOTLAND TR or the head of JOCK TRENCH & moved due N encountering a strong enemy patrol when they had gone about 100 yds from our Trenches - At 1 am 2/LT DARBY & 3.O.R. left the CHALK PIT & reached a point about M.9.c.9.5. 16 the gap in GALWITZ TR & found no traces of either a Trench or wire. The DRY DITCH about this point was much damaged by shell fire - No hostile movement or flares were noticed in this locality | W.D.H. |
| do. | 17. | | Battn in Trenches. Usual enemy shelling of front line O.9.1.2., LE SARS & DESTREMONT FARM - 26TH AVENUE was persistently shelled during the afternoon with 15cm shells. At night the Bn was relieved by the 1/4 OXFORD & BUCKS L.I. Bn H.Q. 'A' & 'D' Coys moved to MARTINPUICH, 'C' Coy to 70TH TR & 'B' to 26TH AVENUE. | W.D.H. |
| | 18. | | Battn in dugouts & Trenches - At night 'A', 'B', 'D' found large R.E. carrying parties, 'C' Coy carried water for the 1/4 OXFORD & BUCKS L.I. | W.D.H. |
| -do- | 19. | | Battn in dugouts & Trenches - At night 'A','B' & 'D' Coys found R.E. working parties. 'C' Coy carried rations. | |
| -do- | 20. | | Battn in dugouts & Trenches - At 6.30 pm the Bn moved up to the front line & relieved the 1/4 OXFORD & BUCKS L.I. after handing over to the 11th PROSTERS the MARTINPUICH dugouts & inspiration - 'A' took over the left front & 'D' the right front. 'B' the left support line & 'D' the right support - The 1/8 WORCESTERS were on our right, the CANADIANS on the left - | W.D.H. |

Army Form C. 2118.

# WAR DIARY
## or
## INTELLIGENCE SUMMARY

(Erase heading not required.)

1st BUCKS BATTN.

| Place | Date 1916 Nov. | Hour | Summary of Events and Information | Remarks and references to Appendices |
|---|---|---|---|---|
| TRENCHES N. of LE SARS. | 21 | | A patrol consisting of 2.LT. P.A. COATES + 1.O.R. left the CHALK PIT at 1 am & proceeded in a N.W. direction along AQUEDUCT R.P. - they could hear talking at a point along M.Q.C.7.1. - 2.LT. J.G. CLARKE + 3.O.R. left SCOTLAND TR about M.15.B.7.8. & moved in a N.E. direction & then patrolled the Bn front ; no sign of the enemy were seen or heard. Bn in Trenches. Apart from the usual shelling, nothing out of the way occurred ; at 3.30 pm however SCOTLAND TR & CHALK TR were heavily shelled for 10 mins A thick mist lasted all through the day & night & no patrols were sent out owing to this — An inter-company relief took place — | M.R. |
| do. | 22 | | Bn in Trenches. At about 5 am an enemy patrol that seemingly had lost its way in the mist approached one of our posts at M.15. c.80.62. - & was driven off by our fire ; they again returned & were driven off - 2.LT. DARBY & 2.O.R. went out to look for any bodies or traces of the enemy patrol but could find none — A fairly quiet day. As night the Bn was relieved by the 1/4 R. BERKS. The relief was memorable owing to the enemy placing a barrage of lachrymatory shells along the S of LESARS & another along the northern side of MARTIN PUICH up to the MILL (M.27.c.1.7) — MARTINPUICH itself was heavily shelled with 15 c.ms especially in the region of the CHURCH. On relief the Bn marched back to | M.R. |

Army Form C. 2118.

# WAR DIARY
## or
## INTELLIGENCE SUMMARY
(Erase heading not required.)

| Place | Date 1916 Nov. | Hour | Summary of Events and Information | Remarks and references to Appendices |
|---|---|---|---|---|
| SCOTTS REDOUBT HUTS. | 23 | | Battn. in Camp. PEAKE WOOD South Bernafay, No 1 Trenches. | PLh |
| | 24 | | 300 men on working parties (250 - 8AM to 3pm). Moved to meet bivouac up 50 - 8pm - 3am | PLh |
| | | | SCOTTS REDOUBT NISSEN huts. | |
| | 25 | | 300 men on working parties by day. | PLh |
| | 26 | | Moved to MIDDLE WOOD Camp | PLh |
| MIDDLE WOOD CAMP | 27 | | Worked on camp during day. Working parties committed moving to huts. | PLh |
| | 28 | | " " " " " " 300 men working party at night. | PLh |
| | 29 | | " " " " " " 300 " | PLh |
| | | | " " " " " " 300 " | |
| | | | Brigadier inspected A.B & C Coys at 3pm & met all officers afterwards. | PLh. |
| | 30 | | Moved to SHELTER WOOD Camp NORTH in afternoon - 300 men on working parties at night. Bttn moved to & huts in SCOTTS REDOUBT. | PLh. |

A Bridget Baker Major
O.C. 1/Border Batt.

WAR DIARY Vol 23

1 BUCKS

From Jan 1st 1919 to May 1919

CONFIDENTIAL

CONFIDENTIAL

Army Form C. 2118

1st Bucks Battn

# WAR DIARY
or
## INTELLIGENCE SUMMARY
*(Erase heading not required.)*

Instructions regarding War Diaries and Intelligence Summaries are contained in F.S. Regs., Part II. and the Staff Manual respectively. Title Pages will be prepared in manuscript.

| Place | Date | Hour | Summary of Events and Information | Remarks and references to Appendices |
|---|---|---|---|---|
| BRESLE | 1/1/17 | | Battn in billets — Companies carried out training | |
| " | 2/1/17 | | do — do | |
| " | 3/1/17 | | do — do | |
| " | 4/1/17 | | do — do | |
| " | 5/1/17 | | do — do | |
| " | 6/1/17 | | do — do. The following Officers & warrant officer awarded New Year honours. Major MITCHELL O.J. (London) Distinguished Service Order | |
| | | | Capt HALL P.A. Military Cross | |
| | | | Capt/Adjt Wright P.L. Military Cross | |
| | | | No 16 C.S.M. SWEET A.G. Military Cross | |
| | | | Revd Ce. REYNOLDS. M.C., D.S.O. Mentioned in Despatches | |
| | | | Capt BIRCHALL E.V.D. D.S.O. (died of wounds) do | |
| | | | " REID N.S. D.S.O, M.C. do | |
| | | | " WRIGHT E.L. (deceased) do | |
| | | | " HUGHES L.E. (R.A.M.C.(T)) do | |
| | | | Revd " NEAVE G.V. do | |
| | | | " HALES J.B. do | |
| " | 7/1/17 | | Battn in billets — Companies carried out training. | |

# WAR DIARY
## or
## INTELLIGENCE SUMMARY

*(Erase heading not required.)*

Army Form C. 2118

1st Bucks B.W.

| Place | Date | Hour | Summary of Events and Information | Remarks and references to Appendices |
|---|---|---|---|---|
| BRESLE | 8/1/17 | | Batt" in billets – Companies carried out training | R.L.b. fut |
| do | 9/1/17 | A.M. 3.25 | Batt" moved by Companies to HEILLY St" and entrained for NEUVILLE-au-BOIS and FORCEVILLE-en-VIMEU. Arrived at OISEMONT 12.0 noon and marched to billets. | R.L.b. fut |
| NEUVILLE au BOIS FORCEVILLE en VIMEU | 10/1/17 | | Batt" in billets – A & B Coys in FORCEVILLE-au-BOIS, C,D Coys & H.Q.rs at NEUVILLE-au-BOIS. Companies carried out training | R.L.b fut |
| do | 11/1/17 | | Batt" in billets – Platoon training etc. – All Coys | R.L.b. |
| do | 12/1/17 | | " | R.L.b. |
| do | 13/1/17 | | | R.L.b. |
| | | | – Officers & Sergts instructed in Jury | |
| do | 14/1/17 | | + War of French Instrs – Officers lecture as evening | R.L.b. |
| do | 15/1/17 | | Church services. Pln Training. | R.L.b. |
| do | 16/1/17 | | A Coy on range. Remainder Platoon Training. Officers lecture 5pm | R.L.b |
| do | 17/1/17 | | B Coy on range. do. Officers bombing class | R.L.b |
| do | 18/1/17 | | Bn H.Q. on Wormwood. Lodom Lectures etc. NCO's lecture N.C.O. | R.L.b |
| do | 19/1/17 | | C Coy on range. Remainder Platoon Training etc | R.L.b |
| do | 20/1/17 | | D Coy doing collective practices on range. C Coy attack practice. Remainder C.O. A & B Company Training | R.L.b |

Army Form C. 2118

1st BUCKS BATTN

# WAR DIARY
## or
## INTELLIGENCE SUMMARY
(Erase heading not required.)

Instructions regarding War Diaries and Intelligence Summaries are contained in F.S. Regs., Part II. and the Staff Manual respectively. Title Pages will be prepared in manuscript.

| Place | Date | Hour | Summary of Events and Information | Remarks and references to Appendices |
|---|---|---|---|---|
| NEUVILLE & FORCEVILLE | 20/1/17 | | Battn in billets. "D" coy doing collective practices on range. "C" coy doing attack practice under C.O. Remarks by Training | P.h. |
| do | 21/1/17 | | All coys musketry. Battn Stephelsen. Bucks Batt 1st. | P.h. |
| do | 22/1/17 | | Bde field day under Div at HALLENCOURT. Paraded 8am possible at 9am. Return to billets 3pm. Funds of Bde training | P.h. |
| do | 23/1/17 | | Coy training. Sum officers of the Bde doing tactical exercise hitherward troops under G.O.C. Division | P.h. |
| do | 24/1/17 | | Battn paraded 12 noon for demonstration of "contact patrol" at HALLENCOURT. Return to billets 4pm | P.h. |
| do | 25/1/17 | | Coy training | P.h. |
| do | 26/1/17 | | do | P.h. |
| do | 27/1/17 | | do | P.h. |
| do | 28/1/17 | | Coys training. Transport left at 9am, marching by road to new area | P.h. |
| do | 29/1/17 | | Battn entrained at OISEMONT at 9am for new area. Very cold journey. Detrained South of SOMME. Marched to billets & Hutty huts in HAMEL CERISY at 6pm | P.h. |
| HAMEL | 30/1/17 | | Battn route marching 10am to 12.30pm | P.h. |
| do | 31/1/17 | | + hills. Coys training | P.h. |

N.F.C. Reynolds
Lieut. Colonel
Comdg. 1/Bucks Battalion.

Vol 24

CONFIDENTIAL

War Diary

of

1st Bucks Battalion

From February 1st 1917 to February 28th 1917

# WAR DIARY or INTELLIGENCE SUMMARY

Army Form C. 2118.

1st BUCKS BATTN.

| Place | Date | Hour | Summary of Events and Information | Remarks and references to Appendices |
|---|---|---|---|---|
| HAMEL (CAMP 8). | 1916 FEBY 1. | | Battn in Adrian huts. Coy training – In the afternoon officers' bombing practice under supervision of G.O.C. 145 Inf Bde. | L.B.M. |
| do. | 2. | | Battn in Adrian huts. At 12 noon the Battn marched to huts in Camp 56 outside CAPPY – route via CERISY – MORCOURT – MERICOURT – FROISSY. | L.B.M. |
| CAMP 56 CAPPY. | 3. | | Coy training in morning. In afternoon Coy Comdrs carried out a road reconnaissance around FRISE & HERBECOURT. | L.B.M. |
| do. | 4. | | The C.O. rode up to see the 1/4 & 3 Inf Bde in the line. In the evening certain officers & N.C.O's went up to the support Bn of the 143 Inf Bde next to a trip to taking over the trenches held by that Bn. | L.B.M. |
| do. | 5. | | At 4.30 p.m. the Bn moved from camp & marched up to relieve the 1/7 R. WARWICKS, the support Bn of the left Bde – Route via ECLUSIER – FRISE & roads in H.21.a. thence by Boyau GUERRIERES to the support trenches – 'A' Coy took over the posts on the RIVER SOMME. 'B' the left & 'C' the right of TR. 191AU – Bn HQ were in the latter trench. 'D' Coy remained at CAPPY in Camp 50 bis as Works Coy. | map FRANCE Sheet 62c N.W. Edition 4.A. 1/40,000 (Kriegskarten) "map A'jm" |
| Support trenches | 6. | | Very quiet day – trench mortar + rifle grenades active on front line. A few trench mortar bombs around SLADEN REDOUBT. | L.B.M. |
| do. | 7. | | Quiet day. Enemy artillery more active in the back areas, also near Bois Bell at KIBORO WOOD (H.36.a). The SOMME was frozen over on REACHES but flowing freely opposite BAZIN COURT FARM. (H.24.G.J). | map A. |
| do. | 8. | | Quiet day – During the morning a few 77mm shells fell near the bridges at BAZIN COURT FARM a in the afternoon a few H.E. shrapnel shells burst over the track adjoining the BOIS DE L'EPEE (H.30.a.v.6) – Two platoons of 'D' Coy came up with dugouts in TR. DESIRÉE opposite KIBORO WOOD. | map A. |

Army Form C. 2118

# WAR DIARY
## or
## INTELLIGENCE SUMMARY
(Erase heading not required)

1st BUCKS BATTN.

| Place | Date 1916 FEBY | Hour | Summary of Events and Information | Remarks and references to Appendices |
|---|---|---|---|---|
| Support Trenches | 9. | | Battn. in support trenches. A quiet day. At night the Bn. handed over its line to the Bns of 143 Inf Bde as follows:— <br><br> 2 left platoons on the SOMME to 1/8 R.WARWICKS. <br> 2 right " + SLADEN REDOUBT } to 1/7 R.WARWICKS. <br> Northern half of TR. 19 LAU }  do <br> Southern " " " } to 1/5 R.WARWICKS <br> Bn H.Q. } <br> 2 platoons in TR. DESIRÉE } 1/6 R.WARWICKS <br><br> On completion of relief the Battn. moved via BOYAU GUERRIERES & TR. SOPHIE approximately in G. 30 b + d + north of the HERBÉ COURT — BULL'S WOOD — CAPPY road. B, C + D Coys were in dugouts in + around TR. SOPHIE + 'A' Coy were similarly situated in HERBÉCOURT. <br> The Bn. was in Bde Reserve to the 145 Inf Bde. — | W.D.— App 'A' W.D. W.D— W.D— W.D— W.D— |
| Bn in Bde Reserve near TR. SOPHIE near HERBÉCOURT | 10. | | Battn. in dugouts. 'D' Coy supplied an R.E. working party of 2 platoons — at night B + C Coys went up to the trenches to work for the 1/5 GLOSTERS. | |
| do. | 11. | | do. — At night A + B Coys supplied working parties for the front line Battns. (1/4 OXF & BUCKS L.I. + 1/5 GLOSTERS) | |
| do. | 12. | | Coys engaged in box respirator drill. | |
| do. | 13. | | do. — In the evening the Battn. marched to trenches via B. ROMAIN DES FOSSÉES + B. VALLOT + relieved the 1/5 GLOSTERS in the line N.E of BARLEUX — 'D' Coy were on the right, 'C' in the centre, 'B' on the left + 'A' in support — 1st BN. R.MUNSTER FUSILIERS (1st DIVISION) were on our right + the 1/4 R.BERKS on our left. — | |

Army Form C. 2118

# WAR DIARY
## or
## INTELLIGENCE SUMMARY

1ST BUCKS BATN.

(Erase heading not required.)

Instructions regarding War Diaries and Intelligence Summaries are contained in F. S. Regs., Part II. and the Staff Manual respectively. Title Pages will be prepared in manuscript.

| Place | Date 1916 FEBY. | Hour | Summary of Events and Information | Remarks and references to Appendices |
|---|---|---|---|---|
| Trenches N.E of BARLEUX. | 14. | | Battn in trenches. A quiet night — enemy intermittently sent over rifle grenades & still bombs — At night 2 Lt. DARBY & 2.O.R. patrolled our wire & found in need of repair — | W.H. |
| do. | 15. | | Between 9 am & 12 noon B. de COSTE, BRISSON, des POMMIERS & CHAMINADE were intermittently shelled with 10 cm & 15 cm shells — no damage done — Between the same hours the R.E. dump adjoining the FLAUCOURT — RIACHES road (N.5a) was very heavily shelled with 15 cm shells, one direct hit being obtained on a dump of French bombs. Heavy horse transport heard between 6pm & 9 pm on the BARLEUX — GARDEN FARM road. (N.86 — 0.13 a & 6 — 0.14.a) A patrol of 1 N.C.O. & 4 men left our lines about N.12.a. 90.10. at 2 am & examined the enemy wire which was found to consist of 2 belts about 7 yds wide & very strong. A second patrol consisting of NEUT G.F. KNIGHT left our lines about 0.7.a. 20.81 but were made to approach the enemy wire owing to a hostile covering party which was screening a wiring party — A third patrol of 1 N.C.O. & 4 men left our lines at 0.7.6. 20.80 at 2 am & found the enemy wire to be about 15 yds deep — enemy sap at 0.7.a. 78-75 was not held — Lights from dugouts could be seen along BENOIT TR. | map. BARLEUX 12° S.W. 2 Section 1a 1/10,000 (Areas calls 'Map B') map 'B'. W.H. |
| do. | 16. | | Enemy Artillery quiet — At 11.15 pm a patrol of 1 N.C.O. & 3 men left our lines about N.12.a. 90.11 & located enemy posts at N.12.b. 42.32 & N.12.b. 52.32. Two other patrols also went out. | W.H. |

**Army Form C. 2118**

# WAR DIARY
## or
## INTELLIGENCE SUMMARY

*(Erase heading not required.)*

**1st BUCKS BATN.**

Instructions regarding War Diaries and Intelligence Summaries are contained in F.S. Regs., Part II. and the Staff Manual respectively. Title Pages will be prepared in manuscript.

| Place | Date 1916. FEB. | Hour | Summary of Events and Information | Remarks and references to Appendices |
|---|---|---|---|---|
| TRENCHES N.E. of BARLEUX. | 17. | | Bn in Trenches. A quiet day & night. In the evening the Bn was relieved by the 1/6 Glosters & marched back to Camp 56 at Cappy. | 1 App. |
| Camp 56 CAPPY. | 18. | | Bn in huts. Coys at disposal of O.C. Coys for interior economy. | 2 App. |
| do. | 19. | | do. Baths for Bn at ECLUSIER. | 2 App. |
| do. | 20. | | do. Company Training – Working parties of 2 officers & 150 men supplied. | P.App. |
| do. | 21. | | do.   do.            "   2   "   150   " | P.App. |
| do. | 22. | | do.   do.            "   2   "   140   " | P.App. |
| do. | 23. | | do.   do.            "   2   "   140   " | P.App. |
| do. | 24. | | do.   do.            "   3   "   200   " | P.App. |
| do. | 25. | | do.   do.            "   3   "   200   " | P.App. |
| do. | 26. | | Starting from Camp at 3.45 pm & marching by platoons by road, Bn moved to support line near BOIS ACHILLE & relieved 7th Worcesters. D Coy in DESIREE walk., A Coy half in BEAUSEJOUR half in Bn HQ trench, C Coy at Batn HQ & B Coy in FLAUCOURT. Relief complete at 9.30 pm. | P.App. |
| Bn in BDE SUPPORT (nr BOIS ACHILLE) | 27. | | Quiet day. 2 coys on working parties. Relieved 1/5 Glosters in front line in evening. Relief complete at 11.30 pm. 1st Div on right. 1/4 R.Berks on left. Artillery bombarded enemies front & support line at 1 AM. Strong patrols out in no mans land. | |
| TRENCHES NE OF BARLEUX | 28. | | Our artillery bombarded enemy front & support line from 5.25 AM – 5.55 AM to assist operations undertaken by XIV Corps on our right. (Men + Q.R. wounded.) (Capt G.R.C. Rough wounded) | 2nd Lt Hall Capt. Pu... killed |

1875. Wt. W593/826 1,000,000 4/15 I.B.C. & A. A.D.S.S./Forms/C. 2118.

WM 25

L.a.
25.S
16 sheet

CONFIDENTIAL

WAR DIARY

of

1/1 Bucks Battalion.

From 1st March 1917 to 31st March 1917.

# WAR DIARY or INTELLIGENCE SUMMARY

Army Form C. 2118

**1/1 BUCKS BATTN.**

| Place | Date 1917 March | Hour | Summary of Events and Information | Remarks and references to Appendices |
|---|---|---|---|---|
| TRENCHES | 1 | | Bn in Trenches. Quiet day - Visibility - good. Trenches drying but still very muddy. Relieved by 1/5th GLOSTER REGT in evening. Relief took place overland + was complete by 9.15 pm. Battn. marched back to BDE Reserve in TR. SOPHIE. A.B.+C coys in TR. SOPHIE. D coy in HARBECOURT. Total casualties during 2 days French tour - 1 Officer (Capt. G.R. CROUCH) + 13 O.R. Ration strength - 23 Offrs. 695 O.R. | P.L.h. |
| TR. SOFIE (M 25 c) | 2 | | Bn in Bde Reserve. All coys supplying working parties in daytime for digging out supports + communication trenches + carrying T.H. bombs etc. Ration strength - 23 Offrs. 696 O.R. | P.L.h. |
| do | 3 | | B.Tn. moved from SOFIE TR at 2 pm into Div Reserve at MARY Camp. Ration strength 23 Offrs. 645 O.R. | P.L.h. Rolls of att.d |
| Bn in Div Reserve at MARY CAMP (ADRIAN HUTS) | 4 | | All coys resting. Ration strength 23 Offrs. 701 O.R. | P.L.h. |
| do | 5 | | Enough during night. Then thaw throughout day. Coys carried out training in huts as far as possible. Lt Col REYNOLDS resumed command 1 B.T.L. Ration strength 22 Offrs. 701 O.R. | P.L.h. |
| do | 6 | | Marched to SOFIE TR by platoons, starting at 1.30 pm. 2 Coys had baths at CAPEY on way through. Ration strength - 23 Offrs. 694 O.R. | P.L.h. |

# WAR DIARY or INTELLIGENCE SUMMARY

Army Form C. 2118.

1/ BUCKS BATTN

| Place | Date MARCH 1917 | Hour | Summary of Events and Information | Remarks and references to Appendices |
|---|---|---|---|---|
| SOFIE TR. | 7. | | Battn in Bde reserve. Training taken up with coy's/trench tools tombing. 2 coys baths in CAMP. Marched up to trenches 1st Coy heading TR SOFIE at 6:30 pm. Relieved 1/7 FORESTERS - Relief completed by 10 pm. Dispositions - Front Line - A coy on right, B coy on left, C coy (1 platoon in CRAPOUNNER, 1 in MAUPAS) in FIELD, 1 in POMMIERS). Reserve - D coy (bottom of ASHIRES) 1/4 R. BERKS on right, 1st ROYAL SUSSEX (1st DIV) on right. 1/4 R. BERKS carried out raid on enemy front line at 12.45 am, but found no enemy. Patrols sent out by us later found enemy occupying their front line strictly to support line very strongly. A further raid carried out by BERKS at 3 am seemed 2 prisoners. Ration strength 22 offr 900 or. | Rly order attached |
| Trenches. | 8. | | Bn in trenches. Enemy active with GRANATEN WERFER during early morning, otherwise quiet day. Some snow + v. cold - visibility fair. Front line coys sent out patrols in evening. Bns reported enemy holding their front line. 143 Bde on left of Divl sector carried out raid at 9 pm. Result not known. Casualties during 24 hours - killed 3 or, wounded 5. All caused by GRANATENWERFER. Ration strength 22 offrs 695 or. | P.L.I |

J.B.C. & A. Forms/C.2118/12

# WAR DIARY
## or
## INTELLIGENCE SUMMARY

*(Erase heading not required.)*

**1/1 Bucks Battn.**

Army Form C. 2118.

| Place | Date | Hour | Summary of Events and Information | Remarks and references to Appendices |
|---|---|---|---|---|
| TRENCHES | MARCH 9 1917 | | Bn in Trenches. Enemy active with GRANATENWERFER, especially about "Stand to", otherwise quiet. Our guns shelled LA MAISONETTE (with persistently all day. C coy relieved B coy in left front line during evening. Casualties for 24 hours — killed — 2 O.R. Wounded 3 O.R. Ration str. 22 offrs 690 OR | P.L.W. |
| do | 10 | | Just about 4 am enemy sent over a gas shell which burst directly in the entrance to the right coy (A) HQ dugout, gassing the occupants, 3 O/rs & 15 OR all of whom were dead by 10 am. Otherwise quiet day. Foggy. Then continued throughout day. Trenches in v. bad condition by evening. Casualties — Killed Officers 3 (Capt J.D.B.WARWICK. 2/Lt S.KISEMAN 2/Lt R.B.COOPER,SMITH) OR - 15. Wounded 4. Missing 1. Ration strength 22 offr 691 OR | P.L.W. |
| do | 11 | | Quiet day. Trenches very muddy. Relieved by 1/5 Glosters in evening. Relief complete by 1 am. Went back to support line. C & D Coys in FLAUCOURT. A & B coys in DÉSIRÉE valley. Ration strength 19 offrs 664 OR | P.L.W. |
| SUPPORT - 2 coys FLAUCOURT 2 " DÉSIRÉE VALLEY | 12 | | Bn in Bde Support. Quiet day. About 300 men in working parties during day. Enemy shelled FLAUCOURT with 59's intermittently throughout afternoon, causing D Coy casualties. Killed 4 O.R. Wounded 2 O.R. Ration str. 19 offrs 664 OR | P.L.W. P.L.W. P.L.W. |

Army Form C. 2118.

# WAR DIARY
## or
## INTELLIGENCE SUMMARY

1/1 BUCKS BATTN

(Erase heading not required.)

| Place | Date | Hour | Summary of Events and Information | Remarks and references to Appendices |
|---|---|---|---|---|
| SUPPORT. 2 coys FLAUCOURT 3 " DESIRÉS VALLEY | MARCH 1917 13 | | Bn in Bde Support. Enemy shelled FLAUCOURT & neighbourhood with 5.9" throughout day with S.9's & some lachrymatory shells. Bth relieved in evening by 1/7" WORCESTERS – Relief complete by 10 pm – Coys marched independently to CAMP 56. Ration Strength 21 offrs 646 OR. | R/M |
| CAMP 56 | 14 | | Bn in Divl Reserve. All coys rest. 2 coys baths in CAPPY in afternoon. Ration Strength 21 offrs 635 OR. | R/M |
| (CAPPY — ECLUSIER Rd) | 15. | | do. Bth supplied 600 OR & 7 RE working parties. 200 for working Corps line. Ration Strength 20 offrs 636 OR. | R/M |
| do | 16 | | do. 2 coys baths at CAPPY. Training. Presentation of medals. by Corps Commander at Divl HQ – 100 OR C coy attended. Following were decorated — CAPT R.A. HALL — MC. CAPT R.L. WRIGHT MC. 1247 CSM BISHOP.S.G. – DCM & Croix de Guerre. 2131 Sgt BALDWIN.G – MM. 1408 CPL GOLDWAIN J – MM. 1392 L/Cpl ODELL G.H. – MM. 1805 Pr HAYNES T4 – MM Ration Strength 20 offrs 642 OR. | R/M |
| do | 17 | | 3 Coys Training. 1 Coy on Working Party. 2 Coys listed lose respirators in the afternoon. Ration Strength 20 offrs 640 OR. | R/M |
| do. | 18 | | All coys resting. Ration Strength 21 offrs 641 OR | R/M |

# WAR DIARY
## INTELLIGENCE SUMMARY

1/1 BUCKS BATTN

Army Form C. 2118

| Place | Date | Hour | Summary of Events and Information | Remarks and references to Appendices |
|---|---|---|---|---|
| CAMP 36. CAPPY - ECLUSIER Rd | 1917 MARCH 19 | | Bn. in Div. Reserve. Battn. Training for all Coys. in the morning. C.O. lectured Officers on Coln. Grenades and Outposts in the evening. Ration Strength 24 officers 641 OR | P.A.H. |
|  | 20 | | Battn. left Camp 36 at 1 p.m. and marched to PERONNE via HERBECOURT – BIRCHES – BAZINCOURT FARM – HALLE. Advance parties were sent ahead to reconnoitre the outpost-line covering PERONNE and for billets. Bn. arrived at PERONNE about 4 p.m. The town had been completely wrecked by the enemy and was still burning in several places. Coys. were billeted in cellars on N.W. side of the Square. Bn. Hqrs were at the Château. Transport were in a field just E. of LA QUINCONCE. Ration Strength 24 officers 639 OR | P.A.H. Reinforcement P. 169 attached |
| PERONNE | 21 | | Outpost-Line. B.C. x D Coys. moved off about 6.30 a.m. to relieve 1/8 R. Warwickshire Regt. in the outpost-line in THREE TUB3 WOOD, DOINGT WOODS and COURCELLES WOOD. A Coy. relieved reserve Coy in the Barracks at PERONNE. Relief complete 10.15 a.m. H.Qrs. moved temporarily to 8th WARWICK Hqrs. in PERONNE. Coys. were disposed as follows:- D Coy. in forward position on E. edge of COURCELLES WOOD. C and B Coy. on line of Resistance along E. edge of THREE TUBS WOOD and DOINGT WOOD holding a line from 500 yds. S. of BUSSU to the COLOGNE RIVER. C Coy. at N. end, A Coy. Southern end. Ration St. 24 officers 637 OR | P.A.H. |

Army Form C. 2118

Instructions regarding War Diaries and Intelligence Summaries are contained in F.S. Regs., Part II. and the Staff Manual respectively. Title Pages will be prepared in manuscript.

# WAR DIARY or INTELLIGENCE SUMMARY

(Erase heading not required.)

1/1 Bucks Batth.

| Place | Date 1917 March | Hour | Summary of Events and Information | Remarks and references to Appendices |
|---|---|---|---|---|
| PERONNE | 21 | | Outpost line. In the afternoon Bn. H.Qrs. moved to DOINGT (1.35.6.9.9.) | P.att. |
| DOINGT | 22 | " | C. Coy. took over from D. Coy. in forward position at 5 a.m. with picquets at RONCES WOOD, COURCELLES WOOD, and quarry in J.32. B. WARDS COLUMN moved forward through outpost line to CARTIGNY. D. Coy. took over position previously held by C. Coy. at 4 p.m. A. Coy. moved up from PERONNE to billet in Maison Dieu, 31 Avenue 638 a.tt. C. Coy. relieved C. Coy. at 5 a.m. in forward position in DOINGT. | P.att. Ref. Frames 62.C.N.E |
| " | 23 | " | B. Coy. withdrawing. C.Coy. withdrawing to position previously held by B.Coy. in Reserve Line. During day D.Coy. dug section B.Coy. trenches in front of 3 Tanks Wood. 2 Platoons of A.Coy. took over portion of Reserve line nearest COLOGNE, now in trenches astride DOINGT — COURCELLES Rd. Remaining 2 Platoons of A.Coy. and Coy. H.Qrs. billeted in E. end of DOINGT. 2nd Lieut. PULLMAN took over command of A.Coy. vice Capt. WOOLERTON to hospital sick. Ration Strength 21 Offr. 653 O.R. | P.att. |
| " | 24 | " | D. Coy. relieved B. Coy. in forward position at 5 a.m. The line was advanced to cover BUIRE, a picquet being established in the village with posts on E. edge. Front covered was also festooned front of | P.att. |

# WAR DIARY
## or
## INTELLIGENCE SUMMARY

*(Erase heading not required.)*

Army Form C. 2118

1/Bucks Battn.

| Place | Date 1917 MARCH | Hour | Summary of Events and Information | Remarks and references to Appendices |
|---|---|---|---|---|
| DOINGT | 24 | Outpost line | COLOGNE RIVER to cover BRUSLE, this portion being taken over from 1/4th R.BERKS. REGT. and held by 2 Platoons of A. Coy. brought up from DOINGT Village. B. Coy. was withdrawn to position vacated by D. Coy. in Reserve line. line runs RED HOUSE (exclusive) – RONCES WOOD, – COURCELLES WOOD – BUIRE – BRUSLE. Lieut. J. B. HALES rejoined Battn. from 145 Inf. Bde. H.Qrs. 5th Cavalry Div. handed over outposts to maintain touch with enemy. Ration strength 20 Officers 644 OR | P.A.A. |
| " | 25 | " | C. Coy. + 2 Platoons of A. Coy. relieved D. Coy. and other 2 Platoons of A. Coy. in forward position at 5 a.m., D. Coy. returning to DOINGT WOOD line, and the 2 Platoons of A. to Trenches astride DOINGT – COURCELLES road. The line was again altered, the portion in front of BRUSLE South of COLOGNE river being handed over to 1/4th R.BERKS. at 8 a.m. Our Outpost line was extended Northwards as far as V.11.c.5.7. so as to cover BUIRE WOODS, and running from then in a straight line to E. edge of BUIRE. | P.A.A. |

Army Form C. 2118

# WAR DIARY
## or
## INTELLIGENCE SUMMARY  1/1 Bucks Battn.
(Erase heading not required.)

Instructions regarding War Diaries and Intelligence Summaries are contained in F.S. Regs., Part II. and the Staff Manual respectively. Title Pages will be prepared in manuscript.

| Place | Date 1917 MARCH | Hour | Summary of Events and Information | Remarks and references to Appendices |
|---|---|---|---|---|
| DOINGT | 25 | | Outpost line. There was a certain amount of shelling of the Outpost line near BUIRE WOOD 9 during the day. Hostile aircraft were very active. Ration strength 21 offr. 646 o.r. | P.A.H. |
| " | 26 | | Heavy rain nearly all day. B.Coy. relieved C.Coy. in forward position at 4.30 a.m. The two halves of A.Coy. again changed over. D.Coy. found working party for R.E. at CARTENY river crossing until 1.30 p.m. Bn. moved to TINCOURT at 5 p.m. handing over to DOINGT area to 4th Ryl. BERKS. Billets at TINCOURT were taken over from 4th OXFORDS. Transport difficulties Mo. delayed Bn. and they were not all in till 10 p.m. Fairly comfortable billets, a village contained civilians and was not much damaged. Capt. N.S. REID rejoined Battn. and took over command of A.Coy. Ration strength 26 offr. 646 o.r. | P.A.H. |

1875. Wt. W593/826 1,000,000 4/15 J.B.C. & A. A.D.S.S./Forms/C. 2118.

# WAR DIARY
## or
## INTELLIGENCE SUMMARY — 1/1 BUCKS BATTN.

Army Form C. 2118

| Place | Date | Hour | Summary of Events and Information | Remarks and references to Appendices |
|---|---|---|---|---|
| TINCOURT | 1917 MARCH 27 | | Outpost line. Bn. moved at 9 a.m. to take over Outpost line from 1/4th OXFORDS. H.Qn. at HAMEL + B Company. D & C Coys holding ROISEL, A Coy. holding line K.3 central to K.10 d.1.2. with Coy. H.Qn. at MARQUAIX. At 5.30 p.m. 5th Cavalry Div. attacked and captured 9 VILLERS - FAUCON, SAULCOURT and GUYENCOURT. At 7 p.m. line covering ROISEL was handed over to 2/4th LINCOLNS (59th Div.) and our right boundary became COLOGNE RIVER. D Coy. were withdrawn to MARQUAIX, and C Coy. to HAMEL. At 9.30 p.m. B Coy. moved up to VILLERS-FAUCON to assist the Cavalry who were holding the edge of the village and southwards along road to K.4.b.3.3. A Coy. moved up a lewis gun to protect flank of Cavalry. Ration strength Offrs. 21 OR 638. | Path. Ref. 62 C. NE. 1/20,000. Definition not attacked D.5. |

Army Form C. 2118

# WAR DIARY
## or
## INTELLIGENCE SUMMARY

1/1 BUCKS BATTN.

*(Erase heading not required.)*

Instructions regarding War Diaries and Intelligence Summaries are contained in F.S. Regs., Part II. and the Staff Manual respectively. Title Pages will be prepared in manuscript.

| Place | Date 1917 MARCH | Hour | Summary of Events and Information | Remarks and references to Appendices |
|---|---|---|---|---|
| HAMEL | 28 | 5 a.m. | Outpost line. D. Coy. relieved A Coy. in outpost line as yesterday. A. Coy. were withdrawn to MARQUAIX. Enemy shelled VILLERS-FAUCON with 77 cms. and 5.9's in the morning. During night 4th R. BERKS. provided working parties to dig craterform posts on outpost line. A few #77's were fired into Eastern edge of HAMEL during the afternoon. Cavalry were withdrawn from VILLERS-FAUCON after dark, and A Coy. were sent up to take their place. At same time C. Coy. relieved B. Coy. the latter returning to billets in MARQUAIX. A very wet and dark night. Telephones were out for several hours, and communication forward entirely broke down owing to difficulty of finding forward Coys. H. Qrs. in the intense darkness. B and C were shelled during relief. Casualties 1 O.R. killed, 9 O.R. wounded. 2nd Lieut Vaughan to Hospital, sick. Ration str. 21 offrs 658 or | P.4.H. Disposition map attached D's |

1875. Wt. W593/826 1,000,000 4/15 J.B.C. & A. A.D.S.S./Forms/C. 2118.

# WAR DIARY
## or
## INTELLIGENCE SUMMARY
### 1/1 Bucks Battn.

*(Erase heading not required.)*

Army Form C. 2118

| Place | Date 1917 MARCH | Hour | Summary of Events and Information | Remarks and references to Appendices |
|---|---|---|---|---|
| HAMEL | 29 | Outpost line. | Dispositions as yesterday. Heavy rain nearly all day. Battn. was relieved by 1/4 GLOSTERS after dark, and marched back to CARTIGNY to billets in cellars. Before relief A Coy. sent out strong patrols to find out if enemy were still holding Ste. EMILIE. This was found to be still held. Bn. all in at CARTIGNY, about 3 am. where they became part of DOBBIN'S COLUMN. Casualties 2 O.R. Wounded. Ration str. 20 offrs. 650 or. | P.A.H. |
| CARTIGNY | 30 | DOBBIN'S COLUMN. | All Coys. resting. Day spent - getting clean and dry. Ration strength 19 offrs. 673 or. | P.A.H. |
| " | 31 | " | Coys. resting. 2 offrs. per Coy at work on roads in village. 2nd Lieut. PASSMORE to Hospital sick. 2nd Lieut. ZIRMINGER to Signalling Course. N.X.C. Ration strength 19 offrs. 624 or. | P.A.H. Lt Col cdg 1/1 Bucks Bn |

S E C R E T.    1/ BUCKS BATTALION.    W/601.

1. The Battalion will move to MARLY CAMP (R.4.b.9.2) to-day, 3rd instant.

2. The leading platoon of each Company will pass SOFIE TR. on the HERBECOURT - CAPPY Road at following times. 300 yards interval between platoons will be maintained.
Dress - Marching Order.
  'A' Coy.   -   1.0  p.m.
  'C'  "     -   1.05  "
  'B'  "     -   1.10  "
  'D'  "     -   1.15  "

3. All cookers (except 'D' Coy) will move in rear of the last platoon of its Company. 'D' Coy's cooker will be moved at dusk.

4. All blankets and valises (except 'D' Coy's) will be dumped at SOFIE TR. at side of main road by 11 a.m.. 1 man per Coy. will remain with them. Mess boxes surplus to those carried on cooker to be dumped by 1 p.m.. Lewis Guns will be loaded on limbers at SOFIE TR. at 12.30 p.m.

5. Horses for O.C. Coys. will be at SOFIE TR. at 1 p.m.

6. O.C. 'A' Coy. will provide 2/Lieut. COOPER-SMITH with a party large enough to move all Coys. Lewis Gun handcarts from Camp 56 to MARLY Camp during afternoon. This party will move independently to the Coy. under 2/Lieut. Cooper-Smith.

*[signature]*
Captain & Adjutant,
1/ Bucks Battalion.

3/3/17.

W/612.

O.C. Companies.
---------------

1. The Battalion relieves 1/7 WORCESTERS in right front line to-night.

2. The line will be held as follows -
'B' Coy. on Left  )
'A'  "   "  Right )  Front line.
'C'  "   In Support.
'D'  "   "  Reserve.

3. Dispositions:
A & B Coys. will each have 3½ platoons in front line and ½ in support at Coy. H.Q.. Coy. H.Q. as before for right and left Coys.
C Coy. - 1 platoon in FIOLLE, 1 in MAUPOIL, 1 in POMMIERS, 1 in CHAMINADE. Support Coy. H.Q. as before.
D Coy. - All platoons and Coy. H.Q. in support line in dug-outs at bottom of ACHILLE close to Support Bn. H.Q..

4. Guides will be at point where VALLOT Trench crosses HERBECOURT - FLAUCOURT Road at 7.15 p.m..

5. Order of going up will be notified later.

6. Officers blankets and mess boxes will be loaded at end of SOFIE at 6.45 p.m., and in the case of 'D' Coy. at their Cooker. The waggons taking these will also carry up fuel and rum. 'D' Coy. will be responsible for meeting these waggons at the Dump on FLAUCOURT - BIACHES Road and delivering the rum and fuel to Companies.

7. A, B & C Coys. will load their Lewis Guns on limbers at SOFIE at 5.30 p.m.. Two men per Company will accompany limbers. Coys. will pick up their guns as they pass Ration Dump. 'D' Coy. will man-handle their guns.

(Sd)   P.L. WRIGHT, Captain & Adjutant,
7/3/17.                              1/ Bucks Battalion.

COPY.

SECRET.   B/691.

## 1/ BUCKS BATTALION.

1. The Battalion, together with Transport and Quartermaster's Stores, will move to PERONNE to-day.
Dress - Marching Order.

2. Companies will march by platoons, the first platoon of each Company leaving Camp at following hours.   Usual distances will be maintained.

H.Q. - 12.55 p.m.
'A' Coy. - 1.00 "
'B' " - 1.05 "
'C' " - 1.10 "
'D' " - 1.15 "

Cookers will move behind the rear platoon of their Company.

3. Transport and Q.M. Stores will join the Column at cross roads, G.28.b.4.3..

4. Route: ECLUSIER - HERBECOURT - BIACHES (outskirts) - BAZINCOURT FARM - HALLE - I.21.c.9.1. - I.21.d.1.6..

5. Valises and 1 mess box per Company will be loaded close to the road, near the Camp Stores at 12 noon.
Blankets will be dumped at same place by 12.30 p.m..   Each Coy. will leave 1 man with their blankets, and 'D' Coy. 1 N.C.O. in addition to take charge.

6. Lewis Gun limbers together with 1 man per Coy. will move at 1.20 p.m.

7. Any kit surplus to that mentioned above must be carried on cooker or dumped in hut at present occupied by C.Q.M.Sgts.

(Sd) P.L. WRIGHT, Captain & Adjutant,
1/ Bucks Battalion.

30/3/17.

# 1ST BUCKS. BATTN.
## OUTPOST DISPOSITIONS.
### MARCH 27th 1917.

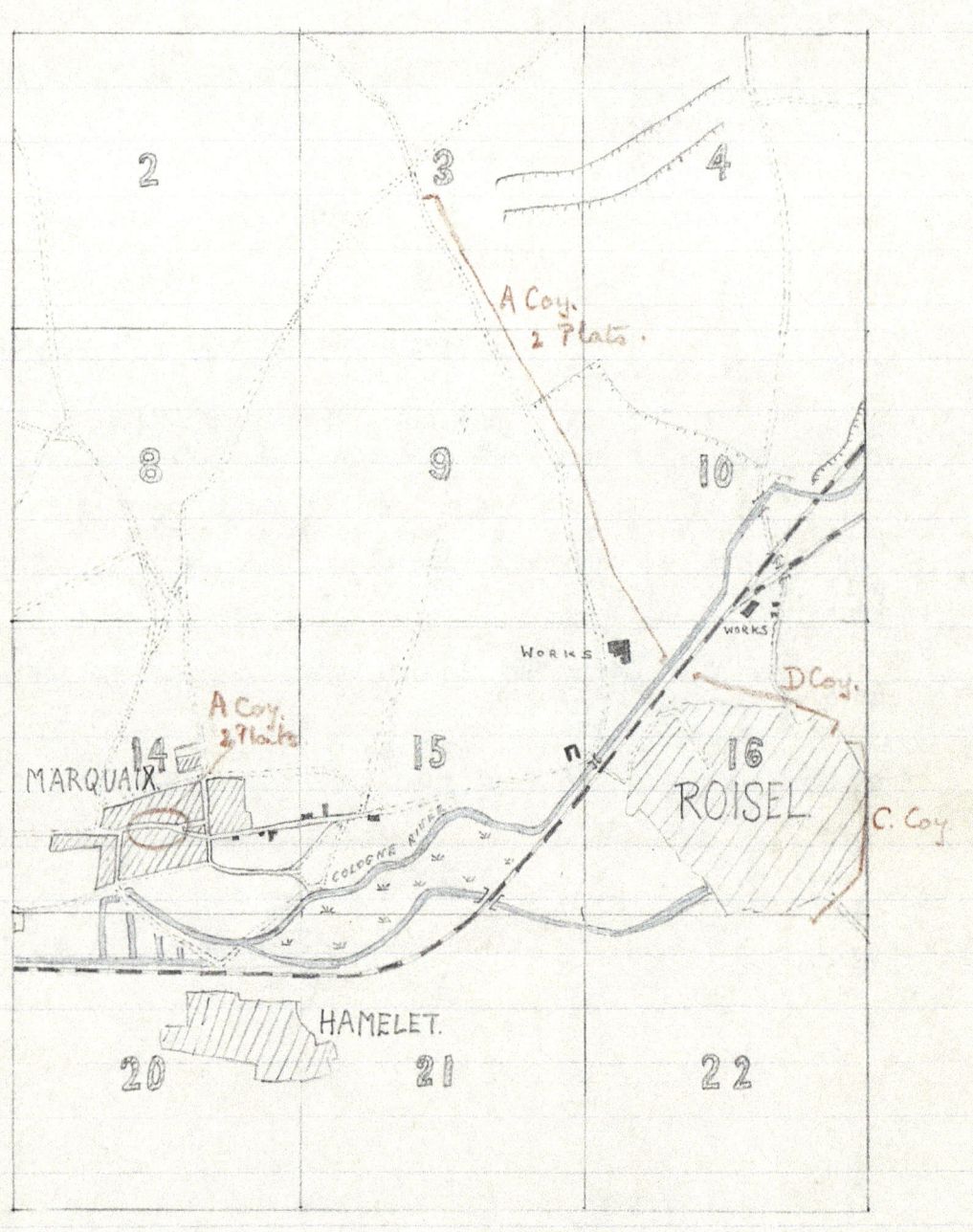

Scale 1/20,000.

1st DCLI BATTN
OUTPOST DISPOSITIONS.
MARCH 28th
1917.

Scale 1/20,000

March 28th
A Coy.

VILLERS FAUCON

March 28th
C Coy.

R.& S.6.

R.J.Cert.

March 28th
D Coy.

March 27th
A Coy.

COLOGNE RIVER

Works   Works

March 27th
D Coy.

March 28th
B Coy.

MARQUAIX

ROISEL

March 27th
C Coy.

To HERVILLY

P A Hall Major

# WAR DIARY or INTELLIGENCE SUMMARY

Army Form C. 2118.

1/1 Bucks Bn., Oxf & Bks. L.I.

| Place | Date 1917 APRIL | Hour | Summary of Events and Information | Remarks and references to Appendices |
|---|---|---|---|---|
| CARTIGNY | 1 | Bn in billets. | Working parts of 400 men worked on roads in & around TINCOURT. Major P.A. Hall proceeded to ENGLAND to attend Senior Officers course. Train departed 14 Bde GAS DR. | RLW |
| do | 2 | do | Working party of 400 men on roads in & around TINCOURT. Train departed 14 Offrs 646 OR. | RLW |
| do | 3 | do | Battn, with Transport, left Cartigny between 8.30 am & 9 am & moved by platoons to LONGAVESNES, relieving 1/5 Glosters in Bde reserve. All ranks in very poor bivouacs & shelters. No cellar accommodation left. B & C Coys in trenches. Parties during evening. Ration strength 19 Offrs 654 OR. | RLW |
| LONGAVESNES | 4 | do | Coys resting & improving billets &c. Ration str. 19 Offrs 653 OR. | RLW |
| do | 5 | do | Battn, less Transport, moved from LONGAVESNES at 2 am to Railway cutting E of VILLERS FAUCON, arr E.23.A.2.4, acting as reserve to remainder of Bde who were to capture down the villages of LEMPIRE, RONSSOY, & BASSE BOULOGNE, by attacking as follows:— 1/4 R BERKS — N & SE of RONSSOY & BASSE BOULOGNE. 1/4 OXFORDS — SW end of RONSSOY. 1/5 GLOSTERS — LA TRAVERELLE, LEMPIRE & BASSE BOULOGNE. Each battn to about 16 cm in Battn reserve. Zero 4.15 am. Attack completely successful, all objectives being taken 1 with 30 prisoners & about 4 machine guns. At 10.30 am Battn moved into selves & billets in VILLERS FAUCON for the day, taking over the left of the new line from 1/5 GLOSTERS, F.10 C 8.2 (excl) to | See Map D. |

Army Form C. 2118.

# WAR DIARY
## or
## INTELLIGENCE SUMMARY.
*(Erase heading not required.)*

| Place | Date 1917 April | Hour | Summary of Events and Information | Remarks and references to Appendices |
|---|---|---|---|---|
| OUTPOSTS LEMPIRE (N°5a) to MALASSISE FARM (F2.D) | 5 | 4 P.M | Full Central. Dispositions – 2 coys in outpost line – A coy on right, B coy on left. (See Map D attd) – C coy in support in cellars in BASSE BOULOGNE – D coy in reserve at F8c.27. Bn HQ under cover in railway cutting abt F8.c.03. 1/6 R. BERKS on right – 1/6 R. WARWICK regt on left. Quiet night. Transport at root crossing abt F23d.22. | Ref Map in all cases 62c NE 1/20000 |
| do | 6 | On Outpost | Enemy shelled MAYE COPSE & MALASSISE FARM intermittently throughout day otherwise quiet. A proposed attack on No 12 copse in F3b, which was to have been carried out by D coy, at 9.30 pm, was cancelled. All coys at work during night digging communication posts along new line of resistance (marked in red on MAP D). – Zone reliefs in evening. C coy relieving A coy on right. D coy relieving B coy on left. Casualties 3 OR (2 slightly wounded). Ration etc 19 offrs 654 OR. | P.t.o. |
| do | 7 | do | Finer full during night. Quiet day in evening. Relief completed by 11.30 pm. Relieved by 1/7 WORCESTERS. to MARQUAIX. Accommodation – Fair – Chiefly cellars, some bivouacs. Ration etc 20 offrs 651 OR. | P.t.o |
| MARQUAIX | 8 | 2. Billets. | All coys resting & cleaning up. Ration etc 20 offrs 647 OR. | P.t.o |

# WAR DIARY
## or
## INTELLIGENCE SUMMARY.
(Erase heading not required.)

Army Form C. 2118.

| Place | Date 1917 APRIL | Hour | Summary of Events and Information | Remarks and references to Appendices |
|---|---|---|---|---|
| MARQUAIX | 9 | | 2. Bullets. Working party of 400 men on roads round MARQUAIX during morning. – Ration etc. 300ft 6.4% o/s. | PW |
| do | 10 | | do Working party of 200 men on roads throughout day. Ration etc. 21 off, 650 o.r. | PW |
| do | 11 | | do do do Ration etc. 20 off 650 or | PW |
| do | 12 | | do do do Ration etc. 20 off 648 o.r. | PW |
| do | 13 | | Battalion moved into Bde support in Camp S.W. of ST EMILIE nr E.29.b.64, relieving 1/5 GLOSTERS. Relief complete by 6 pm. B + C Coy under MAJOR A.B.L. BAKER there down up to ROMILLY WOOD for night in support of 1/4 OXFORDS, who had a long time to kill. Ration etc. 20 off 652 o.r. | PW |
| E.29.b.64. | 14 | | 2 Coy (Bde Support) B + C coys got back to Camp about 7.30 am. Transport moved up from MARQUAIX to EAST end of VILLERS FAUCON 1 coy working on Divl line of resistance (see map D) throughout morning. A coy 9 pm to 1 pm. D coy 1 pm to 4 pm. Ration etc. 20 off 640 o.r. | PW |

# WAR DIARY
## INTELLIGENCE SUMMARY

Army Form C. 2118.

| Place | Date | Hour | Summary of Events and Information | Remarks and references to Appendices |
|---|---|---|---|---|
| | 1917 APR 15. | | Battn relieved 1/5 Glosters in left subsector, from MARASSISE FARM (excl) to cross tracks F17c28 (incl). Dispositions – Two coys in outpost line, B coy on left, C coy on right – A coy in BASSE BOULOGNE. D coy at F8c27. Bn HQ at E13c59. 1/4 R. BERKS on right, 1/5 R. WARWICKS on left. Very dark night. Relieved which was not complete until 1 AM. Quiet night. Enemy attack light. Very active. Received orders that Battn was to attack TOMBOIS FARM. Tomorrow night. Ration etc. 20 [?] 6.35 AM. | Ref Map 62cNE & 57cSE 1/20000 MAP D |
| OUTPOSTS MARASSISE FARM (excl) to X roads F17c28 (incl) | 16 | | OUTPOST LINE. Quiet day. A coy took over whole of outpost line at attack, relieving B & C coys for attack on TOMBOIS FARM, arranged for 11.30 pm. ATTACK ON TOMBOIS FARM. Objectives – TOMBOIS FARM & 100 yards east of TOMBOIS FARM. On our right 1/4 R. BERKS to capture GILLEMONT FARM. On our left 1/5 R. WARWICKS to capture latest copse of LE PETIT PRIEL FARM. Dispositions for attack – C coy on right to attack S & E of FARM. B coy on left to attack W & N of FARM. D coy in echelon behind C coy to occupy enemy trench from abt F11c31 to F11c59 & new one that [?] and defend that leading trench had attained their objective when it would be the 4 cmp from attacking | Pln. SEE MAP E Operation orders attached |

# WAR DIARY
## or
## INTELLIGENCE SUMMARY

Army Form C. 2118.

| Place | Date | Hour | Summary of Events and Information | Remarks and references to Appendices |
|---|---|---|---|---|
| OUTPOSTS. MALASSISE FARM (incl) to X tracks F.17 & 28 (incl) | 1917 APRIL 16th (cont) | | **ATTACK ON TOMBOIS FARM (cont)** | Ref Maps 62c N.E. & 57 c S.E. 1/20,000 MAP. E. |
| | | | **OUTPOST LINE:** 1 coy 1/5 Glosters in support in LEMPIRE. Forming up positions – B coy W. of SART FARM. C " att F.10 d 5.7. D " " F.10 b 6.8. | |
| | | | WEATHER – Pouring rain – Blowing a gale – Very dark. Had blown funnels forming. Zero – 11.30 p.m. | |
| | | | Result: – All coys encountered a thick belt of wire in front of enemy position on frontage of company opposition which had been strongly held. Enemy rifle + M.G. fire very heavy. C + D coys with difficulty penetrated outskirts of TOMBOIS + SART FARM – | |
| | | | **ATTACK ON TOMBOIS FARM (cont)** | |
| | | | to SART FARM & reorganised. B coy, who attacked rather too much in front, penetrated enemy trench abt F.10 b.5.7 by abt 2 am had got possession of farm in spite of considerable opposition in which the bayonet played a leading part. In view of C + D coy's failure to attain objective, watching Bn HQ, Mr coy of 1/5 Glosters in support were sent at 2 am to from touch with + support B coy, if necessary. The remaining 3 coys of B, C + D coys following shortly after Mr 16 supporting them, succeeded in reaching B coy + holding them to their former neighbourhood of Gueneavoy, who were still holding in enemy attacks in ORCHARD immediately South of FARM. By 4 am both FARM + ORCHARD were respectively attacked to Tombois being lying N of the road also N+S of | |

Army Form C. 2118.

# WAR DIARY
## or
## INTELLIGENCE SUMMARY.
*(Erase heading not required.)*

| Place | Date | Hour | Summary of Events and Information | Remarks and references to Appendices |
|---|---|---|---|---|
| OUTPOSTS MAKASSISE FARM (2nd) to X tracks F17c28 (incl) | 1917 APRIL 16th (cont) | (cont) | **ATTACK ON TOMBOIS FARM** (cont) <br><br> OUTPOST LINE. Enemy dead in & round FARM estimated at 30. Captures – 9 prisoners & 1 Machine Gun. <br> 1/4 R. BERKS in right & 1/5 R. WARWICKS on left, both failed to reach their objectives on account of heavy M.G. & rifle and fire. <br><br> Casualties –: Officers Wounded –: CAPT R. GREGSON ELLIS (remains) D coy <br>                                       2/Lt J JACK (slight)        A " <br>                                       2/Lt N.S. FLINT (serious)    A " <br>                                       2/Lt B.C.C. OLIVIER (slight)  B " <br>                                       2/Lt R.F. CHATHAM (slight, at duty) <br><br> O.R. KILLED –: 18 <br> O.R. WOUNDED –: 42 <br> O.R. WOUNDED (Slight, at duty) –: 6 <br><br> Strength of attacking coys    B coy 4 O/s 136 O.R.   Lt M. BOWEN in command <br>                               C " 3 " 175 "   Lt J.B. MALES " <br>                               D " 4 " 134 "   CAPT R. GREGSON ELLIS " <br><br> Reserve Coy 20 O/s 634 O.R. | Refs Maps: 62 NE 57 d SE <br> MAP. E. |

| Place | Date Hour | Summary of Events and Information | Remarks and references to Appendices |
|---|---|---|---|
| OUTPOSTS. X Tracks F4d 99 TOMBOIS FARM. F17 b 88. | 1917 APRIL 17ᵃ | OUTPOST LINE. About 7.30 am Germans were seen coming over ridge in F6a apparently for counter attack. Artillery fire was brought to bear on them, but they did not appear from shellen into which they had descended. At 9 am a patrol of 11 Platoon Acous went out from TOMBOIS FARM to reconnoitre and moving from the FARM to PETIT PRIEL FARM, found the latter unoccupied. A message to this effect was immediately sent back to the 1/5 WARWICKS their troops to relieve us in that front. From about 12.30 pm. Another patrol went out by A coy from the old outpost lines, to reconnoitre road running thro' FIDA & FAC found CATELET COPSE unoccupied. A head was at once sent to nearest post of 1/5 R. WARWICKS who at once sent out to occupy it. It would appear that the enemy withdrew from PETIT PRIEL & CATELET COPSE at dawn, in believing that they had lost TOMBOIS FARM. TOMBOIS FARM & the road running from the FARM to LEMPIRE shelled intermittently during day, causing some casualties. At 5 pm German were reported to be defiling trench in F17 6. | Ref: Maps 62 & NE & 57c SE & Map E |

Army Form C. 2118.

# WAR DIARY
## or
## INTELLIGENCE SUMMARY.
(Erase heading not required.)

Instructions regarding War Diaries and Intelligence Summaries are contained in F. S. Regs., Part II. and the Staff Manual respectively. Title pages will be prepared in manuscript.

| Place | Date | Hour | Summary of Events and Information | Remarks and references to Appendices |
|---|---|---|---|---|
| OUTPOSTS X Tracks F.4.d 99. TOMBOIS FARM. F.17.b.8.8. | 1917 APRIL 17 (cont) | | OUTPOST LINE. At 6 p.m. a bombing party was sent down the trench towards this point but could find no trace of enemy. Batt. relieved by 1/5 GLOSTERS after dark & proceeded to Camp S.W. of St EMILIE at E.29.c.6.4. Capt. R. GREGSON ELLIS died in Field Ambulance of wounds received previous night. 2/Lt. H.J. PULLMAN took over temp. command of 'D' Coy. Ration strength 16 offrs 544 o.r. | Ref/Map 62.c. N.E. 1/20,000 P.L.y P.L.y |
| E.29.c.6.4. | 18 | | IN CAMP. (BDE SUPPORT) All coys resting. Burial parts of 60 or 'A' Coy went up to TOMBOIS FARM to bury dead & salve material. Ration Streng. 14 offrs 549 o.r. | P.L.y |
| | 19 | | do Batt. received hy 7th WORCESTERS about 5 p.m. Huts & billets in VILLERS FAUCON. Officers not allowed in billets on account of numerous mines which have been up lately. Ration Streng. 19 offrs 549 o.r. | P.L.y |
| VILLERS FAUCON | 20 | | HUTS & BILLETS. Coys resting. Ration Streng. 14 offrs 595 o.r. | |
| do | 21 | | do 4 coys on working parties all day. Officer casualty –: Wounded (slight) – Lt EBERY 2/Lt RE CHATHAM. Ration Str. 118 offrs 585 o.r. | P.L.y |

Army Form C. 2118.

# WAR DIARY
or
# INTELLIGENCE SUMMARY.
(Erase heading not required.)

Instructions regarding War Diaries and Intelligence Summaries are contained in F.S. Regs., Part II. and the Staff Manual respectively. Title pages will be prepared in manuscript.

| Place | Date 1917 APRIL | Hour | Summary of Events and Information | Remarks and references to Appendices |
|---|---|---|---|---|
| VILLERS FAUCON | 22 | Hutts & billets | 4 coys. carried out platoon practice all day. Ration strength 19 offrs 594 o.r. | PW |
| | 23 | do | Inspection of the Battn by G.O.C. Divn at 2.30 pm. Battn formed up in line of platoons in depth, each platoon being in section front. Dress - Fighting order. G.O.C. delivered short address after inspection congratulating battn on the part it took in operations of 16th inst. Ration strength 19 offrs 592 o.r. | PW |
| | 24 | do | Breakfasts eaten by 4.15 am after which times Battn stood by during operations being carried out by 144, 2nd Bde. At 5.30 am orders received to stand to. Remained 'standing to' until 3 pm. Result of operations our Divn captured GUISENET FARM, the KNOLL & the SPUR (x30). Enemy recaptured the FARM & KNOLL but our own troops thought to be still holding out in FARM. Further attack by 144 Bde arranged for tonight. Ration strength 21 offrs 582 o.r. | See Map E.  PW |

(P7092). Wt. W12839/M1293. 750,000. 1/17. D.D & L., Ltd. Forms/C2118/14.

# WAR DIARY or INTELLIGENCE SUMMARY

Army Form C. 2118.

| Place | Date | Hour | Summary of Events and Information | Remarks and references to Appendices |
|---|---|---|---|---|
| VILLERS FAUCON | 1917 APRIL 25 | | Huts & billets in Villers Faucon. Breakfast eaten during 4am, after which time Batt. stood to. Roller close to Batt. HQ. At 5am orders received to move to neighbourhood of TEMPLEUX HOOD. This was carried out in artillery formation. The ridge being under enemy observation. Remained there out until 9.30am at which time Batt. was sent back to billets & stood down. Relieved 9th GLOSTERS in BDE Support in enemy trenches Villers at 6.30pm. B & D Coys to in camp in sunken close to ST EMILIE STOP. Batt. HQ & A Coy billeting in LEMPIRE — 2 platoons A Coy holding BROWN LINE (sunken). Enemy Aircraft spotted relief as he shelled the BROWN LINE & neighbourhood of HORNHOUSE PRETTY heavily — Our Recon 27.Oth. 582 CR. | Ref Map 57c NE & MAP E |
| Bn. HQ A Coy } LEMPIRE B Coy } CAMP C } E.III.D.20 D | 26 | | BDE SUPPORT. Enemy "Shelled" to from 4am to 5am. Quiet day. Relieved 4/5 GLOSTERS in left subsector in evening F.II.d.77 to F.I.8.a.99. Line held by 3 coys. B coy on right. D coy in Centre. C coy on right. A coy in northern support in cellars & shelters NE end of LEMPIRE. Bn. HQ in LEMPIRE at F.16.a.95.80. EAST LANCS (42nd Div) on left. Recon Occ. Diff. Off. 582.CR. | |

# WAR DIARY
## INTELLIGENCE SUMMARY

Army Form C. 2118.

| Place | Date | Hour | Summary of Events and Information | Remarks and references to Appendices |
|---|---|---|---|---|
| OUTPOSTS. F11.B.16 - TORBOIS F18a.80.95. | 1917 APRIL 27 | OUTPOST LINE. | At 3.55 a.m. 39th Divn on Right attacked railway & quarry in L.5.d. with COZONE FARM as 2nd objective. 48th Divn arty cooperated by simulating attack on MAISSKOFF FARM. Result - Both objectives reached but counterattack drove us out of COZONE FARM. Quiet day. Between 8 p.m & 9 p.m enemy appeared numerous sending up many rockets mostly red, & putting down barrage on Sunken Road (F11c) & valley in DART FARM (F11c). Rockets during night - Green up action Trenches & make own (our own post) Railway through ?riff. 55yx. A coy relieved D coy in line. | Ref Maps 62c NE & 62c NW 20000 |
| do | 28 | do | Quiet day. Relieved by 1/5 GLOSTERS in evening. Relief complete by 10.45 p.m. MAJOR A.B.L BARNER moved with 3 coy (ABC) to Camp at E.29.6.64. Bn HQ & D coy in LEMPIRE 2 Platoons D coy holding BROWN LINE (see MAP 2) Large fires broke out in ST EMILIE Sugar Factory in evening. Rockets etc ?riff. 585 or. | PK |
| Bn HQ LEMPIRE D coy Camp C " E.29.6.64 D " | 29 | BDE SUPPORT | Enemy started shelling LEMPIRE with 5.9's at 9 a.m. & continued incessantly until 2 p.m. Majority of shells fell about Bn & Coy HQ. Bn HQ to move back to Camp, which was done. Battn relieved by 1/4 GLOSTERS in afternoon at 2 p.m. | PKW |

Army Form C. 2118.

Instructions regarding War Diaries and Intelligence
Summaries are contained in F. S. Regs., Part II.
and the Staff Manual respectively. Title pages
will be prepared in manuscript.

# WAR DIARY
## or
## INTELLIGENCE SUMMARY.
(Erase heading not required.)

| Place | Date 1917 APRIL | Hour | Summary of Events and Information | Remarks and references to Appendices |
|---|---|---|---|---|
| Dainville | | | continuing - Relief of 3 coys in Coup completed by 4.30 pm. Moved to Billets in HAMEL. Relief of D coy complete by 9.30 pm. Casualties - Weather - very fine. Ration strength 31 officers 584 ors. | P.W. |
| HAMEL. | 30 | | Battn moved by cars from HAMEL to MONS EN CHAUSSEE & ESTREES EN CHAUSSEE starting at 2 pm, & reaching destination about 4.30 pm. Battn HQ, Transport, A, B & C coys at MONS - D coy at ESTREES. Billets (chiefly cellars) very indifferent. Weather - very fine & hot. Ration strength 22 offrs 596 ors. | Ref Map 52c 1/40000 P.W. |
| MONS EN CHAUSSEE & ESTREES EN CHAUSSEE | | | | |

J.F.C. Reynolds
Lieut. Colonel
Comdg. 1 North' Regt
1-5-17

O.C. Companies.
Quartermaster.
Transport Officer.
-----------------

1. The Battalion will move from LONGAVESNES to-night 4/5th instant into Support of remainder of Brigade wgo will carry out operations against villages of RONSSOY and LEMPIERE, as explained verbally to O.C. Coys.

2. Position of Battalion during commencement of operations will be Railway Cutting about E.23.d.2.2.

3. Battn. Headquarters will be in cellar of first house W. of westernmost level crossing about E.23.d.25.10.

4. Comapnies will pass fork roads Eastern exit to LONGAVESNES in order - D. B. A. C.. First platoon of 'D' Coy. moving off at 2 a.m.. Transport will march in rear of 'C' Coy.

5. Lewis Gunners who will march with their limbers will rendezvous under Lewis Gun Officer atnthe Transport lines. at 2 a.m.

6. Dress - Fighting Order. Greatcoats will be worn

7. One bombing section per Coy. will rendezvous at the cross roads by the well at 1.15 a.m. under 2/Lieut. CHATHAM.

8. All ranks will be in possession of rations for 24 hours.

9. Transport Officer will arrange for pack ponies with S.A.A. to accompany each Company. In addition one S.A.A. limber, the Grenade limber and Tool cart will move with Battalion.

10. S.A.A. (one box per platoon), Very Lights and Rum will be issued on arrival at Level Crossing. Companies will send sufficient men there to carry same.

11. Blankets and packs will be stored in a hut on the MARQUAIX Road at 7.30 p.m.. Valises will be loaded on G.S. Waggon at Transport lines at same hour. Mess boxes will be loaded before Companies move.

4/4/17.

Captain & Adjutant,
1/ Bucks Battalion.

WO/95
2763

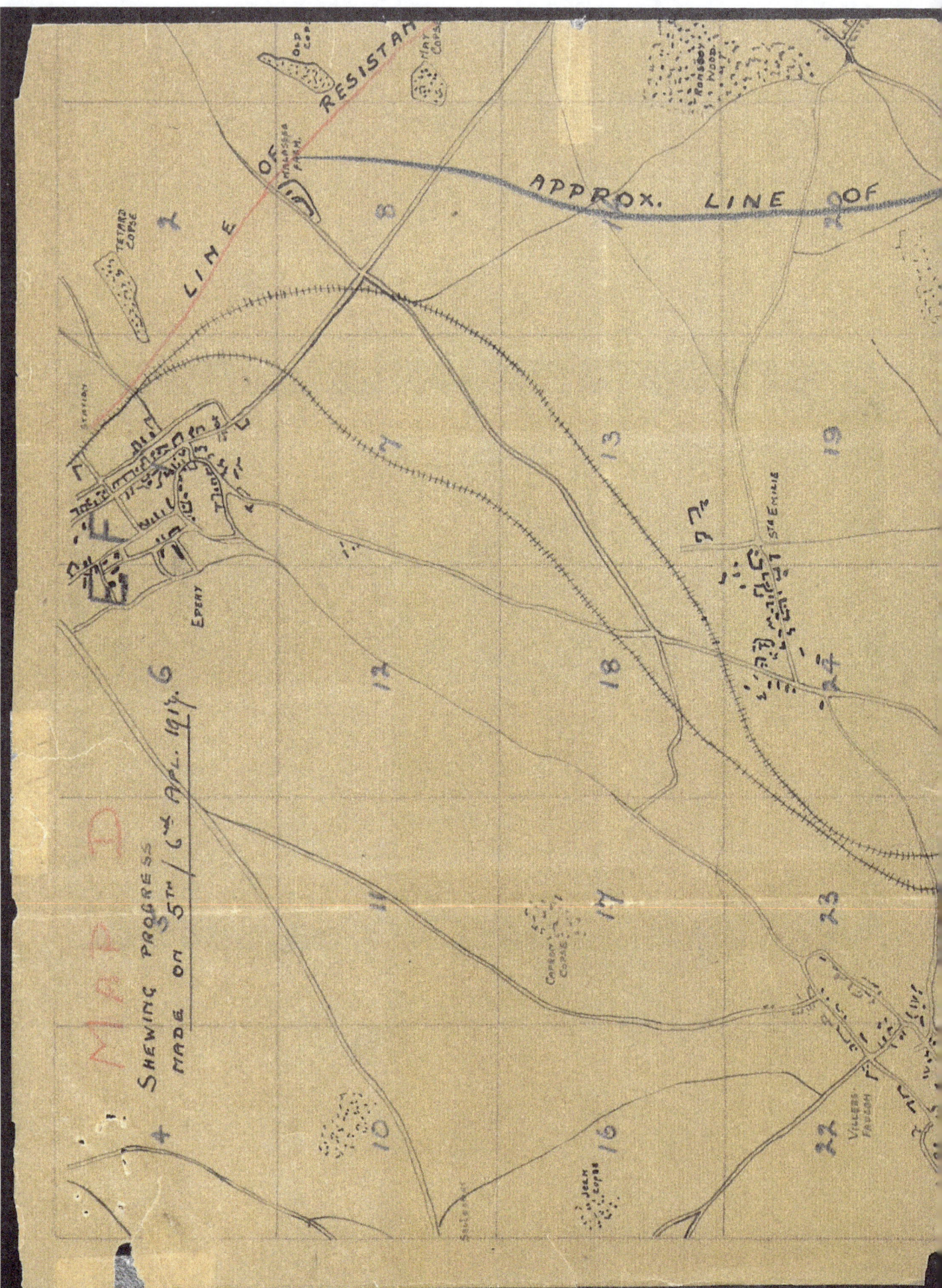

WO 95/
2763

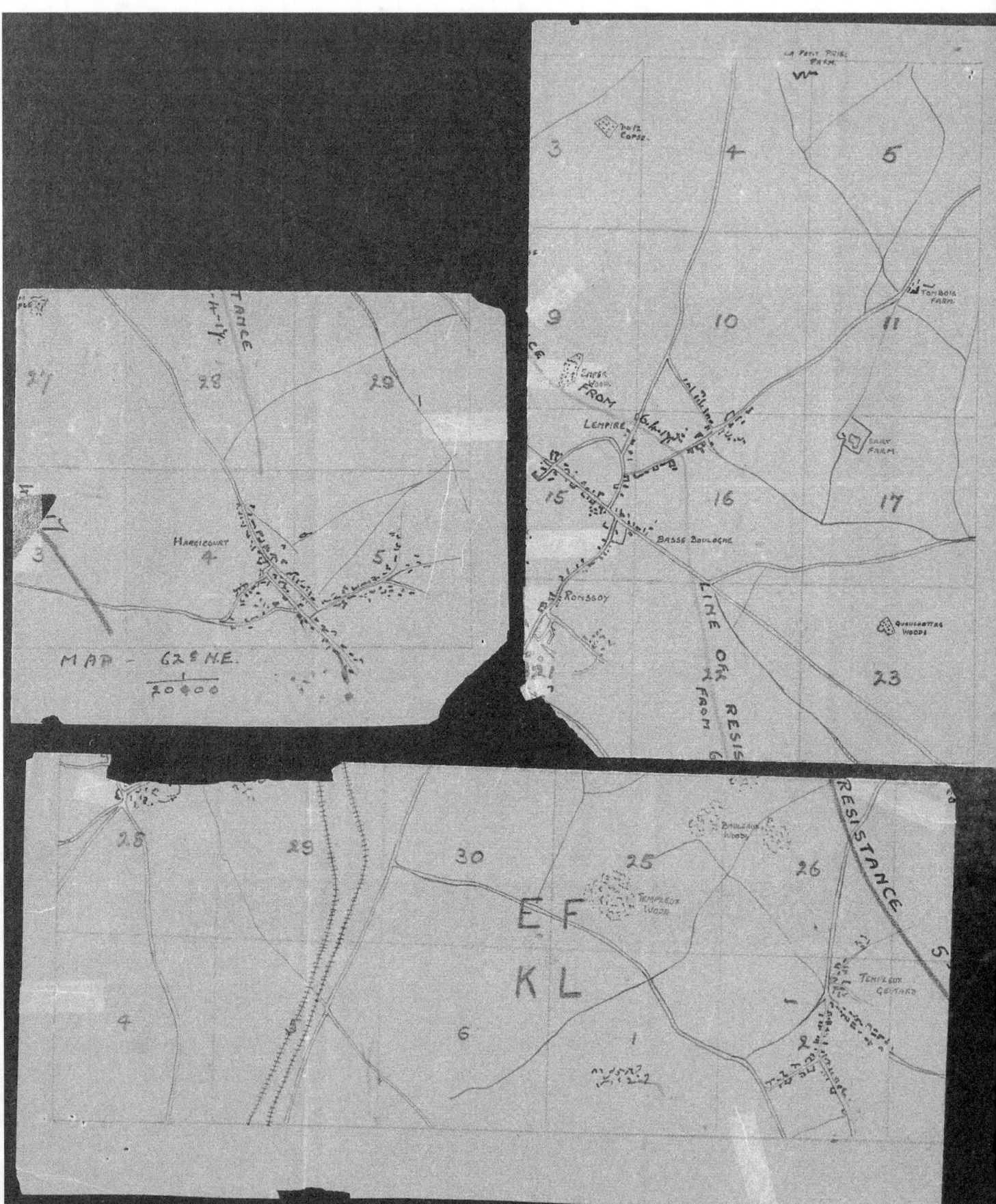

1/ Bucks Battalion.

S/40.

1. The Battalion will relieve 1/5 GLOSTERS in Support position in Camp S.W. of STE. EMILIE, E.30.a.6.7. to-day, 13th instant.

2. Companies will march by platoons, leading platoons of each Company passing cross roads K.14.d.5.5. at following times:

    'D' Coy.   -   3.0  p.m.
    'B'  "     -   3.10  "
    'C'  "     -   3.20  "
    'A'  "     -   3.30  "
    H.Q.       -   3.40  "

Interval between platoons - 200 yards.

3. Route: ROISEL - Cross roads, K.5.b.4.2. - PLEASANT HOUSE.

4. Advance party of 1 N.C.O. per Coy. and H.Q. will report to 2/Lieut. H.J. PULLMAN at Battn. H.Q. at 1 p.m.

5. Blankets and valises will be dumped at Q.M. Stores by 10.30 p.m.. Mess boxes dumped at same place by 3.30 p.m.

6. Lewis Gun limbers will be loaded at Transport lines at 12 noon.

13-4-17.

Captain & Adjutant,
1/ Bucks Battalion.

O.O./2.

## 1/ BUCKS BATTALION.

1. <u>48th Division</u> will continue its advance to-night.
Bucks Battalion will capture TOMBOIS FARM, with a second objective the ridge due E. of the Farm.
4th R. Berks Regt. will capture GILLEMONT FARM.
143rd Infty. Bde. will capture CATALET COPSE and LE PETIT PRIEL FARM.

2. <u>Zero hour</u> - 11.30 p.m.
Zero hour for 143rd Infty. Bde. will be - 10 p.m.

3. Bucks Battalion will attack with three Companies;
'C' Coy. Right, 'B' Coy. Left, with 'D' Coy. in echelon behind 'C' Coy. and will go through to second objective.
'A' Coy. will take over outpost line as early as possible after dusk. One Company 1/5th Gloster Regt. with half section M.G. Coy. will be in support about F.16.b.1.9.

4. <u>Formation</u>. Attacking Companies will be deployed on a two platoon frontage of 150 yards, each platoon in two lines, 25 yards distance between lines and waves, by Zero -30'.
Each of the attacking Coys. will have one Bombing Section equipped as such.

5. <u>Forming up positions</u>.

Right Coy. W. of SART FARM.
Left Coy. about F.10.d.5.7.
Third Coy. about F.16.b.7.6.

6. <u>Objectives</u>.

(a) <u>Right Coy</u>. will direct its attack S. and E. of TOMBOIS FARM.
(b) <u>Left Coy</u>. on W. and N. of TOMBOIS FARM.

Each of the above Coys. will arrange to leave one section at point where its outer flank crosses enemy trench to protect its flank against possible counter attack up trench.

(c) <u>Third Coy</u>. will follow Right Coy. and occupy enemy trench F.11.b.3.1. to F.11.d.5.9. and remain on that line until satisfied that leading Coys. have attained their objectives, retaining its formation (i.e. rear lines not closing up), when it will go through and occupy ridge E. of TOMBOIS FARM, approximately E. of Road running N. and S. through F.12.a..

(7) <u>Consolidation</u>.

(a) <u>Right Coy</u>. on attaining its objective will establish itself from Road F.11.b.3.5. (exclusive) to F.12.c. with support about trench F.11.c.0.5.
(b) <u>Left Coy</u>. will establish itself from Road F.11.b.3.5. (inclusive) to F.5.c. gaining touch with 143rd Infty. Bde. (1/5th R. Warwick Regt) with support about F.10.b.
(c) <u>Third Coy</u>. will establish itself on ridge, extending S. to gain touch with 1/4th R. Berks Regt. in F.12.c. with support dug in on our xxxxx side of slope.

(8) <u>Artillery Barrage</u> as communicated to Coys. this afternoon.

(9) Attacking Companies will carry S.O.S. signal lights, Very Lights & Pistols, Aeroplane Flares. Also every man will carry one extra bandolier S.A.A. Also all available wire-cutters.

(2)

10. <u>Dump for S.A.A.</u> will be formed about road junction F.15.b.9.3. under Regtl. Sergt. Major.

11. <u>Dump of tools</u> will be formed at road junction F.16.a.9.7. Support Company will be prepared to take these forward without delay.

12. <u>Dividing line</u> between the Battalion and 1/4 R. Berks Regt. during attack and after capture of objectives will be line F.17.c.0.0 – A.7.b.0.0.

13. <u>Covering Parties</u> will be pushed forward during the work of consolidation.

14. <u>Countersign</u>ˣ to be made known to all concerned. This has been communicated to 143 Infty. Bde.

15. One Section R.E. and one Platoon R. SUSSEX Regt. will be available to help with work of consolidation.

16. <u>Contact Aeroplane</u> will fly over at about 6.30 a.m., or if misty, one hour after mist lifts. Advanced troops will be careful to answer the call for flares.

17. <u>Battalion Headquarters.</u> F.15.d.9.7. (present 'C' Coy. Headquarters).

18. <u>Report Centre.</u> F.16.a.9.8.

19. <u>Dressing Station.</u> F.15.b.4.0.

16.4.17.
         (Sgd.) P.L. WRIGHT, Capt. & Adjutant,
            1/ Bucks Battalion.

Copies to:

  4 Companies.
  1 Support Coy.
  ? Battn. H.Q.
  1 1/5 Gloster Regt.

ˣ-

O.C. Companies.
----------------

1. Rations for 'B' and 'D' Coys. will be delivered at 'D' Coy. H.Q. about 6 p.m.. Rations for 'A' and 'C' Coys. will be carried up by pack ponies, and will be below ridge just S. of Workhouse at 7.30 p.m.. 'C' Coy. will send carrying party to this place to take ponies up further if necessary.

2. Water will be delivered to 'A' and 'C' Coys. in petrol tins by 'D' Coy. (nine petrol tins per Coy). These will arrive at Workhouse at about 3 p.m.. These tins when empty may be sent back and refilled at watercart at 'D' Coy. H.Q. if required. Petrol tins when empty to be handed in to 'A' Coy. H.Q..

3. Bombs (detonated) will be delivered by 'D' Coy. to 'C' Coy. about 9 p.m. to-night.

4. Telephones.
Signal Stations will be established -

One at Battn. H.Q. (present 'C' Coy. H.Q.)
" " Major BAKER's H.Q. (about F.16.c.9.7)

Wire running between Workhouse and F.16.c.9.7 is being laid double. In addition to this 'B', 'C' and 'D' Coys. will endeavour to run a wire out to positions captured. Signalling Sergeant will arrange to provide them with wire.

Runners.
Battn. H.Q. will man their H.Q. and Major BAKER's H.Q. with signallers and runners. 'B' and 'C' Coys. when sending back runners will not send them further than ~~Major Baker's H.Q.~~ trench at F10d94 which will constitute a relay post.

Captain & Adjutant,
1/ Bucks Battalion.

16-4-17.

1/ Bucks Battalion.

W/30.

1. The Battalion will relieve 8th GLOSTERS in Brigade Support positions this evening.
   Dispositions:

   Battn. H.Q. — Opposite WORKHOUSE, LEMPIRE.
   'A' Coy. — BROWN LINE.
   'B' " —)
   'C' " —) Camp about E.34.c.9.8.
   'D' " —)

2. Guides for 'A' Coy. to be arranged by O.C. 'A' Coy. Billeting party will guide 'B', 'C' and 'D' Coys. meeting them at O.W. entrance to STH. EMILIE.

3. Head of each Coy. will pass VILLERS STATION at following times. Interval between platoons — 200 yards.

   'A' Coy. — 6.40 p.m.
   'B' " — 6.50 "
   'C' " — 7.0 "
   'D' " — 7.10 "

4. Blankets and valises of 'B', 'C' and 'D' Coys. to be dumped at fork roads, E.33.c.3.1., soon as possible. Each Coy. will have one limber for Lewis Guns and Mess Box. This limber will be loaded at Transport.
'A' Coy's valises and blankets will NOT be taken, but will be left with C.Q.M.S who will arrange with Quartermaster for collection and storage.
5. 'B', 'C' and 'D' Coys. will take their Cookers.

6. Dress will be Fighting Order with greatcoats. Packs will be left with Coy. Q.M. Sgts. The Quartermaster will arrange collection and storage.

P.L. [signature]
Captain & Adjutant,
1/ Bucks Battalion.

25-4-17.

CONFIDENTIAL Vol 27

WAR DIARY

OF

1/1st Buckinghamshire Battalion of the
(Oxfordshire & Buckinghamshire Light Infantry)

From May 1st 1917 to May 31st 1917.

# WAR DIARY or INTELLIGENCE SUMMARY

Army Form C. 2118.

1/1 Bucks Batty

| Place | Date | Hour | Summary of Events and Information | Remarks and references to Appendices |
|---|---|---|---|---|
| MONS EN CHAUSEE and ESTREES EN CHAUSEE | MAY 1. | | Overnight - Conform at work on battery positions. Wng Personnel OR's are moved in Military Huts to Quarry and addition to Battery wh attached to TOMBO's FARM in ABU 16 bow 10NW.  26,5195 Sgt WOODMANS S.A.  26,5246 Pte CROSS H.  26,3191 " HERBERT A.  5261 523 " SEMPLE F.A. | Coy |
| do | 2. | | Battery line. Ranges & lengths of wires 640 or. Battery Battery Personnel & 200 men at work at ESTREES EN CHAUSEE from Coy HQ. Remaining at work on Battery position. 1 I.L. RECVES, O.C. from 2nd L Battery to 1st Batty 2nd L DIPPLE T.O. to 1st Batty Minimum & maxim O.Range 700ft. 541 sec. | Coy |
| do | 3. | | do. Wiring an LE 6 services in line at ESTREES EN CHAUSEE. Guns arr & dr. at Battery Remains attached an Company Battery and ammunition hut. Reference Discharged from duty | Coy |

Army Form C. 2118.

# WAR DIARY
## or
## INTELLIGENCE SUMMARY.
(Erase heading not required.)

Instructions regarding War Diaries and Intelligence Summaries are contained in F. S. Regs., Part II. and the Staff Manual respectively. Title pages will be prepared in manuscript.

| Place | Date | Hour | Summary of Events and Information | Remarks and references to Appendices |
|---|---|---|---|---|
| MONS EN CHAUSSÉE and ESTRÉES EN CHAUSSÉE | 4 May | | Working parties. Visit by Gen'l in Chief at ESTRÉES EN CHAUSSÉE. Remainder of Bn at Rest. One Company training and informing of buildings. Weather fine and warm. Rations 250ff 582 OR | Coy. |
| do. | 5 | a.m. 11.30 2.10 | Bath in huts. Battn on Embus'g & march to afternoon. Magazine Burial words the Battn bivouac'd Sheltenbres and Customs Campoute avoiding engaged in movements in the Catacomb. No service an engagement... Weather fine and warm. 25ff 519ok | Coy. |
| do. | 6 | | Battalion towards 10 A.M. Church service at 10 a.m., conducted by the Chaplain. Commanding Officer inspected Squadrons. Rain fell during the night, fine and warm during the day. Rations Strength 25 offrs 549or | Coy. |
| do. | 7 | | Battn at bombing training morning and afternoon. NCOs in attend'ce and wiring from hn RES Bns. Reinforcement Officer arrived from Hn RES Bn. 2/Lt MARSHALL F.C. Weather fine and warm Rations Strength 25 offrs 610 or | Coy. |

A7092). Wt. w12839/M1292. 750,000. 1/17. D. D & L., Ltd. Forms/C2118/14.

Army Form C. 2118.

# WAR DIARY
## or
## INTELLIGENCE SUMMARY.
*(Erase heading not required.)*

| Place | Date | Hour | Summary of Events and Information | Remarks and references to Appendices |
|---|---|---|---|---|
| MONS EN CHAUSEE and ESTREES EN CHAUSEE | 8 | | [illegible handwritten entries] | Ap. |
| do | 9 | | do | Ap. |
| do | 10 | | do | Ap. |
| do | 11 | | do | Ap. |
| PHMICOURT | | | | Ap. |

Army Form C. 2118.

# WAR DIARY
## or
## INTELLIGENCE SUMMARY.
*(Erase heading not required.)*

Instructions regarding War Diaries and Intelligence Summaries are contained in F.S. Regs., Part II. and the Staff Manual respectively. Title pages will be prepared in manuscript.

| Place | Date | Hour | Summary of Events and Information | Remarks and references to Appendices |
|---|---|---|---|---|
| FLAMICOURT | 12 | | [illegible handwritten entries] | |
| | 13 | | [illegible handwritten entries] | (A) |
| LE TRANSLOY | | | [illegible handwritten entries] | (A) |

# WAR DIARY
or
## INTELLIGENCE SUMMARY

*(Erase heading not required.)*

Army Form C. 2118.

| Place | Date | Hour | Summary of Events and Information | Remarks and references to Appendices |
|---|---|---|---|---|
| OUTPOST LINE | 14 | | [illegible handwritten entries - very faded] | |
| do | 15 | | | |
| do | 16 | | | |

*[Page content is largely illegible due to faded handwriting. Visible fragments include references to "Disposition of Columns", company listings C, B, A, D, E with coordinates/grid references (KV A, KV B, J17 D30, etc.), "TRANSPORT A.T.", "QUARTERMASTER STORES", "ENEMY SHELLED", and "DERNANCOURT".]*

Army Form C. 2118.

# WAR DIARY
## or
## INTELLIGENCE SUMMARY.

*(Erase heading not required.)*

Instructions regarding War Diaries and Intelligence Summaries are contained in F. S. Regs., Part II. and the Staff Manual respectively. Title pages will be prepared in manuscript.

| Place | Date | Hour | Summary of Events and Information | Remarks and references to Appendices |
|---|---|---|---|---|
| OUTPOST LINE | 16 | | (Outpost line) [illegible] | Coy |
| do | 17 | | [illegible handwritten entry mentioning DEMICOURT, FRENCH, MORTARS, OBSERVERS, ARTILLERY] | Coy |
| do (RESERVE) | 18 | | [illegible handwritten entry mentioning ENEMY ARTILLERY, RESERVE LINE, MICHIGAN, GLOUCESTERS, BATTALIONS, A Coy] | 57/S/R/E |
| | | | | (B) |

Army Form C. 2118.

# WAR DIARY
## or
## INTELLIGENCE SUMMARY.
(Erase heading not required.)

| Place | Date | Hour | Summary of Events and Information | Remarks and references to Appendices |
|---|---|---|---|---|
| RESERVE LINE | 19 | - | RESERVE LINE. A/C went. Black C Coys dug outs. Carrying Parties not used. Work on dug outs on Suffolk Road continued the day. B Coy HQ and Inns ENEMY ARTILLERY rather quiet. Our BATTERY reported not firing. Jungle down the road to our front. Cloudy throughout day. CO and MO by car in. Reserve Line. 2nd B. No Train. Jacob working hard and moving about. Weather fine. Roll in strength 28 offr 590 o.r. | (a) |
| | 20 | - | RESERVE LINE. Cloudy day. All troops quiet, one or two ENEMY AIRCRAFT over. ENEMY Artillery Langton quiet 5pm AA. guns and machine guns. Railway (areas 50.0x 50.0x). | (a) |
| | 21 | - | do. ENEMY guns and ARTILLERY. Blankets issued. ditto our lines. SAUSAGE BALLOONS. Men's dinners and The day passed quiet. 2nd offr arrived 30th May. | (a) |
| | 22 | - | do. The day January quiet ... our orders ... night, and ... Tunnels and ... 5 Gloucesters 11th Oxford and Bucks carried out a OPERATIONS ... a Gas Attack ... | (a) |

Army Form C. 2118.

# WAR DIARY
## or
## INTELLIGENCE SUMMARY.
(Erase heading not required.)

| Place | Date | Hour | Summary of Events and Information | Remarks and references to Appendices |
|---|---|---|---|---|
| RESERVE LINE | 22nd | | Taken Joined Battalion. Marched up to the Reserve Line. AERIAL activity very marked. | Coy |
| do | 23 | | Our Artillery shelled enemy front lines during afternoon. Enemy Aviators very active throughout day. One balloon shot down at 3 p.m. in our sector. Our attack on the ENEMYS line at 6 p.m. unfortunately broken down. Weather broken. | Coy |
| do and OUTPOST LINE | 24 | | Raining throughout. Men wet. Quiet day. Relieved by men of the RIGHT BATT SECTOR coming out, and proceeded to OXFORD on the 13/0113 with 2 platoons at the 4th OXFORD BUCKS the entirety. At 9 p.m. Battalion taken over Outpost Sector without incident. Formation Disposition as follows:- D. Coy. RIGHT SUB SECTOR from J.36.b.5.5.t and to K.26.a.93 S.H.H. with Coy. Hq at T.36.b.2.t. B. Coy. CENTRE SUB SECTOR from K.26.a.9.3 mot to K.19.c.9.1 2nd plat. with Coy. Hq at K.25.b.5.6. C. Coy. B.LEFT SUB SECTOR from K.19.c.7.1. and K.14.c.B.9 with main Coy Hq at K.19.a.8.5. | |

# WAR DIARY
## or
## INTELLIGENCE SUMMARY

Army Form C. 2118.

Instructions regarding War Diaries and Intelligence Summaries are contained in F. S. Regs., Part II. and the Staff Manual respectively. Title pages will be prepared in manuscript.

(Erase heading not required.)

| Place | Date | Hour | Summary of Events and Information | Remarks and references to Appendices |
|---|---|---|---|---|
| OUTPOST LINE | 24. | | OUTPOST LINE at 12a 15.5.6. Weather wet. Relief completed without incident. CAPTAIN G. CROUCH proceeded from the ARRAS front. Wounded ... and ... Ration strength Offrs 5 ORs ... | (a) |
| do. | 25. | | do. ... heavy enemy shelling ... ARTILLERY of both sides unusually active. AIRCRAFT of both sides were particularly active and in two cases engaging took place between one of our planes and one of the enemy, both times the enemy plane driven back. HROEN ... MCO. and 1 Other Rank of 1 NCO and 2 men and 3 ORs wounded but his squad ... and 3 ORs wounded on way up to their line and the ... of discovery an enemy listening post. Patrols reconnoitered ... of the enemy's front. Later. An OBSERVERS noted that the enemy was holding TREES on the main BAPAUME - CAMBRAI road and white craters in HAVRINCOURT. Working parties of 1 Offr. and 40 ORs arrived from BASE. Reinforcements of 1 Offr. and 110 ORs arrived from BASE. Officer 2/L MASON. N. Rank and File and men Ration strength | (a) |

**Army Form C. 2118**

# WAR DIARY
## or
## INTELLIGENCE SUMMARY
*(Erase heading not required.)*

Instructions regarding War Diaries and Intelligence Summaries are contained in F.S. Regs., Part II. and the Staff Manual respectively. Title Pages will be prepared in manuscript.

1917 MAY

| Place | Date | Hour | Summary of Events and Information | Remarks and references to Appendices |
|---|---|---|---|---|
| OUTPOST LINE | 26 | | ENEMY ARTILLERY more active than usual. Round Bastion Hy. was mainly shelled with 5.9. One COOKER being knocked out. Special attention was also paid to HERMES the roads being intermittently shelled. On the front line some BLUE PIGEONS and RIFLE GRENADES were fired at the 3 foot D Cup, but without doing any damage. E. 29.d had been Our OBSERVERS noticed that 4 trees on road in been fell during the night. ENEMY MOVEMENT was much quieter than usual. On our patrols looked in an ENEMY post in a COPSE at K.20.c.3.0. One of our posts who were fairly active in front of SPOIL HEAP AEROPLANES of both sides were fairly active OUR ARTILLERY carried out WIRE CUTTING in front of SPOIL HEAP at K.20 culta. Ration Strength. 73 off 632 or Weather very warm | MAP REF 57c NE |
| do | 27 | | ENEMY ARTILLERY rather Quiet OURS shelled the SLAG HEAP and wire in front OUR OBSERVERS reports the usual movements of the enemy, no news SUPPORT LINES. An officers patrol went out with the object of locating a COPSE Known at K.20 C.B.O. they the covered RIFLE PITS and enemy wire but reports that no such COPSE exists You will notice that no opposition was offered laterly. ENEMY MACHINE Guns were active also their AEROPLANES. Work on our posts was proceeded with during the night Weather very warm Ration Strength 73 off 614 or | (a) 57c NE (a) |

1875  Wt. W593/826  1,000,000  4/15  J.B.C. & A.  A.D.S.S./Forms/C. 2118.

# WAR DIARY / INTELLIGENCE SUMMARY

Army Form C. 2118.

| Place | Date | Hour | Summary of Events and Information | Remarks and references to Appendices |
|---|---|---|---|---|
| OUTPOST LINE. | 28. | | During the day the ARTILLERY of both sides was very quiet. D Coy HQr was shelled in the early hours but squadie was wounded. No real ENEMY movement was seen at Ysn. HAVRINCOURT CHATEAU was blown up. A German Signal message to RATIONS was translated only figures of AEROPLANES. A number of ENEMY were seen flying off by our A.A. guns. Our officer patrol went out at night with the object of locating our recovering ENEMY trench at Kroc and 2 on their discreet signal RIFLE PITS but no enemy were encountered and the patrol returned safely. During the night the furnishing redistribution of the line took place. 1 Platoon withdrawn from the line to neighbour post D Coy Hqrs. 2 platoon HQr. B Coy Cheographive Hq at Kopes also 1 platoon in SUPPORT and remainder holding No. 3R, 4R, 5R, 6R posts C Coy Hq as at present with 1 platoon in outpost and remainder holding No. 6 R.S. 8.R. of posts. Work on posts was carried out during the night. Trench Strength / Ration Strength. | 57c 7E (W64 attached)  57c 7E  Coy |

2449 Wt. W14957/Mgo 750,000 1/16 J.B.C. & A. Forms/C.2118/12.

# WAR DIARY or INTELLIGENCE SUMMARY

Army Form C. 2118.

| Place | Date | Hour | Summary of Events and Information | Remarks and references to Appendices |
|---|---|---|---|---|
| OUTPOST LINE + RESERVE | 29 | OUTPOST LINE. | At 2 am the ENEMY'S LINE was bombarded with Gas shells. The attack in which the ARTILLERY co-operated, was an intermittent affair for about 10 minutes followed by an actual GAS ATTACK bombardment lasting about 2 hours. A number of VERY LIGHTS were put up also a GREEN STAR SHELL. the ENEMY did not pay much attention to it and attempted no retaliation. The number of the day passed very quietly. ARTILLERY of both sides kept very quiet about 9.0 pm Severe barrage shells were put into BEAUMETZ. About 11 pm the Bosch retired by the 1/5th GLOSTERS and came back to YELU WOOD about J31 & 8/5. who which was underneath heavy shell fire by them. Trench strength 24 Offrs 613 OR. | 570 ME. |
| RESERVE | 30 | RESERVE. | Men relaying and cleaning up. Trench strength 23 Offrs 606 OR. | Coy |
| do | 31 | do | Companies on Company training. Officers Lewis Gun Companies carried out practice in Rifles Wiring Bombing and Manner. Trench strength 23 Offrs 605 OR. | Coy |

J. C. Reynolds
Lieut Colonel
Comdg 1/7 Worcester Regt

2449 Wt. W14957/M90 750,000 1/16 J.B.C. & A. Forms/C.2118/12.

1/ Bucks Battalion.                                   A/9.
------------------

1. The Battalion will relieve 7th South Staffordshire Regt. in the Outpost Line this evening.

2. The Battalion will move to Transport lines of 7th Sth. Staffordshire Regt. by ~~platoons at 300 yards interval~~ about I.36.c. by platoons at 300 yards interval for teas.

    'A' Coy. will move at 2.30 p.m.
    'B'  "    "    "   " 2.45  "
    'C'  "    "    "   " 3.0   "
    'D'  "    "    "   " 3.15  "

3. Guides, 1 per platoon, ~~1 Coy. H.Q.~~, 1 Battn. H.Q. will be at VELU CHATEAU at 2.30 p.m.. Further instructions later.
*Each platoon passes by. H.Q.*

4. Battalion Headquarters - J.18.d.4.9.

5. All plans, maps, photographs and intelligence will be handed over by relieved to relieving Companies.

6. Blankets, shoemakers material and Orderly Room boxes will be dumped at side of road opposite Battn. H.Q. by 2 p.m. A loading party of 1 man per Coy. will be detailed and will proceed on the lorry.
    Officers' valises and mess boxes must be dumped at Transport Lines by 2 p.m.

7. Lewis Gun limbers will not proceed further than Transport Lines, where they will be unloaded and the guns, equipment and ammunition carried from there.

8. Distribution in the line - 3 Coys. in front line ('A' Coy. Right, 'B' Coy. Centre, 'C' Coy. Left), 1 Coy. ('D') in Reserve close to Battn. H.Q..

9. Completion of relief to be notified to Battn. H.Q. in Code.

10. Acknowledge.

                                A.B.L.Baker
                                Major fa
14-5-17.                          Lieut. Colonel,
                              Comdg. 1/ Bucks Battalion.

Issued at 11.30 a.m.

Copies to: 4 Coys.
          Q.M.
          T.O.
          H.Q.

SECRET.                                                       W.64.

1/ Bucks Battalion.

Following redistribution of the line will take place to-night, 28/29th instant.

1. 'D' Coy. less 1 Platoon will be withdrawn from the line and will be situated in the neighbourhood of Battn. H.Q. Lieut. FIRMINGER will allot billets.

2. Present 'D' Coy. garrison (less the extra (5th) Lewis Gun Section) will remain holding No. 3 Post under command of O.C. 'B' Coy.

3. 'B' Coy. will take up dispositions as under:
    1 Platoon  -  No. 4 R. Post.
    1   "       -  No. 5 & 6 R. Post.
        (Two sections each)
    1   "   (less L.G. Section) - No. 3 R.S. Post.
        This L.G. Section to relieve the extra L.G. Section of 'D' Coy. in No. 3 R. Post.
    1 Platoon  -  Coy. H.Q.
    Coy. H.Q.  -  As at present.

4. 'C' Coy. will take up dispositions as under:
    1 Platoon (less 1 section) - No. 7 R. Post.
    1 Section  -  No. 8 R. Post.
    1 Platoon  -  No. 9 R. Post.
    1   "      -  No. 6 R.S. Post.
    1   "      -  Coy. H.Q.
    Coy. H.Q.  -  As at present.

5. The relief of the 'D' Coy. platoon in No. 3 R.S. Post will take place at earliest possible moment, as this platoon is required for work.

6. The Battalion will be relieved to-morrow night, 29/30th instant, by 1/5th GLOSTERS.

                                                Captain & Adjutant,
                                                1/ Bucks Battalion.

26-5-17.

CONFIDENTIAL.

WAR DIARY
of
1/1st BUCKS BATTN
June 1st to June 30th
1917

**CONFIDENTIAL**

Army Form C. 2118.

# WAR DIARY
## or
## INTELLIGENCE SUMMARY

*(Erase heading not required.)*

1/1 BUCKS BATT'N

Instructions regarding War Diaries and Intelligence Summaries are contained in F. S. Regs., Part II. and the Staff Manual respectively. Title Pages will be prepared in manuscript.

| Place | Date | Hour | Summary of Events and Information | Remarks and references to Appendices |
|---|---|---|---|---|
| IN RESERVE | JUNE 1918 1 | | Battn in Reserve. Companies engaged in Company training during the evening. OFFICERS Classes in musketry in Ration Stores and room. Weather fine & warm. 2 X Offr 606 O.R. | Weather hot |
| do | 2 | | Companies in Company training at 3.30 pm. the BRIGADIER GENERAL inspected the OFFICERS in the foregoing - FIGHTING DRESS - BOOKS - SALVING - WIRING. The Commanding Officer went to AUXI LE CHATEAU to witness demonstration in TACTICAL MANOEUVRES. Weather fine and warm. | Cpl. |
| do and in OUTPOST LINE | 3 | | HOLY COMMUNION at 8 am. SERVICE at 10.30 am. During the night 3/st the Battn relieves the 1/5th GLOSTERS in the OUTPOST LINE moving by Platoons from J.31.d. and taking over the foregoing disposition. D Coy Right front Company falling 3 posts from K.26.A.8.9 inclusive such Coy H.Q. at K.25.b.4.5. to K.30. C.2.5. inclusive. A Coy Left front Coy holding 4 posts from K.20.C.35.1. inclusive from K.14.C.2.5. to K.15.C.4.5. B Coy in support at J.30.B. C " " " " at J.29.K. in reserve. | See ME APPENDIX B. No. 1. |

# WAR DIARY
## INTELLIGENCE SUMMARY
*(Erase heading not required.)*

Army Form C. 2118.

| Place | Date | Hour | Summary of Events and Information | Remarks and references to Appendices |
|---|---|---|---|---|
| OUTPOST LINE | June 1917 3. | | The relief was carried out without interruption and no Cas/ялись by 12. Dawn up. Ration strength 23 off. 599 o.r. | Coy. |
| do | 4 | | The day passed quietly. An attempt was made at 12 mn to locate + capture an enemy post reported at K 26 a 92 35. The patrol located the post who opened fire on the patrol - showers of rifle grenades were thrown also fired on them from the other side of the track owing to the enemy being in greater strength than anticipated, the officer i/c of the party (2nd Lt W. O'B. RIGDEN) decided to withdraw. Ration strength 22 off. 603 o.r. Casualties 2 o.r. wounded. | M.A.P. Sheet 57c NE. |
| do | 5 | | Very fine + visibility good. Gun Fire reconnaissance made by 2/Lt FAWCETT + 2-R of the firing locate start myself. Scouts + men to to an attack being made on it. Ration Strength 23 off. 601 o.r. | Coy. |
| do | 6 | | Heavy Rain - C Coy reduced. A Coy in left sector. Ration strength - 21 off. 599 o.r. | Coy. |

Army Form C. 2118.

# WAR DIARY
## or
## INTELLIGENCE SUMMARY.
(Erase heading not required.)

| Place | Date | Hour | Summary of Events and Information | Remarks and references to Appendices |
|---|---|---|---|---|
| | June 14/17 | | in them our men threw down the bombs to them. No attempt at a counter attack was made, but rifle grenades were fired from the opposite bank & from under the CANAL bank further North, at intervals for the rest of the night. With the help of a R.E. Officer & 1 platoon 5/R. Sussex, the work of consolidation was quickly started & continued without interruption until 2.30 am when it became very light. Besides the platoon of 5/R. Sussex, 2 platoons 'A' Coy & the support platoon B Coy were sent up to help with the work. A position was dug at K.26.c.92.35. with a traversed trench abt 30 yds long facing NORTH & a zig zag trench 35 yds long under the canal bank facing EAST, the South end being connected up by a CT to the CAGE trench. The new front line patrolled by 1 L.G. section & 1 Bombing section & | MAP 57C/N.E. |

# WAR DIARY
## INTELLIGENCE SUMMARY

Army Form C. 2118.

| Place | Date | Hour | Summary of Events and Information | Remarks and references to Appendices |
|---|---|---|---|---|
| OUTPOST LINE K26 central to KM39. (57cNE) | JUNE 7 | 1917 | Rather a Quiet day. 3 coy carried out an attack on enemy post situated K26a 92 35. Zero 12 m. Attack carried out in accordance with O.O. 22 attached. The attack started at 12.3 am after a few minutes bombardment by 1 section of F.M.M. Guns according to programme. The enemy opened fire rifle gun before the assault took place but then retreated they scale from here from trench in front of "CAGE". This is confirmed by statement made by their officers taken prisoner that the machine gun fire forced them behind the parade & that the noise knew they knew that the English were on top of them. There was concentric trench there in front of the enemy held little difficulty having experienced in dragging it out of the way. After the assaulting platoons got in there was a bunch of fight for a few minutes, but the enemy soon gave | Sheet 57cNE X APPENDIX A APPENDIX No. 1. X Map Sheet |

# WAR DIARY or INTELLIGENCE SUMMARY

Army Form C. 2118.

| Place | Date June 1917 | Hour | Summary of Events and Information | Remarks and references to Appendices |
|---|---|---|---|---|
| OUTPOST LINE K 26 c n d 6 K 14 c 39. | 8 | | Batt in line – Quiet day. Rear posts on CANAL BANK worried by GRANATENWERFER & rifle grenades, replied during early morning & evening. Casualties – 1 OR killed, 5 OR wounded. Strength 71 Offs 596 OR. | PAK |
| | 9 | | Batt in line – Enemy artillery slightly more active. + Batt relieved by 1/5 Gloucesters in evening. Relief completed by 12.45 am. 1 A & D Coys on relief became garrison of R. RESERVE line. HQ & B & C Coys to shelters & bivouacs in sunken roads just S. of BEAUMETZ. Casualties – K.C. Wounded – 71 Offs 589 OR. | APPENDIX A No. 2. PAK |
| | | | 2nd Lt K.C. REYNOLDS proceeded on leave. Major H.B. BAKER assumed Command. Strength – 71 Offs 583 OR. | PAK |
| 2 Coy Reserve 2 Coy & Bn HQ BEAUMETZ | 10. | | Bn in Bde Reserve. Coys resting. | PAK |
| " | 11 | | do – Baths for B & C Coys at NEUVILLE in afternoon. Reinforcement of 20 OR arrived. Ration Strength 18 Offs 563 OR. | PAK |

# WAR DIARY
## or
## INTELLIGENCE SUMMARY.

Army Form C. 2118.

| Place | Date | Hour | Summary of Events and Information | Remarks and references to Appendices |
|---|---|---|---|---|
| | | | is rifled on the creek & commands all ground up to SLAG HEAP (K20 central) - Prisoners captured — 11. of the 41st IR. They state that the Regt had consisted of 2 groups of 1 NCO & 8 men. 4 were killed during our advance. Our Casualties — 2 OR Killed, 9 OR Wounded. Name of Officer i/c of Attacking Force. — 2/Lt G.H. FAWCITT. | Copy Report attached GS&I SR |

Army Form C. 2118.

# WAR DIARY
## or
## INTELLIGENCE SUMMARY.
(Erase heading not required.)

| Place | Date 1917 | Hour | Summary of Events and Information | Remarks and references to Appendices |
|---|---|---|---|---|
| 2 Coys/Reserve Line 2 Coys BEAUMETZ B-HQ | June 12 | | Batln in Reserve. Following interior relief took place in Reserve line — 'B' Coy relieved 'D' Coy. 'C' Coy relieved 'A' Coy. Very quiet. Ration strength 18 offrs 543 OR. | Ph- |
| do | 13 | | do. A & D coys resting. Very fine. Ration strength 18 offrs 543 OR. | Coy |
| do | 14 | | do. 1 officer & 1 NCO from each of A & D Coys sent to the several O.B. & 82nd HAVRINCOURT Wood, to have a look at what advanced trenches strength up to CANAL behind SPOIL HEAP in S.20. — D Coy sent up to Sunken Road in K.7.c. to extend the Mine while 1/6 OXFORDS carried out raid on enemy trench about K.2.630. Zero 1.30 a.m. 15". No call was made 12.30 am 15". Zero 1.30 am 15". No call made on Raiders by Men to Villers Plouvigny at 3.40 a.m. — Ration strength 19 offrs 545 OR. | 57c ME Coy |

Army Form C. 2118.

# WAR DIARY
## or
## INTELLIGENCE SUMMARY.
(Erase heading not required.)

Instructions regarding War Diaries and Intelligence Summaries are contained in F. S. Regs., Part II. and the Staff Manual respectively. Title pages will be prepared in manuscript.

| Place | Date | Hour | Summary of Events and Information | Remarks and references to Appendices |
|---|---|---|---|---|
| 2 Coy Reserves Line 2 Coy Supports line and Posts 10A and 11A | June 15 | 12/17 | [illegible handwritten entry] | * APPENDIX A. No 3. 15/6/18 Coy |
| OUTPOST LINE Posts 6 and 8 Post c 3.0. | 16 | | do. | Coy |
| do. | 17 | | do. | Coy |
| do. | 18 | | do. | Coy |
| do. | | | do. | Coy |

WAR DIARY
or
INTELLIGENCE SUMMARY.

Army Form C. 2118.

Instructions regarding War Diaries and Intelligence
Summaries are contained in F. S. Regs., Part II.
and the Staff Manual respectively. Title pages
will be prepared in manuscript.

(Erase heading not required.)

| Place | Date JUNE | Hour | Summary of Events and Information | Remarks and references to Appendices |
|---|---|---|---|---|
| OUTPOST LINE K36 central to K1t 3.9. | 19 | | Both artillery much more active both during day and night 1920. Particular attention being paid to HERMIES. K25 a 16 being much shelled. Machine gun fire was fairly active. Much enemy movement noted. The well in outskirts of HERMIES gave trouble as patrols went out to obtain water. Weather very wet during night. Patrol strength 22 OR 60 OR. Casualties 3 OR | Caj |
| do. | 20 | do. | The day was fairly quiet. Enemy artillery not so active as usual. Unusual amount of enemy movement observed. B Coy relieving on right. A — C — on left. Enemy aeroplanes were active than usual. Patrols out (1) reconnaissance WIRE across road at K20 b o. 65 (2) Reconnoitre TRENCH about K20 o b. Weather fine and warmer. Relieving strength 22 off 605 OR. | Appendix A No. 4. Caj |

Army Form C. 2118.

# WAR DIARY
## or
## INTELLIGENCE SUMMARY.
(Erase heading not required.)

Instructions regarding War Diaries and Intelligence Summaries are contained in F. S. Regs., Part II. and the Staff Manual respectively. Title pages will be prepared in manuscript.

| Place | Date | Hour | Summary of Events and Information | Remarks and references to Appendices |
|---|---|---|---|---|
| OUTPOST B-L-H-E | 21 | | Enemy Artillery rather more active than usual attn ta Havry Road to HERMIES and the HERMIES-HAVRINCT ROAD. Naval aeroplane went over us. Another aeroplane reported, but not sighted. | 57c M.2. |
| K15B3 Central 1/10 | | | X Two Battalions were relieved at night by the 15th Glosters. the relief being carried out without incident and completed by 4.30 am 22. The Battn went by Road to RESERVE at NEAU WOOD K12.a.3 on arrival from there S.W. of NEAU WOOD. Commanding Off. Lt. Col. L.H.C. REYNOLDS. 2nd in Command Major G. Ratcliffe. Captains 22/4f/6/4am Battn on engaged in Cuverey & Lewis Gun training Section training 22/4f/6/14 am | APPENDIX A No 5 Ouf |
| BATTN in RESERVE | 22 | | " " | |
| do | 23 | | do | Retired 22.9/5/3 am Rations 22.9/5/3am |
| do | 24 | | do | do 22.9/5/3am |
| do | 25 | | do | do in way of |
| do | 26 | | do | |
| do and OUTPOST | 27 | | Brigadier General inspects all officers and Cadres & and reports loading of the Battn. Returned strength two. X the Battn Relieved the 15th Glosters in outpost line to-night. Distressing officers carrying out formation Probably in K12b K3 as Section in form of Outpost. R.H. flank Capt. A. Rawtl of D Eng. 4 Rawre. B " Ray Rawre. Return strength 22/4f/5.30am | Ouf |
| LINE K12b Central 63.9 K12B3 9 | | OUTPOST. | | APPENDIX A No 6 Ouf |

# WAR DIARY
## or
## INTELLIGENCE SUMMARY.

*(Erase heading not required.)*

Army Form C. 2118.

| Place | Date | Hour | Summary of Events and Information | Remarks and references to Appendices |
|---|---|---|---|---|
| OUTPOST LINE H26 Central to K4.c.5.9. | 28 June | - | Be thro in line. Enemy Artillery normal - Shored amount of movement seen. Machine and M.Gun fire along our posts at intervals. Great number of flares up. Enemy seen at FONTAINE and HAVRINCOURT. Two Patrols sent out to reconnoitre roads. No enemy encountered. Branches active. Rations Strength 22 off. 64 OR | NONE |
| do | 29 | - | Enemy artillery and own arm more active than day. Branches active. Enemy T.M. active, own arms. Aeroplanes very active, own not. Machine Gun & Rifle normal. Flares profuse but not numerous. Branches active. Enemy snipers killed Post R.Q. Rations arrived normally. Strength 22 off 368 OR | Cay |
| do | 30 | - | Battalion Brigade Artillery and own are very quiet. Great amount of equipment found. T.M. and Machine Guns active. X Paragra Reliance taken out 1/5th Wingolping Regt British Division in forward D Coy fronting machine Guns (J20 c.8.6 and J20 c.5.b) (Rels 6.17pm) A and B Coys fronting machine gunsions to RR Line C Coy fronting machine Guns J22 b.9. (Rels RR Line to RDH) 340 HQ C.O.S. do (Rels RR line to RDH) 340 HQ C.O.S. Relief completed by 1.30 am 1st July Rations through as usual French Machine Guns taken over. | APPENDIX A No 7. Cay |

W.C. Reynolds
Lieut Colonel
Comdg. 1 Bn/160 Battn.

Army Form C. 2118.

# WAR DIARY
## or
## INTELLIGENCE SUMMARY.
(Erase heading not required.)

Instructions regarding War Diaries and Intelligence
Summaries are contained in F. S. Regs., Part II.
and the Staff Manual respectively. Title pages
will be prepared in manuscript.

| Place | Date | Hour | Summary of Events and Information | Remarks and references to Appendices |
|---|---|---|---|---|
| | June 1917 | | Officers who have been with Battalion during month of June. | |
| | | | Commanding Officer — — — — Lt Col. H.C. Reynolds DSO | |
| | | | Second in Command — — — — Major A.B. Lloyd Baker | |
| | | | Adjutant — — — — — Lt. P. Wright | |
| | | | Quartermaster — — — — Lt Nicol | |
| | | | Transport Officer — — — 2/Lt M. Major | |
| | | | Intelligence Officer — — — 2/Lt Leggeston | |
| | | | Signalling Officer — — — Lt Ye Learnons | |
| | | | Medical Officer — — — Capt L.C. Hughes | |
| | | | Company Comm anders {Capt O.R. Cough (A) Capt M. Rowan (B) | |
| | | | {Capt Y.B. Field (D) a/Capt O.B. Price (C) | |
| | | | Platoon Commanders 2/Lt O.C. Reeve | |
| | | | " R. Norman | |
| | | | " Brad Taylor | |
| | | | Lt ORG Knight 2/Lt N O.B. Roblin | |
| | | | Lt Glew Lieut Rannow | |
| | | | Lt 2/Lt Putman L.C. Martin | |
| | | | 2/Lt 2/Lt Mason | |
| | | | 2/Lt O.B. Roadby | |
| | | | 2/Lt Ra. Conrie 2/Lt L.R. Dodge | |

Copy

# APPENDIX A

| NUMBER | DATE | REMARKS |
|--------|------|---------|
| 1 | 7th | Orders for capture of enemy position |
| 2 | 9th | Orders for Relief. |
| 3 | 15th | Orders for Relief. |
| 4 | 19th | Orders for Relief (Inter Company.) |
| 5 | 21st | Orders for Relief |
| 6. | 27th | Orders for Relief |
| 7 | 30th | Orders for Relief. |

SECRET.          O.O./33.

## 1/ Bucks Battalion.

No. 1.

1. The Battalion will capture enemy position on Canal Bank between K.36.a.93.35. and K.26.a.95.55. on night 7/8th instant.

2. 'B' Company will carry out the attack.

3. The attack will be made with two Platoons, with one Platoon in support and one Platoon forming a left flank guard about K.36.a.6.8..

4. ZERO will be 12 midnight.

5. **Formation.**

The assaulting platoons will assemble in new trench W. and N.W. of the CAGE. At Zero they will leave their trenches and form up on a line parallel to Canal Bank in one wave, each platoon in two lines at 15 paces distance and on a frontage of 50 yards; the right-hand man of the right platoon being in line with the N.W. corner of the CAGE and 50 yards N. of it.

They will advance at Zero + 5, and as barrage lifts they will charge with the bayonet.

6. **Artillery.**

The Artillery will place a barrage on enemy position from Zero to Zero + 5, when it will lift to trenches on East bank until Zero + 40, when it will slow down.

A Box Barrage will also be placed round the area of operations. The Southern limit of this barrage on W. side of Canal will be a line drawn West from K.26.d.10.35.

7. **Trench Mortars.**

Trench Mortars will place a barrage on enemy position from Zero to Zero + 4½, when it will lift to trenches on East bank.

8. **Consolidation.**

After capture of the position -

(a) A trench 50 yards long will be dug along Canal bank facing East,

(b) A trench 30 yards long at right angles to (a) facing North, and

(c) A Communication Trench from S. end of (a) to N.E. corner of CAGE.

Care will be taken to site this post far enough North to command ground up to SLAG HEAP.

R.E. and Pioneers will assist with this work.

9. During the work of consolidation great care will be taken to protect left flank against a possible counter attack. A Bombing Post will be established to command tow-path, and a Lewis Gun to command approach from North.

10. Advanced Battalion Headquarters will be situated at present Divisional O.P., K.35.a.5.2..

11. Watches will be checked at Advanced Battn. H.Q. at 10.30 p.m..

12. If enemy interfere with work of consolidation the S.O.S. will be sent up.

13. No troops engaged in the operation will carry maps or any documents likely to afford information to the enemy.

14. The greatest care will be taken that all ranks thoroughly understand the part they have to play, especially the details for forming up for the attack.

15. Company in Battalion Reserve ('A' Coy) will take up a position in the neighbourhood of present Support Coy. H.Q., J.30.b.9.3., by 11.30 p.m.

16. Advanced Dressing Station - J.30.b.6.4..

17. White Distinguishing patches will be worn on the backs by all troops of the attacking Company and by troops holding No. 3 Post.

7-6-17.

Lieut. Colonel,
Comdg. 1/ Bucks Battalion.

Copies to:
    4 Companies.
    1 145 Inf. Bde. H.Q.
    1 240 Bde. R.F.A.
    1 145 M.G. Company.
    1 145 T.M. Battery.
    1 Battn. H.Q.
    1 War Diary.

SECRET.    No. 2    W/72.

1/ Bucks Battalion.
-------------------

1. The Battalion will be relieved by 1/5th GLOSTERS on night 9/10th instant.

2. On relief Companies will move to positions as follows -
   'A' Coy. - Dispositions as per para. 2 attached. Coy. H.Q. - J.22.b.9.9..
   'B' "    - J.20.c.9.8..
   'C' "    - J.20.c.6.7..
   'D' "    - Dispositions as per para. 1 attached. Coy. H.Q. - K.19.c.0.5.
   Hd. Qrs. - J.20.c.8.6.

3. 'D' Coy. will form a Fourth Platoon to enable the dispositions given on attached to be carried out.

4. 'A' and 'D' Coys. will each send 1 Officer and 4 N.C.Os (1 per Platoon) to reconnoitre dispositions, etc., to-night. These N.C.Os must be capable of guiding their platoons to their correct positions to-morrow night.
    Information as to whether and where cookers are required, position of Coy. Ration Dump and how water is obtained will be sent to Battn. H.Q..

5. 'B' and 'C' Coys. will each send out 1 senior N.C.O. at 3 a.m. to-morrow to take over their accommodation. An additional party may be sent after dark if wished.

6. Guides, 1 per Platoon, will meet incoming unit at a time and place to be notified to-morrow. 'B' Coy. guides will be sent out at dawn to-morrow with their rations. 'C' Coy. guides must be kept at Coy. H.Q. during daylight to-morrow.

7. 1 Limber will be at disposal of each of 'A', 'B' and 'C' Coys., and two pack ponies will report to O.C. 'D' Coy. 'C' Coy's limber will be loaded at Battn. H.Q., and 'B' Coy. Limber at STATION.

8. All petrol tins will be brought out. 'A' and 'D' Coys. will each retain 16 if required.

9. The following reliefs will probably take place on night 12/13th instant -
   'B' Coy. will relieve 'D' Coy.
   'C'  "      "      'A'  "

Captain & Adjutant,
1/ Bucks Battalion.

8-6-17.

Copies to: 4 Companies.
           Quartermaster.
           Transport Officer.
           Battn. H.Q.
           War Diary.

No. 3.

SECRET.

## 1/ BUCKS BATTALION. W.82.

O.C. COMPANIES.

1. The Battalion will relieve 1/5th Bn. GLOSTER Regt. in the line tomorrow night 15th/16th instant.

2. Dispositions:-

   C Coy. on Left.
   B  "     Right.
   A  "     ~~Support~~ — Forward Reserve
   D  "     Reserve.

3. Officers Commanding 'B' and 'C' Coys. will tonight arrange guides direct with the Officers Commanding Gloster Coys. from whom they will take over and will notify Battn. H.Q. of the place and time arranged. Detailed dispositions will also be taken over.

4. Guides for 'A' and 'D' Coys. as follows:-

   A Coy. - Station HERMIES.
   D  "     Gloster Bn. H.Q.

5. 'A' and 'D' Coys. will move off as soon as they are in possession of their rations.

6. Transport arrangements will be notified in the morning.

Captain & Adjutant,
1/ Bucks Battalion.

14.6.17.

No. 4.

SECRET              W/97.

## 1/ BUCKS BATTALION.

1. My W/95 hereby cancelled.

2. Following reliefs will take place to-night:

    'D' Coy. will relieve 'B' Coy. on the Right.
    'A'  "    "    "    'C'  "   "   "  Left.

3. On relief 'B' Coy. will move to the Forward Reserve position (E. of HERMIES), and 'C' Coy. will move into Reserve position close to Battalion Headquarters.

4. 'C' and 'D' Coys. rations and water will both be delivered at Battalion Headquarters. 'A' and 'B' Coys. rations will both be delivered at the Forward Reserve Coy's H.Q., J.30.b.84.

5. ACKNOWLEDGE.

Captain & Adjutant,
1/ Bucks Battalion.

19/6/17.

No. 5.

SECRET.                                                         W/100.

1/ Bucks Battalion.

1. The Battalion will be relieved by the 1/6th Bn. GLOSTER REGT. to-morrow night, 21st/22nd June.

2. On relief Companies will proceed to CAMP at O.6.b.9.9., moving via SLAG HEAP in J.34.d. and ration track as far as S.W. corner of VELU WOOD, where guides will meet.

3. Time and place at which guides must meet incoming unit will be notified later.

4. 1 Limber for Lewis Guns, urns, and petrol tins, etc. will be at disposal of each Company at places undernamed.

       'A' & 'C' Coys.  - Battn. H.Q.
       'B' Coy.        - Coy. H.Q.
       'D'  "          - STATION.

5. A billeting party of 2 O.R. per Company will rendezvous at Orderly Room at 4 a.m. Ø 21st instant.

6. All petrol tins will be brought out.

                                            Captain & Adjutant,
                                            1/ Bucks Battalion.

20-6-17.

SECRET.    1/ Bucks Battalion.    W/107/A.

No. 6

Reference my W/107.

1. Companies will leave Camp at the following times; 200 yards interval being maintained between platoons.

    'D' Coy. — 9.20 p.m.    'C' Coy. — 9.40 p.m.
    'A'  "  — 9.30  "    'B'  "  — 9.50  "

    Route: via SLAG HEAP in J.34.d..

2. No cookers will be taken up to the line.

3. 1 Limber will be at disposal of each Company for Lewis Guns, mess boxes, etc. Two additional limbers will carry all Companies' urns. 1 to be shared by 'A' and 'B' Coys. and 1 by 'C' and 'D' Coys.

4. Watercarts will visit the usual places in HERMIES to supply cooks with water to-night.

5. Packs will be dumped at Q.M. Stores, Companies being marched down so as to reach the Stores at following times:

    'A' Coy. — 6.0 p.m.    'B' Coy. — 6.15 p.m.
    'C'  "  — 6.30  "    'D'  "  — 6.45  "

Lieut. & Adjutant,
1/ Bucks Battalion.

27-6-17.

SECRET.   1/ Bucks Battalion.   W/115.
─────────────────

1. The Battalion will be relieved in the line to-morrow night, 30th/1st inst. by 1/5th GLOSTER REGT.

2. On relief Companies will move to positions as under:-
   'A' Coy.  -  BEAUMETZ (Coy. H.Q. about J.20.c.88)
   'D'  "    -  BEAUMETZ (Bde. Rd. Boy. H.Q. about J.20.c.58).
   'C'  "    -  Finding nucleus garrisons for R.R. line, (Posts 6 to 17 both inclusive).
                Coy. H.Q. - J.22.b.99.
   'B'  "    -  Finding nucleus garrisons for R.R. and R.D. lines (Posts R.R.1 to R.D.4).
                Coy. H.Q. - about K.19.c.05.

3. Os.C. 'B' and 'C' Coys. will to-night visit the Company Commanders, 1/5th GLOSTERS, whose posts they will take over to-morrow night, and ascertain latest dispositions, and arrange guides if necessary. 1 N.C.O. per platoon may also be taken to reconnoitre dispositions, if desired.

4. Time and place for guides to meet incoming unit will be notified later.

5. 'A' and 'D' Coys. will each send out 1 senior N.C.O. at 3 a.m. to-morrow to take over accommodation at BEAUMETZ. An additional party may be sent after dusk.

6. Rations and water to-morrow night will be delivered as follows:-
   'A' & 'D' Coys.  -  BEAUMETZ.
   'B' & 'C'  "     -  Present positions, before relief.

7. All reaping hooks and empty water tins will be brought out and sent back to Transport Lines. 'B' and 'C' Coys. will send their tins to Battn. H.Q., handing them over to R.S.M.

8. 1 Limber for Lewis Guns and articles mentioned in (7) will be at disposal of 'A' Coy. at Battn. H.Q. and 'D' Coy. at STATION.
   2 Pack ponies will be at disposal of each of 'B' and 'C' Coys.

9. Completion of move to be reported to Battn. H.Q. at BEAUMETZ in addition to the usual completion of relief report.

Lieut. & Adjutant,
1/ Bucks Battalion.

29-6-17.

## APPENDIX B

| NUMBER | DATE | REMARKS |
|---|---|---|
| 1 | 1st | Map of dispositions of Battalion front line. |

O.C.Battalions,
   145 M.G.Company,
   145 T.M.Battery.

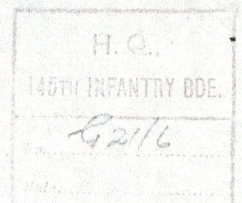

     The nucleus garrisons of the Reserve Line will be as follows:-

       P.C. - Platoon Commander.   L.G. - Lewis Gun.

1. **1 Company.**

| Post | Garrison | Note |
|---|---|---|
| R.R.1. | ½ Platoon (L.G.) | Lives in sunk road at cemetery. Finds a sentry group by night on bridge in K.31.b. New post being made and when finished garrison will live in sunk road near it. |
| R.R.2. | ½ Platoon (P.C.) | |
| R.R.3. | ½ " (P.C.) | Lives in Bank in rear. |
| R.R.4. | ½ " (L.G.) | Present post is in 2nd line of Reserve Line and a new one is being got ready. |
| R.D.1. | ½ Platoon (L.G.) | ( Will live in bank at |
| R.D.2. | ½ " (L.G.) (P.C.) | ( K.19.a.0.5. when vacated. |
| R.D.3. | ½ " | Lives in Sunk Road, DEMICOURT. |
| R.D.4. | ½ " (P.C.) | |

                    Coy. H.Q. in QUARRY K.19.c.05.

2. **1 Company.**

| Post | Garrison | Note |
|---|---|---|
| R.R.5. | Nil. | |
| R.R.6. | ½ Platoon (P.C.) | New site. Lives in bank of Quarry. |
| R.R.7. | ½ " (L.G.) | |
| R.R.8. | Nil. | |
| R.R.9. | ½ Platoon (P.C.) (L.G.) | |
| R.R.10. | ½ " | |
| R.R.11. | 1 V.G. | Lives in Bank. |
| 12. | Nil. | |
| 13. | ½ Platoon. | ) Live in Sunk Road. |
| 14. | ½ " (P.C.) | ) |
| 15. | ½ " (L.G.) | |
| 16. | ½ " (L.G.) | |
| 17. | ½ " (P.C.) | |
| 18.) | ½ " 1-V.G. | |
| 19.) | | |

                    Coy. H.Q. J.22.b.9.9.

3. Garrisons except where <u>not</u> otherwise noted will live in their posts.

                                    Captain, Brigade Major,
4.6.1917.                                 145th Infantry Brigade.

S E C R E T.

To all Recipients of
1/ Bucks Battn. O.O. No.22.
-----------------------------

      Reference 1/ Bucks Battn. O.O. No.22, para. 13.
Delete the following words -

      "any"

   "likely to afford information to the enemy"

7-6-17.

                                  Captain & Adjutant,
                                  1/ Bucks Battalion.

## 1/ Bucks Battalion.

W/74.

1. Rations and water will be delivered to 'A' and 'D' Coys. at their present Coy. H.Q. before they are relieved. Water for both Companies being sent up in tins. All empty tins will be sent back.

2. To-morrow night and in future rations will be delivered to these advanced Companies as follows -

(a) HERMIES - DEMICOURT Coy. ('D').
Rations with 16 tins water brought up on 1 limber, and dumped as follows -
For 2 Platoons holding Southern Posts - J.30.b.7.3..
For 2 Platoons holding Northern Post - J.24.b.0.9.
(200 yds S. of SUGAR FACTORY)
Two men from each post will manhandle the rations from these dumps.
Cooking water for Southern posts will be drawn from HERMIES.
Cooking water from Northern posts drawn from a watercart which will call at approx. J.18.a.7.6. at 11 p.m..

(b) DOIGNIES Coy. ('A').
Rations and 16 tins of water brought up on 1 limber and dumped as follows -
For 2 Platoons holding Southern Posts - at Coy. H.Q.
J.22.b.9.9.
For 2 Platoons holding Northern Posts - at a spot in DOIGNIES to be selected by O.C. 'A' Company.
A watercart will supply cooking water and be at Coy. H.Q. soon after dark as possible.

3. Transport Officer will arrange for all above roads to be reconnoitred beforehand if he considers this necessary.

Captain & Adjutant,
1/ Bucks Battalion.

9-6-17.

CONFIDENTIAL

# WAR DIARY

## OF

### 1st Bucks Bn of the Oxfordshire & Buckinghamshire Light Infy

From 1st July 1917 to 31st July 1917

2nd August 1917

CONFIDENTIAL  1/1 BUCKS BATTALION

Army Form C. 2118.

# WAR DIARY
or
## INTELLIGENCE SUMMARY.
(Erase heading not required.)

Instructions regarding War Diaries and Intelligence Summaries are contained in F. S. Regs., Part II. and the Staff Manual respectively. Title pages will be prepared in manuscript.

| Place | Date July | Hour | Summary of Events and Information | Remarks and references to Appendices |
|---|---|---|---|---|
| FORWARD RESERVE | 1. | | Battn moving to Forward Reserve. Strength 22 offs 693 o.R. Found artillery very active. Wounded fire and warm Vickers fire on pools improving trenches. | an 57c M.E. [J.J.] |
| do. | 2. | | Forward Conj. working on pools improving trenches. Enemy artillery active in back area. Vickers fire but calm. | [J.J.] |
| do | 3. | | do do  Officers of the 1st Royal Fusiliers 9th Brigade went up to reconnoitre the line with a view to taking over the following night. Infantry did no damage. One coy left by 12 cy.  Ration Strength 22 offs 693 o.R. | Retaine Strength do |
| do at VELU | *3. | | do Quiet during the day. Neither fire. At night the Battalion was relieved by the 1st R.F. and moved to transport lines where they remained. Ration Strength 75 offs 640 o.R. | Appendix A No. 1 [J.J.] |
| VELU and BIHUCOURT | *4. | | Battn in transport lines.  Young Bath moved to transport at about 9.10 am and marched 9.2.30 p.m. Bath moved 300x with  Lt Cunningham A.D.C.B. and transport to BIHUCOURT. (57o M.E.) When the Bath arrived at about 12.30. Some Battn had not yet to Rural Baths were being in opts and began to dig out their tents and huts which they took over that evening. Weather cold. Ration Strength | Appendix A No. 2.  [J.J.]  73 offs 639 o.R. |

# WAR DIARY or INTELLIGENCE SUMMARY

Army Form C. 2118.

| Place | Date July | Hour | Summary of Events and Information | Remarks and references to Appendices |
|---|---|---|---|---|
| BIHUCOURT and BAILLEULVAL | 5 | Battn on the march. | At 8.10 am the Commanding Officer and Adjutant attended a Conference at Bn HQ. at 5.30 pm the Battn moved out of camp. D.C.R.A Conference and Luncheon preceded by the 4/5th Oxfords. Major A.B. LLOYD BAKER in command of the Column and Captain HALL in command of the Battn. Battn marched to BAILLEULVAL via ACHIET LE GRAND – ADINFER – BIDLAINZEVELLE – AYETTE – ADINFER – RAMPART – and arrived at 11.9 pm. Also in billets tonight Appt. Weather during day fine and cool. 2 H.G. & RATIONS 2 Lt. Officers. Rations strength 73 offs. 639 or. | 51.c Appendix A No 3. OY |
| BAILLEULVAL | 6 | Battn in billets. | During the morning Officers were given to Company and in the afternoon Conferences were Coy Company training Musketry and within the Battn. Rations strength 75 offs 830 or. training | OY |
| do. | 7 | do. | Battn engaged in Company instruction. Musketry. Captain HALL attached to 1/4th Oxfords as 2nd in Command. Ration strength 76 offs. 634 or. | OY |
| do. | 8 | Sunday | Motor lorries arrived at 10 am. A number of men went over to GOMMÉCOURT WOOD and HÉBUTERNE. Weather cooler. Enemy quiet. Ration strength of 50 or. attached. 76 offs. 634 or. | OY |
| do. | 9 | do. | Battn Strength Journals. MAJOR LLOYD BAKER departs for U.K. on 7 days leave in the evening arrived at 4:50 am. BRIGADE ordered exercise. Weather fine. Battn not in the operations until 5pm to BIENVILLERS | OY |

Army Form C. 2118.

# WAR DIARY
## or
## INTELLIGENCE SUMMARY.

(Erase heading not required.)

Army Form C. 2118.

| Place | Date | Hour | Summary of Events and Information | Remarks and references to Appendices |
|---|---|---|---|---|
| BAILLEULVAL | 9. | Battn in billets | The weather during the day was variable with wet and sunny periods. Ration strength 75 offrs. 693 o.r. | (a) |
| do | 10 | do | Battalion engaged in Company training. Weather fine and warm. Battalion strength 75 offrs. 693 o.r. | (a) |
| do | 11 | do | Ration Staff attended a Staff ride. Battalion strength 75 offrs. 693 o.r. | (a) |
| do | 12 | do | Battalion engaged in field exercises from 8 am to 12 noon. Individual training carried out in the afternoon. Weather fine and warm. Ration strength 75 offrs. 684 o.r. | (a) |
| do | 13 | do | Battalion engaged in Company training in morning and in the afternoon. Weather fine and warm. Reinforcements of 106 O.R. arrived. Battalion strength 75 offrs. 884 o.r. |  |
| do | 14 | do | Battalion paraded at 1/30 am for a Route March to GOMMECOURT via BERLES au BOIS.— BIENVILLERS — FONQUEVILLERS — GOMMECOURT and back at 2.10 pm. MAJOR A.B. LLOYD BARRAX arrived & assumed command. (It. OXFORD Vice MAJOR PA.HALL arrived. MAJOR P. A. HALL appointed 2/Command. Arriving at 9.45 a.m. Ration strength 74 offrs. 845 o.r. | (a) |
| do | 15. | do | Battalion engaged in Coy training. Officers of H.Q., B.Coy, C.Coy Brigade in the evening playing 75 offrs 884 o.r. Weather fine and warm. from 8 pm. Sunday Service at 8 am. (best sharmo) Magicke fine and warm. Reinforcements of 4 O.R. arrived. 74 offrs. 883 o.r. | (a) |

**WAR DIARY**
or
**INTELLIGENCE SUMMARY.**

Army Form C. 2118.

| Place | Date July | Hour | Summary of Events and Information | Remarks and references to Appendices |
|---|---|---|---|---|
| BAILLEULVAL | 16 | | Battalion engaged in Field Firing practice in the morning and Individual Training in the afternoon. Weather fine and warm. Ration Strength 24 offrs. 931 OR. | App 5th Etc |
| do | 17 | | Battalion paraded at 10 to 50 a.m. — much turnout — to take part in Brigade Field exercise which crossed up at attack on DOUCHY LES AYETTE. The Battalion arrived back at 7pm. Weather fine which occasionally showers. Ration Strength. 24 offrs 933 OR. | App |
| do | 18 | | Battalion engaged in Company training Battalion attack in afternoon, in Coy in attack by MAJOR HALL, lectures by MAJOR HALL at night. G.O.C. divn inspected. Weather showery. Ration Strength. 24 offrs 1979 OR. | App |
| do | 19 | | Battalion engaged in individual training all day. Weather fine and warm. Ration Strength. 24 offrs 927 OR. | App |
| do | 20 | | do. Lectures by MAJOR HALL in afternoon to officers N.C.O. Weather warm with wind. Ration Strength. 24 offrs 921 OR. | App |
| do | 21 | | Battalion packing & preparing to moving to 18th Corps area do not day, wine and running. Weather fine & warm. Ration Strength. 23 offrs 750 OR. | App |

Army Form C. 2118.

# WAR DIARY
## or
## INTELLIGENCE SUMMARY.
*(Erase heading not required.)*

Instructions regarding War Diaries and Intelligence Summaries are contained in F. S. Regs, Part II. and the Staff Manual respectively. Title pages will be prepared in manuscript.

| Place | Date JULY | Hour | Summary of Events and Information | Remarks and references to Appendices |
|---|---|---|---|---|
| BAILLEULVAL and HOUTKERQUE | 22. | | Battalion and Brigade marched from BAILLEULVAL at 5 am and entrained at MONDICOURT arriving there at 8.30 am and left for GODEWAERSVELDE (HAZEBROUCK) where they arrived at 10.30 pm. Same rations and day. Wandered about, marched to HOUTKERQUE via WATOU where they arrived at 12.30am. Billets consist of huts and barns. | HAZEBROUCK 7000x (A) |
| HOUTKERQUE | 23. | | Batallion Musketry and machine Ration Strength 73 offrs 911 ort. | (A) |
| do. | 24. | | Battalion Musketry Range 23 offrs 911 ort. Battalion took part in Brigade Route March manoeuvring. Ext. the 10.30 am Brigade moved merely the 18th CORPS Commander Col. G. SILVERMINE KORSOWORD inspected the Brigade do. at Bt. HS from Ration strength 23 offr 911 ort | (A) |
| do. | 25. | | Battalion engaged in Divisional sawings Nyachin South part warm Ration strength 23 offr 908 ort. | do. Ration strength 23 offr 908 ort |
| do. | 26. | | do. | do. 23 offr 909 ort |
| do. | 27. | | do. | do. 23 offr 909 ort |
| do. | 28. | | do. do of 2 officers and 3 other ranks attached 2/Lt VAN GYAN. E.G. 2/Lt. MOY-E. R.A.T. from 4th RES. BATTN. Munchen Rin and man. Kensington. | do. 24 offr 908 ort |
| do. | 29. | | do. Sunday and nothing Ration strengths Whyache Chanmel Rapen trooped to Camp & & & | (A) |
| do. | 30. | | do. Kingsale and Mandheft hosperlung. ST. JANS TER BIETZEN (HAZEBROUCK) 10000ri 7.1 Q.3.) | (A) |

Army Form C. 2118.

# WAR DIARY
or
## INTELLIGENCE SUMMARY.
(Erase heading not required.)

Instructions regarding War Diaries and Intelligence Summaries are contained in F. S. Regs., Part II. and the Staff Manual respectively. Title pages will be prepared in manuscript.

| Place | Date JULY | Hour | Summary of Events and Information | Remarks and references to Appendices |
|---|---|---|---|---|
| HOUTKERQUE and ST JAN TER BIEZEN | 30. | | Battalion duty and standing to at ST JAN TER BIEZEN. Further line and no further shelling. Rations up 8.49 pm – 9.13 pm. | |
| ST JAN TER BIEZEN | 31 | do. | Rations and ammunition drawn at ST JAN TER BIEZEN at about 5. At noon there was news received that the attack on the ground along the XIX Corps on the Corps (XVIII) front was carried out satisfactorily and the NORTH and SOUTH. By 11 am the second line was reached and fighting was continuing. Reports were being received the Divisions during the day that the CORPS front was quite up to schedule. The trenches during the day were quite unimportant and at targets. Normal during the night. Rations up 7.24 pm - 9.05 am. | SHEET 28. C.N.w 5. v. to C.11.c.0 A.23.b C.22.c.2.6. C. |

E.R.E Reynolds
Lieut. Colonel,
Comdg 1/ Fourth Yorkshire

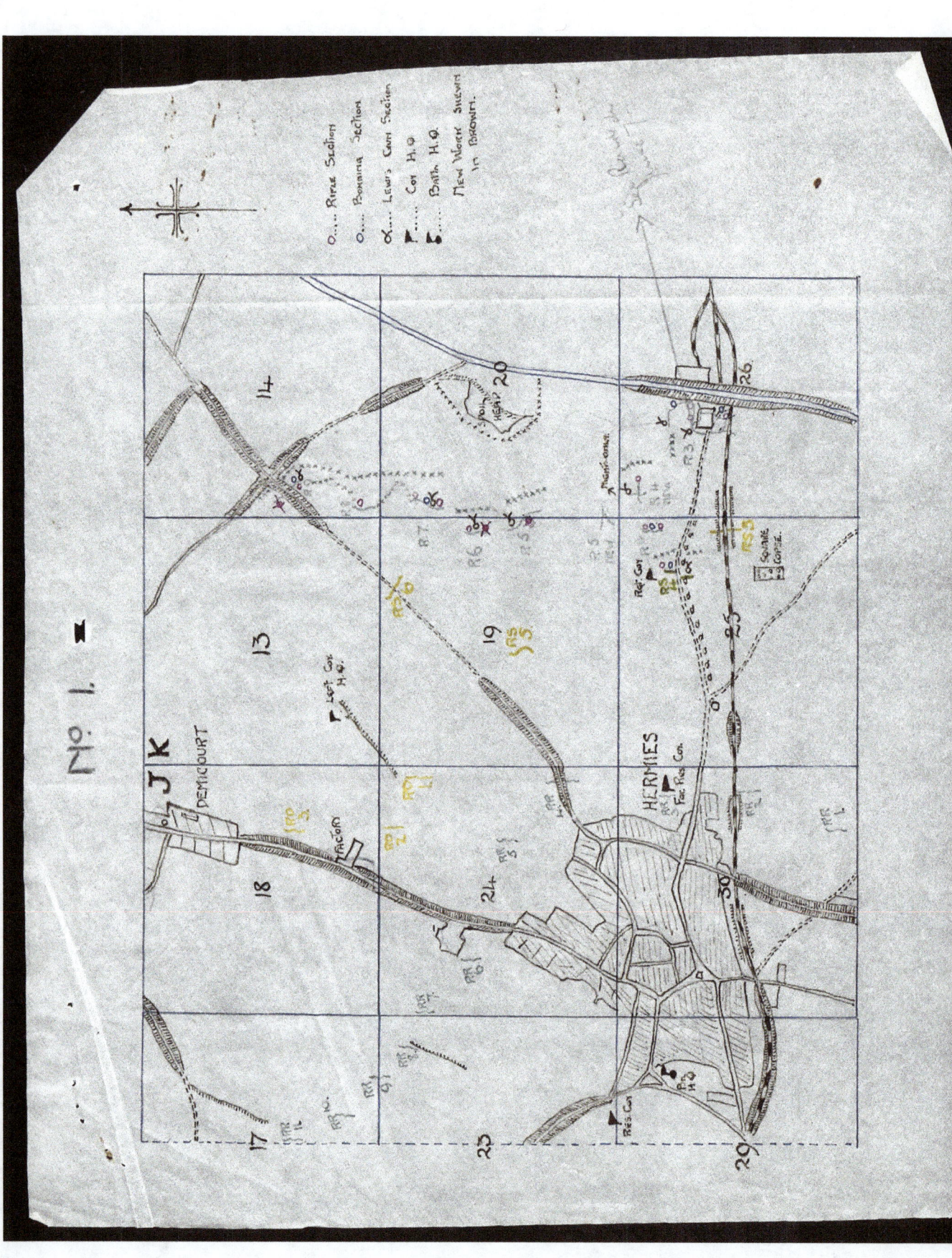

JK

CONFIDENTIAL

APPENDIX "A"
to
WAR DIARY
of

1/1st Bucks Bn. A. the Oxfordshire & Buckinghamshire L.I.

From 1st July 1917 to 31st July 1917

2° August 1917

S E C R E T.                                                        X/780.

                    1/ Bucks Battalion.
                    _____

                    W A R N I N G   O R D E R.
                    =========================

    1.   The Battalion will march to BAILLEUVAL on
July 5th.

    2.   Probable hour of start - 9 a.m.


                                        [signature]
                                        Lieut. & Adjutant,
3-7-17.                                 1/ Bucks Battalion.

## APPENDIX A

| No. | Date. | Remarks. |
|---|---|---|
| 1 | July 3. | Relief. |
| 2 | July 4th | March to BIHUCOURT. |
| 3 | do 5th | March to BAILLEULVAL |

SECRET.     1/ Bucks Battalion.                    W/121.
            ---------------------

1. The Battalion will be relieved on night 3rd/4th instant by 1/4th Bn. ROYAL FUSILIERS as follows:-

    4th R.FUSILIERS 'X' Coy. relieves 'B' Coy.
    "    "     "    'Z' "     "      'C' "
    "    "     "    'W' "     "      'A' "
    "    "     "    'Y' "     "      'D' "

2. 1 Guide per platoon from 'A' and 'D' Coys. will meet incoming unit at VELU CHATEAU Gates (opposite R.E. Dump) at 9.15 p.m. 3rd instant. Two guides from Battn. H.Q. will meet the Companies relieving 'B' and 'C' Coys. and guide them -

    Coy. relieving 'B' Coy. to STATION, HERMIES.
    "    "      'C' "      " Coy. H.Q.

where 1 guide from each post will meet them. Each of these post guides will be in possession of a chit stating for what post he is the guide.

3. On relief Companies will proceed to the Transport lines, where they will bivouac until about 2 p.m. when the Battalion will move to the BIHUCOURT Area.

4. All maps (except those already mentioned), sketches, aeroplane photographs, water tins and bivouac sheets will be handed over and receipts obtained. Duplicates of lists handed over and receipts obtained will be forwarded to Orderly Room. All Very Pistols and Guns will be retained and carried out.

5. All tents, bivouac sheets, furniture, etc. will be left in site.

6. Trenches, huts and shelters must be left perfectly clean and inspected by an officer 1 hour before probable time of relief. A certificate that this has been done will be forwarded to Orderly Room.

7. 1 Limber will be at disposal of each Company at their Coy. H.Q. for conveyance of Lewis Guns, etc. to Transport lines. 'B' Coy. limber will be at STATION, HERMIES.

8. Reports of relief complete and arrival at Transport lines to be reported to Battalion Headquarters.

9. ACKNOWLEDGE.

                                                    Lieut. & Adjutant,
                                                    1/ Bucks Battalion.

2nd July, 1917.

SECRET.                                                    W/122.

                    1/ Bucks Battalion.
                    -------------------

   1.   The Battalion will march to BIHUCOURT on
July 4th.

   2.   Route:  HAPLINCOURT - BANCOURT - BAPAUME -
BIEFVILLERS.

   3.   Starting Point  -  Road Junction O.5.d.87.

   4.   Order of March  -  A. D. C. B. Transport.
Time of passing starting point will be notified later.

   5.   200 yards interval will be maintained between
Companies, and 200 between rear Coy. and Transport.

   6.   Units will halt independently at 10 minutes before
each clock hour.

   7.   A billeting party of 1 N.C.O. per Coy. and H.Q.
will report to Captain P.A. HALL at Battalion Headquarters
at Transport Lines at 10 a.m. to-morrow.  Bicycles will
be provided.

                                          Lieut. & Adjutant,
3-7-17.                                   1/ Bucks Battalion.

SECRET.        1/ Bucks Battalion.                    W/125.

1. The Battalion will march to BAILLEULVAL to-morrow 5th instant.

2. Route: Notified later.

3. Starting point - Fork Roads G.17.d.48.

4. Order of Coys. - D. C. B. A. Transport. Leading Company will pass starting point at ~~8.5~~ 5.45 a.m. 200 yds interval between Companies.

5. Dress - Marching Order. Box Respirators will be carried slung over right shoulder. Special attention to be paid to the fitting of equipment.

6. Units will halt independently at 10 minutes before each clock hour. ~~There will be 1 long halt from 11.50 p.m. to 1 p.m.~~

7. Companies will render a certificate to Orderly Room that billets were inspected by an officer before moving off and found clean. In addition to this 1 sanitary man and 1 other man per Coy. will remain behind to clean up the whole/ Camp. An Officer to be detailed by O.C. D Coy. will supervise this and bring the party on. Party to report to the Officer at Battalion Headquarters at ~~8~~ 5.30 a.m.

8. Mess boxes and valises will be ready for loading just S. of the Officers' lines at ~~8.30~~ 5.0 p.m.

4-7-17.

Lieut. & Adjutant,
1/ Bucks Battalion.

CONFIDENTIAL

# WAR DIARY

of

1st Bucks Battalion of Oxford & Bucks L.I.

From 1st August to 31st August 1917.

ORIGINAL

Vol 30

30.S.
42 sheet

Dated 20 Sept 1917.

# WAR DIARY / INTELLIGENCE SUMMARY

**AUGUST 1917 — 1/1 Bucks Batt'n**

Army Form C. 2118.

| Place | Date 1917 August | Hour | Summary of Events and Information | Remarks and references to Appendices |
|---|---|---|---|---|
| ST JAN TER BIEZEN | 1 | | Batt'n ——— out of the line & engaged in Company training but trying to extremely wet weather made little use of it. OR were sent into front line to escort wounded & carry rations. Strength 34 ofr. 903 or. Batt'n engaged in Company training & was visited by the Bde. Gen'l. | PMZ |
| do | 2 | | do. E/Coy under 2nd/Lieut NEAVE joined up to C.III & 43rd Bde. 39th Div. in carrying out a raid. The Germans had since evacuated their outposts on a line south of the STEENBEEK. Wounded and not located. Batt'n engaged in Company training. Weather changed. | 28. M.W. |
| do | 3 | | Coy. ordered to POPERINGHE and by Corps Commander (Sir C. FERGUSSON) and motor lorries to marched to our DIVISION. Batt'n march 15½ m & ridn. ½m. | MZ |
| do | 4 | | Batt'n and transport marched to DANDRE CAMP (1 mile north of VLAMERTINGHE) via POPERINGHE leaving Col. Hartner other rng. party abt 6:30 am. Arrived at DANDRE camp abt 12:45 pm when the men signed tea. Guides reported camp & tents being pitched. from about 3:30 Billeting on | PMZ |

# WAR DIARY
## or
## INTELLIGENCE SUMMARY.
*(Erase heading not required.)*

Army Form C. 2118.

| Place | Date | Hour | Summary of Events and Information | Remarks and references to Appendices |
|---|---|---|---|---|
| | | | OFFICERS WITH BATTN. ON AUGUST 1ST 1917. | |
| | | | OFFICER COMMANDING    Lt. COL. L.G. REYNOLDS D.S.O. | |
| | | | SECOND IN COMMAND    MAJOR P.R. HALL M.C. | |
| | | | ADJUTANT    Lt. P.L. WRIGHT. M.C. | |
| | | | INTELLIGENCE OFFICER    2/Lt G.A. JOHNSTON. | |
| | | | QUARTERMASTER    Lt. E. MICHOL | |
| | | | TRANSPORT OFFICER    2/Lt W. MAGGS | |
| | | | SIGNALLING    2/Lt J.E. PIRNINGER | |
| | | | COMPANY COMMANDERS (A.) Lt. KNIGHT. G.R.F. | |
| | | | (B.) CAPT. M. BOWEN. M.C. | |
| | | | (C.) CAPT. NEAVE. G.V. | |
| | | | (D.) CAPT. J.B. HALES | |
| | | | Lt. H.J. PULLMAN    Lt. B.L. TROUTBECK | |
| | | | 2/Lt F.D. OLLARD    2/Lt H.C.B. MASON    2/Lt A.R. DARBY | |
| | | | 2/Lt F.G. VAUGHAN    2/Lt R.E. MORMAN    2/Lt E.H. FAWCITT | |
| | | | 2/Lt C.A. REEVES    2/Lt F.M. PASSMORE    2/Lt P.G. MARSHALL | |
| | | | 2/Lt W.D.Q. RODEN    2/Lt T.D. DIPPLE | |
| | | | 2/Lt M.T. MOYLE | |
| | | | CAPTAIN L.E. HUGHES R.A.M.C. | |
| | | | CAPTAIN M. NOTT (CHAPLAIN) | |

Army Form C. 2118.

# WAR DIARY
## or
## INTELLIGENCE SUMMARY.
(Erase heading not required.)

Instructions regarding War Diaries and Intelligence Summaries are contained in F.S. Regs., Part II. and the Staff Manual respectively. Title pages will be prepared in manuscript.

| Place | Date 1917 AUG | Hour | Summary of Events and Information | Remarks and references to Appendices |
|---|---|---|---|---|
| DAMBRE CAMP [B27d] | 4 | | BATTN IN CAMP. Weather rather unsettled, cold. Ration strength 76 offrs 918 OR. | M.L. |
| do | 5 | | Particulars relieving 1/1 HERTS Regt 17 CHESHIRE Bn of 9th DIVISION in the line during the afternoon taking over the following disposns | 20 men to ST JULIEN 12 cods |
| | | | IN RESERVE | |
| | | | Bn HQ. C.22.b. 70 HS. | |
| | | | A Coy HQ. C.22.b. 55 55. | |
| | | | B " HQ. C.22.d. 9. | |
| | | | C " NO. 1 Camp – BANK "CALIFORNIA SUPPORT" | |
| | | | D " NO. 3 CHEDDAR VILLA C.17c. with 2 platoons 1 platoon CALIFORNIA DRIVE REDOUBT C.17.a. 8.5. | |
| | | | 1 plat in FARM THAYER CASUALTY 2/Lt DIOPRE WOUNDED | |
| | | | Relief completed 9/15pm. O.R. | |
| do | 6 | | IN THE LINE Enemy Artillery very lively during the night & our ENEMY artillery shelling our [...] line and [back] areas intermittently during the day. Our snipers took a toll of 5 Germans. Wilhelm shelly the [...] and under CASUALTIES 1 [...] our guns. | M.L. |
| | | | [...] communication trench [...] | |
| do | 7 | | do IN THE LINE Artillery [...] [...] firing at [...] [...] [...] HOSTILE [...] at night. Enemy shelling [...] LANGEMARCK LINE in the Army of the Ypres [...] S.O.S. [...] 9 [...] [...] [...] [...] | M.L. |
| | | | Enemy fire [...] [...] CASUALTIES [...] 2 or [...] [...] out [...] and 7 OR [...] trenches but [...] by Enemy [...] [...] | |
| | | | 11/pm the Battn [...] taken by 1/1 HERTS Regt [...] [...] 1 platoon to Pan H.Q. VAN HEULE FARM 1 pl at [...] C.11A 95 40 [...] 1 platoon C.11A 85 55 | M.L. |

# WAR DIARY
## or
## INTELLIGENCE SUMMARY.

Army Form C. 2118.

| Place | Date 1917 AUG | Hour | Summary of Events and Information | Remarks and references to Appendices |
|---|---|---|---|---|
| IN THE LINE ST JULIEN W hm w/ STEENBEEK | 7. | | IN THE LINE. B. Coy. HQ C.17 th. O.8. 16.3d. 17.50. 1/1.60. 10 men (sigs & R.) at C.12.c. 35.32. Patrols 1 NCO 10 min out at 2.6. to Lt [Jackson's] Guards St JULIEN bridge on W.bank. Remainder of Coy in dugouts out... at C.13. 15. 90. D. Coy. HQ. and 1 [section] CARDER VILLA 2 platoons CALIFORNIA DRIVE. 3 [section] HALFENHAVEN REDOUBT SITE 08. C. Coy. HQ. C.17 & V.S. 2 platoons SERIOUS TRENCH 2 platoons CAMBERI TRENCH | Ref. Map Sheet 28 N.W. 1/10000 7/1/20000 |
| do | 8 | | RATION strength 22 off 808 or. During the day our artillery carried on almost incessant firing any [?] Hostile artillery again active on forward [areas] and roads were [?] During the day the ENEMY shewn f.o. [?] own from line with rifle [?] and M.g. ammunition our front line observation Alt. 8 [?] R WARWICKS ...Anning the [night] [?] ........ 8 [?] R. WILTS [?] up... [?] Coys. B. [?] down spring STEENBEEK at [?] PT. at C.12.c. 15. 50 and L.9. & at C.12.c.10.75. Y.S. D'I. Cock's were carried out during day and [?] were conducted to and from 7 am till 9 pm at DAMBRE Battalion [?] to carry RATION STRENGTH 23 off 855 or CASUALTIES. 3 or RATION for missing 53 or wounded duty... very net. | PR |
| DAMBRE CAMP. (B.27.d.) | 9 | | IN CAMP Ration strength. 23 off. 855 or. Men were awakes [?] | PR |
| do | 10. | | do Battalion [?] Carried out [?] Patrols officers and NCOs [?] [?] Lectures were given during the morning [?] other [?] own [?] to [?] holding [?] afternoon [?] on to group Commander manoeuvre [?] were carried out in [?] Ration strength. 23 off. 803 or. | PR |

# WAR DIARY or INTELLIGENCE SUMMARY

Army Form C. 2118.

| Place | Date 1917 AUG | Hour | Summary of Events and Information | Remarks and references to Appendices |
|---|---|---|---|---|
| DAMBRE CAMP (B 27 d) | 11 | IN CAMP | During the day the Battalion carried out a practice attack in conjunction with the coming operations. Weather rather cloudy with heavy showers. | 14h |
| do | 12 | do | SUNDAY. Church Parade. Service by the CRA in the afternoon. During the afternoon OFFICERS and selected SERGTS. attended a lecture re examination of captured areas, for becoming familiar with an E.A. and better use of the E.A. Brought down by KITE BALLOONS. Tuf. Grafn. was brought down by the Huns at night. Off we no 16. OR wind was the line to renovere apparently positions in conjunction with the forthcoming operations. Returning at 3 a.m. Weather fine. Artillerie Barrage 22½ hr. 20h 30. | 14h |
| do | 13 | do | Rations sent out in batteries carts in buckwagons. Ration strength 22 offrs 20h 30. | 7hr |
| do | 14 | do | Repeated practice attack w/ previous day during morning. Ration strength 22 offrs 805 OR. | 7hr Ref Map Sheet 28 1/20000 |
| do | 15 | do | Batt marched by coys at 200 yards intervals to CANAL BANK, interviews H11.W.3.X. leaving DAMBRE CAMP at 11 A.M. Dinners & Teas eaten there. Men made to rest the whole afternoon. Started moving from CANAL BANK at by Platoons at 11 p.m. Route up to Jumping up position - CORDUROY track past HAMMOND'S CORNER - JULIET FARM. | X APPDX A |

Army Form C. 2118.

# WAR DIARY
## or
## INTELLIGENCE SUMMARY.
*(Erase heading not required.)*

Instructions regarding War Diaries and Intelligence Summaries are contained in F. S. Regs., Part II. and the Staff Manual respectively. Title pages will be prepared in manuscript.

| Place | Date | Hour | Summary of Events and Information | Remarks and references to Appendices |
|---|---|---|---|---|
| | AUGUST 1917 | 16th | Considerable delay at HAMMONDS CORNER, owing to Lewis gun limbers not arriving in time, they having been blocked on the road. Zero hr 4:45 am, 16th inst. Network ration strength 22 Offrs 505 OR.  A. B. & D. coys formed up [HQ Infantry] trench by Zero. Only 1 casualty. C coy late owing to above mentioned Lewis Gun limbers, & heavy enemy shelling which they encountered on way up. Dispositions. The Battalion in four lanes - each company on a two platoon front. A coy on left & B coy on right forming 1st two lanes & D " " " " " " 2nd two lanes. C " " " " " " Battn HQ at C.12.c.0.3 - 1/5th GLOSTER REGT on right. 1/4th OX & BUCKS LI on left. 1/4th R. BERKS Regt in support. | Ref Map Sheet 28NW (ST JULIEN) |

# WAR DIARY or INTELLIGENCE SUMMARY

Army Form C. 2118.

(Erase heading not required.)

| Place | Date | Hour | Summary of Events and Information | Remarks and references to Appendices |
|---|---|---|---|---|
| | August 1917 | 16th | Objectives. 1st wave - ANZAC HILLOCK FARM & line of gunpits to its right. | Ref map Sheet 28 NW VIMY (ST JULIEN) |
| | | | 2nd wave - *Green line (SPOT FARM - SPRINGFIELD - LANGEMARCK RD) | *See map & Appendix B |
| | | | 3rd wave - *Red line - | |
| | | | 4 wave - *Blue line - Right coy - STROPPE FARM | |
| | | | Left " - GENOA & HÜBNER FARM | *Appendix A |
| | | | For detailed objectives see OO 25 - Paras 8, 9, 10, 11, 12. | |
| | | | Artillery. See OO 26 | |
| | | | Narrative. Soon after leading company (A) reached its forming up position N of the STEENBEEK, enemy commenced to shell ground about 150 yds behind. To keep all companies clear of this, the leading companies were sent forward close to the stream. Two leading companies (A & B) crossed stream at Zero - 7. 1 platoon C coy arrived about this time |

| Place | Date | Hour | Summary of Events and Information | Remarks and references to Appendices |
|---|---|---|---|---|
| | August 1917 16th | | Narrative (cont) Remaining 3 Platoons did not arrive until Zero + 20 & losing direction to the left, were, as far as this Battn was concerned, no further assistance in the attack. The right of the leading Coy was lost a few mins from own barrage, but others pushed on before they could reach the ridge E of the STEENBEEK and they came under very heavy machine gun fire while topping the ridge. The fire was very rapidly reinforced by considerable rifle fire from trenches to the sides & front of numerous concrete blockhouses out of which the M.G.'s were firing - The leading wave of the right company was almost entirely annihilated by this fire. The second wave closed up & engaged the enemy with fire, while | Ref Map Sheet 28 NW (1/10000) ALSO Map Appx 3 |

| Place | Date | Hour | Summary of Events and Information | Remarks and references to Appendices |
|---|---|---|---|---|
| | August 1917 | 16th (cont) | Narrative (cont) Parties worked round the flanks. But the enemy kept up a very strong resistance & until the 3rd Wave joined in & closed on them with a rush they showed no signs of giving in. After this charge, there was about 50 or so of the enemy is a around our men to hand fighting before the enemy's in & around our men put up their hands. This was at about 6 a.m. After this the other garrison soon followed suit. The left leading company met with less resistance at first, but after going about 150 yds E of the STEEN BEEK they came under a very heavy cross fire from Machine Guns at a distance & the front wave received the gun fire there until about 16 min. The second wave closed up but the left platoon was absolutely stopped by gun from the left. Gun fire to a trench immediately NE of it, & also from MAISON DU HIBOU & TRIANGLE FARM. The right half of the | Ref map Sheet 28NW 1/10,000 Also Map 1 APPX B |

Army Form C. 2118.

# WAR DIARY
## or
## INTELLIGENCE SUMMARY.
*(Erase heading not required.)*

Instructions regarding War Diaries and Intelligence Summaries are contained in F. S. Regs., Part II. and the Staff Manual respectively. Title pages will be prepared in manuscript.

| Place | Date | Hour | Summary of Events and Information | Remarks and references to Appendices |
|---|---|---|---|---|
| | August 1917 | | | |
| | 16th (cont) | Narrative (cont) | Second team went right through, passing SE of HILLOCK FARM, apparently taking with them the remains of the right platoon of the 1st team, altogether about 25 strong, & reached SPRINGFIELD & road to left of it about 6.45 a.m. Several of these have seen to fall on route especially by fire of gun pit about GERMAN C12a87. Six of our men were seen at SPRINGFIELD about 9 a.m. & four seen not above by Germans about 9.30 a.m. At about 7 a.m. Battn HQ moved forward to Blockhouse at C12.a.51. At that time, situation was as follows. (a) CAPT PULLMAN, REEVES, 2/2T RUDGE, with about 25 men & 2 LGs holding line from C12c96 — 78. (b) Abt 15 men & 1 Lewis Gun C12c65 — 58. (c) Abt 20 men astride road in neighbourhood of HILLOCK FARM | Ref Map Sheet 28 NW Vimy Map 1 Appx D |

# WAR DIARY or INTELLIGENCE SUMMARY

Army Form C. 2118.

| Place | Date | Hour | Summary of Events and Information | Remarks and references to Appendices |
|---|---|---|---|---|
| | | | Narrative (cont) (A) 1 offr & 6 O.R. at GUNPIT C.12.a.3.4.<br>(C) 4 men under a Cpl. at C.12.a.6.2.6.5.<br>(B) About 25 men & 1 Lewis Gun reported to have got through to SPRINGFIELD.<br><br>2/Lt PASSMORE, although slightly wounded was commanding half of the line & CAPT PULLMAN original half of the line.<br><br>On the night it was impossible to get on as there was a large sheet of water in front & the ground all round was little short of a morass, also a blockhouse & gunpits the Jn side held by enemy, Machine Guns & a number of snipers. Every attempt at movement was replied to in casualties. 2/Lt JOHNSTON was wounded here in trying to get touch with the party of D coy. Several attempts were made to get word and on the 14/4? 10/R? stopped by enemy M.G. fire. | Ref Map Sheet 28 NW Also 1/10000 Trench Map 1 APX B |

Army Form C. 2118.

# WAR DIARY
## or
## INTELLIGENCE SUMMARY.
(Erase heading not required.)

Instructions regarding War Diaries and Intelligence Summaries are contained in F. S. Regs., Part II. and the Staff Manual respectively. Title pages will be prepared in manuscript.

| Place | Date | Hour | Summary of Events and Information | Remarks and references to Appendices |
|---|---|---|---|---|
| | August 1917 | | | |
| | 16th (cont) | Narrative (cont) | At this time there was no connection with the Battalions on either flank. About mid-day, considerable fire from enemy snipers, & M.G. on the left flank had become so numerous that our troops forced to withdraw from HILLOCK FARM & take up a position immediately to the South of it. The enemy proceeded to take a slight improvement in enemy fire from TRIANGLE FARM & MAISON DU HIBOU soon stopped them from the TRIANGLE – ST JULIEN Rd & the ground to either side of it. Finally, at dusk the left withdrew to a line C12 a 23 – C12 a 72 – C12 c 88. The whole consolidated their position. Enemy Counter attacks. By evening it was evident he did not hold SPRINGFIELD tonight. A patrol went there during night but not seen any. About 8 am the enemy were seen to be coming over the ridge N of SPRINGFIELD in threes & fours & dropping into a trench just SE of X rds C6d 21. This continued for some time. About 9 am, | Ref Map Sheet 28 NW 1/10,000 also Map 1 APPX 3 |

# WAR DIARY
## INTELLIGENCE SUMMARY

| Place | Date | Hour | Summary of Events and Information | Remarks and references to Appendices |
|---|---|---|---|---|
| | August 1917 16th (cont) | | Enemy counter attacks - Two or three lines of men were seen over the ridge & moved down towards TRIANGLE FARM. There was also an attempt made to reinforce the gun pit. opposite our right - By this time a Vickers Gun had been mounted on top of one of the blockhouses close to Battn HQ & two other arrived about this time & were quickly got into action in a track about C.12.a.30. All available men round Battn HQ were sent up to reinforce the line round HILLOCK FARM. 1 platoon 4" R. BEANS, was asked for & 4th Platoon into position about C.12.a.25, to protect left flank. This platoon were in position by 10 am. Our fire stopped the enemy advance about TRIANGLE FARM & after about 20 minutes many of them were seen returning over the ridge. About 7.30 p.m. the enemy attempted to mass the ramparts at about C.12.a.24 but were stopped & suffered heavily. At 9.30 p.m. he again attacked from direction of TRIANGLE FARM & reached our posts with bombs & succeeding in driving them in further | Ref. Map Sheet 28NW 1/10000 Also Map 1 App. B |

Army Form C. 2118.

# WAR DIARY
## or
## INTELLIGENCE SUMMARY.
(Erase heading not required.)

| Place | Date | Hour | Summary of Events and Information | Remarks and references to Appendices |
|---|---|---|---|---|
| | August 1917 | | | |
| | 16th | | **Enemy Barrage:** Enemy could not be said to have put down a barrage, but a few minutes after Zero, the shells (chiefly 5.9) which had been bursting behind us appeared to shorten range & burst of on both sides of the STEENBEEK, but casualties from shell fire there not numerous. | |
| | | | **General.** Ground v. wet. Lewis Guns especially got a muddy & in some cases unworkable. Barrage had no effect on concrete blockhouses, which had not previously been knocked down by heavier. A large number of Germans were killed. Enemy belonged to 7th BAVARIAN INF REGT. | |
| | | | **Captures.** abt 80 Prisoners (wounded & unwounded) 1 Field gun 3 Machine Guns. | |

**Army Form C. 2118.**

# WAR DIARY
## or
## INTELLIGENCE SUMMARY.
*(Erase heading not required.)*

Instructions regarding War Diaries and Intelligence Summaries are contained in F. S. Regs., Part II. and the Staff Manual respectively. Title pages will be prepared in manuscript.

| Place | Date | Hour | Summary of Events and Information | Remarks and references to Appendices |
|---|---|---|---|---|
| | August 1917 | | | |
| | 16ᵗʰ | | Strength of Battⁿ (Bayonets) before going into action | |
| | | |                                     Offrs    O.R. | |
| | | |        Bn HQ  - - -  4    42 | |
| | | |        A Coy  - - -  3    148 | |
| | | |        B   "  - - -  3    130 | |
| | | |        C   "  - - -  3    142 | |
| | | |        D   "  - - -  7    152 | |
| | | | Names of Officers who went into action:- | |
| | | | Bn HQ ......... LT COL J.L.C. REYNOLDS D.S.O | |
| | | |                  CAPT. M. BOWEN (injury 2ⁿᵈ in command) | |
| | | |                  CAPT. P.L. WRIGHT (ADJUTANT) | |
| | | |                  2/LT G.A. JOHNSTON (INT. OFF) | |
| | | |                  LT    J.E. FIRMINGER (Sig. Off) | |
| | | |                  LT    F.D. OLLARD | |
| | | | A Coy ......... CAPT G.R.F. KNIGHT (c4y) | |
| | | |                  2/LT F.M. PASSMORE | |
| | | |                  "     F.G. MARSHALL | |
| | | | B Coy ......... 2/LT E.H. FAWCITT (cdy) | |
| | | |                  "     F.G. VAUGHAN | |
| | | |                  "     R.E. NORMAN | |

Army Form C. 2118.

# WAR DIARY
## or
## INTELLIGENCE SUMMARY.
(Erase heading not required.)

| Place | Date | Hour | Summary of Events and Information | Remarks and references to Appendices |
|---|---|---|---|---|
| | August 1917 | 16th | Names of officers who went into action (cont) | |

'C' Coy    CAPT G. V. NEAVE (O.C.)
         2/LT W. O'B. RIGDEN
         "   A. T. MOYLE

'D' Coy    CAPT H. J. PULLMAN (O.C.)
         2/LT C. G. REEVES.

CASUALTIES.

OFFRS :-    1 Killed.
          6 Wounded.

Names of officer casualties :-

CAPT G. V. NEAVE ...... killed
  "   G. R. F. KNIGHT ... Wounded (severe).
                         Died of wounds 17·8·17
LT. F. D. OLLARD .... Wounded (slight)
2/LT G. A. JOHNSTON ... Wounded (severe)
  "   E. A. FAWCITT .. Wounded (severe)

OTHER RANKS :-
     43 Killed
     49 Missing
    189 Wounded (slight)
     5 Wounded (so slight remained at duty)

2/LT R. E. NORMAN ... Wounded (severe)
  "   F. M. PASSMORE — Wounded (slight)
  "   F. G. MARSHALL ... Wounded (slight)
  "   A. T. MOYLE .. Wounded (slight)

# WAR DIARY
## or
## INTELLIGENCE SUMMARY.
*(Erase heading not required.)*

Army Form C. 2118.

| Place | Date | Hour | Summary of Events and Information | Remarks and references to Appendices |
|---|---|---|---|---|
| IN THE LINE (JUST NE/ST JULIEN) 4th C12498 - C12862 - C12944 | August 1917 17th | | Day passed without incident of importance. Enemy shelled ground E of STEENBEEK remarkably little, but enemy shelling N of the river has continued, especially on the ST JULIEN - CHEDDAR VILLA Rd & the old KITCHENER LINE. Enemy Machine Guns & snipers active especially from direction of TRIANGLE FARM. Relieved by 8 R. WARWICKS at night, who took over white tape lilt 6 platoons. Relief commenced about midnight & did not take long, but owing to darkness of night & continuous enemy shelling of back areas, the moved out via a lengthy and [signature] | Ref map BELGIUM Sheet 28 N.W. 1/20000 |
| | 18th | | Breakfast eaten at REIGERSBURG CAMP (N6d) on return not, when cookers had been sent. Camp P about 7 am. Remainder of day spent resting. Every one v. tired, but men wonderfully cheery. [signature] | |

Army Form C. 2118.

# WAR DIARY
or
## INTELLIGENCE SUMMARY.
(Erase heading not required.)

| Place | Date | Hour | Summary of Events and Information | Remarks and references to Appendices |
|---|---|---|---|---|
| DAMBRE CAMP B 27 d (Map - BELGIUM Sheet 28 NW 1/20000) | 19 | | Rest, resting & reorganising. Baths during morning. Church Parade for 2 1/5 GLOSTERS & ourselves at 3 pm, attended & read following letter from Divl Commander — "To GOC 145. 2nd 73rd Bde. "In view of the exigencies of the service present me from visiting "your battalions today, please tell them that I appreciate very much "the stubborn & determined fighting spirit shown by N.C.O. & "Officers & men in the Battles on 16th. Although the fortunes of "war with the form of concrete dugouts & an unexpectedly strong "preliminary position prevented us from gaining more than a "portion of the objectives we sought, the made a very valuable "improvement to our positions for future progress. "Besides the capture of 1 min. 100 prisoners, very severe loss was "inflicted on the Germans, one small group & several machine guns "have captured. It is not the mere capture of positions which "is going to bring us the final victory, but determined fighting | Brigadier General Commanding — |

# WAR DIARY or INTELLIGENCE SUMMARY

Army Form C. 2118.

| Place | Date | Hour | Summary of Events and Information | Remarks and references to Appendices |
|---|---|---|---|---|
| DAMBRE CAMP | August 1917 19/7 | | "In spite of all difficulties, like that of the Bucks Battn, which when the enemy think he is beaten I cannot hope to beat in & must give in. I know the fullest confidence in your Brigade & know that they will continue to fight with the same spirit with which they have always done in spite of difficulties." | Athmile |
| " | 20th | | 9.2 a.m. Self and Brig. Staff at Divl reinforcement Camp at HOUTKERQUE inspected Battn., together with Capt J.B. HAZES & 2/Lt P.A. COATES. Capt CROUCH rejoined Battn from hospital. Tour training. Tour we made into 2 Platoons down to strength. 7 men. Major P.A. HALL rejoined Battn from HOUTKERQUE. Ration strength 16 offs. 533 o.r. | Athmile Athmile |
| " | 21st | | Tour training — Ration strength 16 offs 542 o.r. Capt H.V. COMBS, now 23rd D.M.S. Officer rejoined Battn. | Athmile |

# WAR DIARY
## or
## INTELLIGENCE SUMMARY.

Army Form C. 2118.

| Place | Date | Hour | Summary of Events and Information | Remarks and references to Appendices |
|---|---|---|---|---|
| DAMBRE CAMP B27d 1/20,000 MAP BELGIUM SHEET 28 N.N. | August 1917 22 | | Coys training – 3 Platoon commanders sent by lorry to a place close to ST OMER to witness demonstration of method of capturing concrete M.G. emplacements. | Phone |
| | | | CAPT G.E.N. BOWYER Bn STAFF CAPT 184. Inf. Bde, visited Bn. Ration strength 16 Off's 574 OR | Phone |
| " | 23 | | Coys training – Platoon officers reported Batt'n from HOUTKERQUE 2/Lt A.P. DARBY, 2/Lt H.M. FLEEMING (not officer) Ration strength 17 Off's 529 OR | Phone |
| " | 24 | | Coys training – 19 Off's 574 OR Ration strength | Phone |
| " | 25 | | do 19 Off's 579 | |
| " | 26 | | Battn moved from DAMBRE CAMP at 2.15 pm & marched by coy at 200 yds interval to REIGERSBURG CAMP (M6d), preparatory to operations tomorrow – all 90 OR, together with MAJOR P.A. WALL & 2/Lt A.P. DARBY were sent back to Divl reinforcement camp at MOUTKERQUE Ration strength 17 Off's 516 OR | Phone |
| " | 27 | | Heavy rain during night, making ground & trenches | |

Army Form C. 2118.

# WAR DIARY
## or
## INTELLIGENCE SUMMARY.
(Erase heading not required.)

| Place | Date | Hour | Summary of Events and Information | Remarks and references to Appendices |
|---|---|---|---|---|
| | 1917 August | | most difficult. Further showers throughout morning. Zero at 1.55 pm. 144 Inf Bde attacked on left of Divl front with 2 battns on right each with 2 battns 145 Inf Bde in reserve until Zero + 5. 11th Div cooperating on left, 61st Div on right. Objectives. 143 2/1 Bde:- 1st Objective - Red dotted line × (WINNIPEG - SPRINGFIELD) Pause for 30 minutes 2nd Objective - Solid Red line × (Southern portion GHELUVELT - LANGEMARCK line) 144 Inf Bde Objective - N portion of GHELUVELT - LANGEMARCK line (including GENOA) 145 Inf Bde Objective Dotted Blue line × Line of Farms - VAN TRIPOT STROPPE - HUBNER. | × Map 2 Appx B |

# WAR DIARY or INTELLIGENCE SUMMARY

Army Form C. 2118.

| Place | Date | Hour | Summary of Events and Information | Remarks and references to Appendices |
|---|---|---|---|---|
| | 1917 August 27 | | Orders 1/4 R. BERKS & 1/4 OXFORDS to assume CANAL BANK at Zero & move to assembly positions E. of STEENBEEK & to be ready to carry out attack on 3rd objective (DOTTED BLUE LINE X) at Zero + 5 hours. 1/5 GLOSTERS & 1st BUCKS BN to leave CANAL BANK at Zero + 3 hours & move to assembly positions vacated by 1/4 R. BERKS & 1/4 OXFORDS respectively. 145 Inf Bde HQ at Zero — HILL TOP at Zero + 5 — CHEDDAR VILLA. Narrative Head of Bath marching by platoons passed CANAL BANK at Zero + 3 hours. 6.55 p.m. Trekking of back areas wonderfully slight STEENBEEK & ground between the STEEN & the | X Map 2 APPX 75 GWh |

| Place | Date | Hour | Summary of Events and Information | Remarks and references to Appendices |
|---|---|---|---|---|
| | 1917 August 27 | | Narrative (cont). With the ground in this state it was decided that further progress was not possible. Alt. [Alternative] orders were received to the effect that the OXFORDS were to take over from the advanced troops of 1/4th 2nd Batt. & that he was to move up to the positions vacated by OXFORDS. These positions were in most cases difficult to find & consisted [coming?] mostly of Themselves in front kept Dist Today S & E of road LANGEMARCK — X rds C6c8.6 — M126.6.12 6.11.7.11. | Ref map BELGIUM Sheet 28 NW ST JULIEN 1/20000 |

[signature]

# WAR DIARY
## or
## INTELLIGENCE SUMMARY

Army Form C. 2118.

| Place | Date | Hour | Summary of Events and Information | Remarks and references to Appendices |
|---|---|---|---|---|
| | 1917 August 27 | | Narrative (cont) of ST JULIEN – TRIANGLE FARM road was being heavily shelled when we arrived. Battn HQ arrived at MON DU HIBOU at 6.30 pm. Situation v. obscure. So far as could be ascertained from 1/4 OXFORD, 1/7 WORCESTERS, & 1/8 WORCESTERS (all of whom had their HQ at HIBOU) very little, if any, progress had been made. Thus being due in [?] to state of ground which was in most places up to knees in mud, & still hopes for advance. As 1/4 OXFORDS had not succeeded their assembly Trenches, there were ordered to hold on line 300 E of STEENBEEK & dig in in front an available cover. At 9.55 pm, SPRINGFIELD was reported to have been taken by 1/8 WORCESTERS. The French covered | Ref [?] ST JULIEN 1/100,000 Attd Map 2. APPDX III [?] |

Army Form C. 2118.

# WAR DIARY
## or
## INTELLIGENCE SUMMARY.
(Erase heading not required.)

| Place | Date | Hour | Summary of Events and Information | Remarks and references to Appendices |
|---|---|---|---|---|
| | August 1917 | 27 | CASUALTIES<br><br>OFFRS —<br>   KILLED   Nil<br>   WOUNDED   2<br>   MISSING   Nil<br><br>OTHER RANKS —<br>   KILLED   12<br>   WOUNDED   71<br>   MISSING   Nil<br>   Wounded (Remain at Duty)   8<br><br>Names of Officer Casualties<br>   2/Lt. P. A. COATES (wounded)<br>   2/Lt. W. H. FLEEMING (wounded) | |

Army Form C. 2118.

# WAR DIARY
## or
## INTELLIGENCE SUMMARY.
*(Erase heading not required.)*

Instructions regarding War Diaries and Intelligence Summaries are contained in F. S. Regs., Part II. and the Staff Manual respectively. Title pages will be prepared in manuscript.

| Place | Date | Hour | Summary of Events and Information | Remarks and references to Appendices |
|---|---|---|---|---|
| | August 1917 | | | |
| | 27 | | Strength of Battn. (bayonets) before going into action 27.8.17 | |
| | | | Bn. H.Q. — 6 Officers 35 other ranks | |
| | | | A Coy — 2 " 62 " | |
| | | | B " 2 " 70 " | |
| | | | C " 2 " 72 " | |
| | | | D " 2 " 83 " | |
| | | | Names of Officers who went into action 27.8.17 | |
| | | | Bn. H.Q. — Lt. Col. L.C. REYNOLDS D.S.O. (=.O.) | |
| | | | Capt. G. R. CRUDEN. Supng 2nd in Command | |
| | | | " P. L. WRIGHT. Adjutant | |
| | | | 2/Lt C. G. REEVES. Int. Off. | |
| | | | Capt. L.E. HUGHES R.A.M.C.(T) Attached (Bn.) | |
| | | | H MOKE. Chaplain (C.F.) | |
| | | | Lt J. E. FIRMINGER | |
| | | | 2/Lt P. A. COATES | |
| | | | 'A' Coy — Capt. M BOWEN | |
| | | | 2/Lt F. G. VAUGHAN | |
| | | | 'B' Coy — Capt. H.J. PULLMAN | |
| | | | 2/Lt H.O'B. RIGDEN | |
| | | | 'C' Coy — Capt. J.B. HALES | |
| | | | 2/Lt W.H. FLEEMING | |
| | | | 'D' Coy — | |

# WAR DIARY or INTELLIGENCE SUMMARY

Army Form C. 2118.

| Place | Date | Hour | Summary of Events and Information | Remarks and references to Appendices |
|---|---|---|---|---|
| IN THE LINE SUPPORT POSITIONS | August 1917 28 | | At 4.50 a.m. orders were received that Battn. was to move from BDE to 'B' of STEENBEEK & to move Battn HQ to ALBERTA. Withdrawal 2 coys to be as follows:— Bn 9 am disposition A + D coys holding line in support 1/4 OXFORDS from C16.a.5.3 to C17.a.5.4. B + C coys in dugouts & shelters between ALBERTA & STEENBEEK. Artillery throughout day was practically nil. Battn. relieved by 2 coys 2/7 LONDON Regt by 11pm. Marched back to REIGERSBURG CAMP (H6d) Ration Strength 15 off 465 o.r. | Ref Map BELGIUM Sheet 28 N.W. 1/20000 & ST JULIEN 1/10000 |
| REIGERSBURG CAMP (H6d) | 29 | | Moved by lorry to DAMBRE CAMP (B27d) between 10 am & 12 noon. Remainder of day spent resting & cleaning up. Lt Col. A.C. REYNOLDS arrived on leave. Capt G.R. CROUCH assumed temp command | Although |

# WAR DIARY
## or
## INTELLIGENCE SUMMARY.

Army Form C. 2118.

| Place | Date | Hour | Summary of Events and Information | Remarks and references to Appendices |
|---|---|---|---|---|
| ON MOVE | August 1917 30 | | at 6.30 am Batt. moved out remainder of Bde. 1/7 to DAMBRE CAMP to ROAD CAMP ST JAN TER BIEZEN according to road cct. W17 X. About 9 Q.M.S. and men took part in Divl. Reinforcements camp. Prior to operations reported batts., together with Major R.A. Hall & 2/Lt A.P. DARBY. Following reinforcements also arrived :- R4 Nos 106 D.R. Maws & Mins :- 2/Lieut. B.C. TRIGDEN R.J., Lieut. N.J.H NEWTON, 2/Lt J.A. McNISH, 1/Lt P.R. MORFEY. Major R.A. Hall assumed command on arrival. Ration strength 14 Offrs 589 | X APPX A. Arkwright |
| | 31 | | Coys. on disposal of O.C. Coys for inspection, Training etc. - Passes for POPERINGHE issued. Ration Strength 14 Offrs 541 OR | Arkwright |

R.A. Hall Major
Commdg 11 Bucks Bn.

Vol 31

War Diary

1/1 Bucks Bn, Oxf. & Bucks Lt Infty

September 1914

CONFIDENTIAL

CONFIDENTIAL    WAR DIARY 1/1 BUCKS BATTALION

**WAR DIARY** or **INTELLIGENCE SUMMARY**
Army Form C. 2118.
(Erase heading not required.)

| Place | Date 1917 SEPT | Hour | Summary of Events and Information | Remarks and references to Appendices |
|---|---|---|---|---|
| ROAD CAMP ST JAN TER BIEZEN | 1 | | Baths for 250 men during morning at HOUTKERQUE. Bath at disposal of 1/1C Bn for 2 hours collective training. Rations received 140 offrs 541 ors. | Ph knull |
| do | 2 | | Sunday – Bn parade service at 10.30 am on ground just NORTH of Camp. Before service Brig Gen 183 (D.M. HATT DSO) presented Military Medal ribbons to the following who had been on duty on the 16th August 1917. | Ph knull |
| | | | 265923 Sgt ROGERS SG [Bay] Not present Scholan<br>255853 Cpl HINES W [Transport]<br>267533 Cpl SEWARD F.G. [D coy] | Ph knull |
| | | | Ration strength 16 offrs 649 ors. | |
| | 3 | | Coy training – Preparing for coming attack – Collective 8.30 am to 1 pm<br>Individual 10 am to 1 pm<br>Individual training - Classes. Lewis Guns all specially trained + 24 untrained junior, under 2/Lt N.P. DARBY + 2 NCOs + 24 NCOs + ors. | |

Bn strength 1/17 12 Jun ceys Lt. Hutchinson 2/Lt H.F.M NEWTON 268203 Lcl JERICOLE E 267578 Pte MADOX A 268110 Pte LITTLER B.J. Pte Smith W.

Army Form C. 2118.

# WAR DIARY
## or
## INTELLIGENCE SUMMARY.
(Erase heading not required.)

| Place | Date | Hour | Summary of Events and Information | Remarks and references to Appendices |
|---|---|---|---|---|
| ROAD CAMP | 1917 Sept. | | Classes (cont) Lewis Gun Bearers class. All existing SB's & 7 men made to make up to 8 per Coy. | |
| St JAN TER BEIZEN | | | Signalling class all existing signallers + 2 sick men per Coy | Abbrieville |
| | | | Bombing 5/pltn under Sgt A.L. Fountain | |
| | | | Junior NCO's class 3 men per coy under RSM Vincent. | |
| | | | Ration Strength 16 offr 583 or | |
| " | 4 | | Training carried out as per programme (see 3rd inst) | |
| | | | Chaplin + 25 or 1 month NCO's went to seaside by lorry, starting from camp at 7 am. Returned abt 8 pm. | |
| | | | Following officers went to Special course at B XVIII Corps VALKERINGHOVE | |
| | | | Capts G.T. Crouch - J.B. Hales - H.T. Pullman - Lts. J.E. Firminger, H.J.A Newton, | |
| | | | 2/Lts F.A Vaughan, B.L. Trigden, P.A. Mortey. | |
| | | | Tho. 1 offr and 4 7 men with Baths, incl of Mo + TO. | Abbrieville |
| | | | Ration Strength 4 offr 545 or | |
| " | 5. | | Training carried out as per programme. Hostile aeroplanes dropped number of bombs between 10 pm and 11 am. No damage done. | Appdx 11 |
| | | | Ration Strength 4 offr 538 or | |

# WAR DIARY or INTELLIGENCE SUMMARY.

Army Form C. 2118.

| Place | Date 1917 | Hour | Summary of Events and Information | Remarks and references to Appendices |
|---|---|---|---|---|
| ROAD CAMP ST JAN TER BIEZEN | Sept 6 | | Training carried out as per programme Ration strength 44 off. 541 O.R. | Rep full |
| " | 7 | | 25 O.R. sent to seaside by lorry for the day. Following four officers joined the Battn. from "ESSEX":- 2nd Lieut. FISHER, G.A. BROWN,F.N., CAULFIELD, R.C.F., SMITH,C.V.S. Ration strength 48 off. 564 O.R. | Rep full |
| " | 8 | | Coys. remained in Camp for Interior Economy &c. All Lewis Gunners fired on 30 yds range under 2nd Lieut. A.P.DARBY. Nearly 200 Lewis Gunners now fully trained. Ration strength 48 off. 101 O.R. | Rep full |
| " | 9 | | Sunday. Bat. Parade service at 10.30.am. on Camp football ground. Following decoration awards were notified. Lieut. Col. L.L.C.REYNOLDS, D.S.O.  Bar to D.S.O. 2nd Lieut. G.A. JOHNSTON, Military Cross 265094 Sgt. GOLDING, T. D.C.M. H.Q. Coy 166100 " BRIDGES, E. D.C.M. D Coy 266477 L.Cpl. BUCKLAND, W. D.C.M. A " All Coys. and hutments were inspected by C.O. during the morning. The following officers joined the Battn. from 6th Bn. E. BUFFS:- 2nd Lieut SANDERS, C.H.E. 2nd Lieut CLOTHIER, C.E. STANWAY, P.A. SEAGO, G.W.E. Ration strength 16 off. 101 O.R. | Rep full |

# WAR DIARY
## INTELLIGENCE SUMMARY

Army Form C. 2118.

| Place | Date 1917 | Hour | Summary of Events and Information | Remarks and references to Appendices |
|---|---|---|---|---|
| ROAD CAMP ST JAN TER BEIZEN | Sept. 10 | | Companies training. Programme for ensuing week:- Collective Training 8.30 a.m. – 1 p.m. Monday Platoon Training Tuesday Company " Wednesday Platoon " Thursday Company " Friday Platoon " Classes. Senior N.C.Os Class 12 N.C.Os under R.S.M. VINCENT Observers Class 16 men under Capt. G.R.CROUCH Signallers " All partially trained signallers under Sgt. ORCHARD Buglers " 8 Buglers under Sgt. FOUNTAIN. Ration strength 21 Offs. 599 O.R. | Pt Hall |
| | 11 | | Companies Training in field work according to programme. Following awards of decorations were notified:- 265036 Sgt. A.J. HART. } Military Medal 265046 Sgt. G. RICHARDSON } 265292 L.Cpl. G.W. WALLINGTON } 265733 " S.G. STONE } 185074 Pt. F. MOORE } 265473 " F.T. CRIPPS } Ration Strength 20 Offs 592 O.R. | Pt Hall |
| " | 12 | | All Companies training according to programme. Ration strength 21 Offs. 600 O.R. | Pt Hall |

Army Form C. 2118.

# WAR DIARY
## or
## INTELLIGENCE SUMMARY.
(Erase heading not required.)

| Place | Date | Hour | Summary of Events and Information | Remarks and references to Appendices |
|---|---|---|---|---|
| ROAD CAMP MANTER BEIZEN | 1917 Sept 15. | | The following award of decorations were notified:- <br> Capt. H.J. PULLMAN — Military Cross <br> 2nd Lieut. C.G. REEVES — " <br><br> The following officers joined the Battn. on first Commission from 14th Battn. Artists Rifles. <br><br> 2nd Lieut. F.B. BATES — posted to C. Company <br> " " F.N.A. CORFIELD — " B " <br> " " C.B. ELLWOOD — " D " <br> " " V.C.P. COWLISHAW — " D " <br> " " W.V. STOKES — " A " <br><br> Ration strength 24 offrs. 580 or. | Pullman |

# WAR DIARY or INTELLIGENCE SUMMARY

Army Form C. 2118.

| Place | Date | Hour | Summary of Events and Information | Remarks and references to Appendices |
|---|---|---|---|---|
| ROAD CAMP ST JAN TER BIEZEN | 1917 Sept 13 | | A,B, and D Coys training in the morning. C Coy on the range. Two practices fired by whole company; grouping and mad minute. D Coy carried out the same practices in the afternoon. All Lewis Gunners armed with revolvers, also fired in the afternoon. Ration strength 31 off. 594 o.r. | Pt Hill |
| " | 14 | | All Companies training. Ration strength 31 Off. 599 o.r. | Pt Hill |
| " | 15 | | Companies continued training. All companies had baths during the day starting at 11 a.m. Advance billeting party under Capt. G.R. CROUCH left at 6.30 am for training area N.W. of St OMER. The portion of Battn Transport which was not to be entrained left at 9 a.m. This consisted of 2 G.S. Wagons, 1 Grenade limber, 1 S.A.A. limber and spare horses. In the afternoon, numbers of men from 2nd Bucks Battn visited the camp, and a football match was played in which the 1st Bn were successful by 3 goals to 2. This was the first occasion on which the two Battalions had had an opportunity of visiting each other. | Pt Hill |

Army Form C. 2118.

# WAR DIARY
## or
## INTELLIGENCE SUMMARY.
(Erase heading not required.)

Instructions regarding War Diaries and Intelligence Summaries are contained in F. S. Regs., Part II. and the Staff Manual respectively. Title pages will be prepared in manuscript.

| Place | Date 1917 | Hour | Summary of Events and Information | Remarks and references to Appendices |
|---|---|---|---|---|
| S.S. VAN TER RAVEN – LICQUES | Sept 16 | | Transport detained at AUDRUICQ at 11 p.m. Horses were watered and fed. Marched to LICQUES arriving about 6 a.m. Ration strength 24 off: 549 mn. | Part II |
| LICQUES | 17 | | All Companies rest. Billets very bad - Mud + Cow being more than 4 kms. from C. + D. Billets quite good and apparently not used as such before. Country and weather perfect. Comdg. Officer, Adjt., and O.C. Companies attend conference under Divisional Commander at GUÉMY in the afternoon. Ration strength 24 off: 549 mn. | Part II |
| " | 18 | | All Companies did field firing practice on GUÉMY range. Very good shoot, with junk good results. First Company commenced firing 10.30 a.m. Last Company finished about 4 p.m. C. Coy hit score with 427 hits. D. Coy second with 2,418 hits. Ration strength 24 off: 549 mn. | Part II |

(A7092). Wt. W12859/M1293. 750,000. 1/17. D. D. & L., Ltd. Forms/C.2118/14.

**Army Form C. 2118.**

# WAR DIARY
## or
## INTELLIGENCE SUMMARY.
(Erase heading not required.)

| Place | Date 1917 | Hour | Summary of Events and Information | Remarks and references to Appendices |
|---|---|---|---|---|
| ST. JAN TER BEZEN to LICQUES. | Sept. 16 | | Batt. & transport paraded at 6 am. and marched to ABEELE station, about eight miles. After some delay, the Batt. entrained at 10.30 am. and moved to AUDRUICQ (N.W. of ST OMER) where they detrained at 4 pm. The Batt. were met by a guide and marched to the LICQUES area arriving about 10 pm. after a 12 mile march. Packs were carried on lorries. Batt. was disposed as follows:- <br><br> Bn. HQrs. & Transport   LICQUES <br> A Company              CAHEN <br> B    "                 { CANEHY <br>                         { LE BREUIL <br> C    " <br> D    "                 HERBINGHEM. <br><br> Transport moved at 9 am. to entrain at PROVEN (about 23 miles). All trains were late, and transport was not entrained till 3.45 pm moving out about 4.10 pm. | |

Army Form C. 2118.

# WAR DIARY
## or
## INTELLIGENCE SUMMARY.
*(Erase heading not required.)*

Instructions regarding War Diaries and Intelligence Summaries are contained in F.S. Regs., Part II. and the Staff Manual respectively. Title pages will be prepared in manuscript.

| Place | Date 1917 | Hour | Summary of Events and Information | Remarks and references to Appendices |
|---|---|---|---|---|
| LICQUES | Sept 19 | | Hold Batt. onto Brigade Exercise near TOURNEHEM. Batt. returned to billets about 4.30 pm after about 9 hours work. Lieut. TROUTBECK rejoined from 3rd Army School. Strength 43 offrs. 864 ors. All Coys. did about ½ hour of training in vicinity of Billets. Strength 44 offrs. 873 ors. | Ref |
| " | 20 | | | |
| " | 21 | | Held Batt. on Divisional Exercise near TOURNEHEM. Left billets about 5.30am returning about 4 pm. Strength 75 offrs. 893 ors. | |
| " | 22 | | All Coys. did ½ hour training in the vicinity of Billets. The following officers of the WEST KENT Regt. joined the Battalion:— 2nd Lieut. L.W.G. HORNS<br>" H.C. BOCKING.<br>" L. McCRACKEN | |

Ration Strength 76 offrs. 603 ors.

(A7090). Wt. W12539/M1295. 750,000. 1/17. D. D. & L., Ltd. Forms/C-2118/4.

# WAR DIARY
## or
## INTELLIGENCE SUMMARY

Army Form C. 2118.

| Place | Date 1917 Sept. | Hour | Summary of Events and Information | Remarks and references to Appendices |
|---|---|---|---|---|
| LICQUES | 23 | | 300 O.R. had baths during the morning, the remainder of the Battn. attending Church parade. A Brigade Horse Show was held during the afternoon. Recco 1:15 sight 25 yr 6:12 m. | Pistol |
| " | 24 | | All Coys on the range near ARDINGHEM. A&B in the morning. C&D in the afternoon. They practised 5 rd. application 7 200 yds., ditto at 300 yds. and rapid practice at 300 yds. Ration sheet 9:00 5:55 pm. | Pistol |
| " | 25 | | A. B. & D. Coy. training emable Coy. Centre. C. Coy. fired field firing practice. Regimental Batto. on completion for best Coy. in the Division. Ration sheet 16:00 5:47 pm. | Pistol |
| " | 26 | | All Coys. resting preparatory to moving. Ration sheet 2:54/5 6:45 pm. | Pistol |
| " | 27ᵗʰ | | Battn. moved at 2 am. by entrained at AUDRICQUES station. Entraining complete by 7:30 a.m. Arrived & detrained BRIELEN about 12:30 p.m. Marched to CANAL BANK, per rear reserve to Bde. remainder of Bttn. into wooden frame huts dummy with - Transports travelled by |  |

Army Form C. 2118.

# WAR DIARY
## or
## INTELLIGENCE SUMMARY.

(Erase heading not required.)

Instructions regarding War Diaries and Intelligence
Summaries are contained in F. S. Regs., Part II.
and the Staff Manual respectively. Title pages
will be prepared in manuscript.

| Place | Date | Hour | Summary of Events and Information | Remarks and references to Appendices |
|---|---|---|---|---|
| CANAL BANK | SEPT 1917 28" | | Separate Train (M.T. train) at PESELHOEK STATION – Transport moved to Camp just behind RESVRSBURG, ASHIP + Q.M Stores to MARSHES FARM. Ration strength R. officer 37 o.m. Quiet day - Ration Strength 25 offs/ 545 o.m | |
| — | 29. | | Quiet day. All cars on trenches. Batln. move to ST JULIEN in evening. Ration strength 25 offr/ 517 o.m | |
| — | 30. | | Quiet day. Batlk Relieved 1/4 OXFORDS in Reserve at night (D-Tules where Behind Bn 147). Ration stg. 22 offr. 549 o.m | |

K.R.F.C Reynolds
Lt. Col
O/4/Bucks Bn

CONFIDENTIAL

WD 32

WAR DIARY
OF
1st Bucks Bn. Oxfd & Bucks L.I.

From 1st Oct to 31st Oct 1917

CONFIDENTIAL

Army Form C. 2118.

# WAR DIARY
## or
## INTELLIGENCE SUMMARY
(Erase heading not required.)

1/1 Bucks Battalion

Instructions regarding War Diaries and Intelligence Summaries are contained in F. S. Regs., Part II. and the Staff Manual respectively. Title Pages will be prepared in manuscript.

| Place | Date | Hour | Summary of Events and Information | Remarks and references to Appendices |
|---|---|---|---|---|
| LINE V25c96 to D1d47 (PEICAPPELLE YPRES See Appx B) | 30th Sept/1st Oct. | | Started leaving CANAL BANK at 6.30 pm to take over front line (left subsection of BDE front) from 1/4 OXFORDS. Relief complete approx 10-30 pm.<br><br>Disposition:- Battn HQ at MON DU HIBOU<br>Left front 'D' Coy. Coy HQ in STROOM TR. V25d16<br>2 platoons CEMETERY TR (V25c78) 7 posts from there to QUEBEC FARM.<br>2 platoons in support<br><br>Right front 'A' coy. Coy HQ at HUBNER FARM.<br>3 platoons holding line of posts from QUEBEC FM to D1d47.<br>1 support platoon abt D1c98.<br><br>Left support 'C' coy. Coy HQ at C6b84<br>2 platoons in trench C6b7535.<br>2 platoons in shell hole from D1c25 to D1c1585.<br><br>Right support 'B' coy. Coy HQ at HUBNER FARM.<br>All platoons round FM<br><br>11th Div on left. 1/4 R. Berks regt on right | Ref Map POELCAPPELLE EDN 3. 1/10000 Appx B<br><br><br><br><br><br><br><br><br><br><br><br><br><br><br><br><br><br><br><br>Appendix |

# WAR DIARY
## or
## INTELLIGENCE SUMMARY
(Erase heading not required.)

Army Form C. 2118.

| Place | Date | Hour | Summary of Events and Information | Remarks and references to Appendices |
|---|---|---|---|---|
| THE LINE V25 c 9 6 to D.1.d.4.7. | OCT 1917 1 | | D Coy withdrawn from left front at dawn & sent back to ALBERTA, owing to a bombardment by our Heavies of concrete blockhouse at C.25.d.1.9 took in place during day. Very fine. visibility good. 'C' Coy shelled intermittently throughout day. Also HUBNER F.H. From time very quiet, with good deal of sniping at rifle chiefly owing to very bright moonlight. Patrols sent out at moonset by each front coy. D Coy took up their old positions in evening & Thorne moved Casualties — 8 other ranks Killed 3. Wounded 4. Wounded slightly (at duty) 1. Ration Strength 15 off. 549 or. | Ref map PASSCHENDAELE Belgn. 3 1/10,000 Sc. APPX D. Blockhouse |
| | 2 | | Very fine. Good visibility. Enemy shelling rather heavier. Enemy Tangle 'C' Coy Front & coy HQ – also TRIANGLE – ST JULIEN Rd. Sniping active during night. Capt. M. BOWEN wiped whilst going round night cois too – wounded dangerously. & base of lung. 2 patrols sent out by each of A & D coys Capt. G.R. CREWEN reported from down. Removed to Bn HQ as 2nd in Command Sometime during night. Casualties – 1 wounded (Capt M. BOWEN) [illegible] – 3 Killed – 9 wounded O.R. Ration Strength 15 off. 542 o.r. | [illegible] [illegible] |

2449 Wt. W14957/Mg0 750,000 1/16 J.B.C. & A. Forms/C.2118/12.

# WAR DIARY or INTELLIGENCE SUMMARY

Army Form C. 2118.

| Place | Date | Hour | Summary of Events and Information | Remarks and references to Appendices |
|---|---|---|---|---|
| THE LINE V25c 9.6 to D1d 4.7 (N E of ST JULIEN) | Oct 1917 3 | | 'C' coy shelled intermittently all day. Also HUBNER FM & the TRIANGLE - ST JULIEN Rd. For four hours enemy shelled D.40 in CEMETERY + SPREE TRENCHES, some 8" 150m shell falling in this vicinity. 2 coys 1/6 R. WARWICKS to right of 1/7 WARWICKS came up in evening passing HIBOU abt 8 p.m, preparations to journey up along our front for attack in morning. Guides supplied by us. Gas discharged from projectors on our front. TRIANGLE - WELLINGTON FM. Sniping less than on previous nights, but enemy shelling increased considerably. Usual patrols sent out - Some light rain fell about 2 a.m & continued until 5 a.m. Visibility excellent for journey up. Casualties - nominal 5 O.Rs. Ration Strength 25 Offrs 566 ORs. | Appendix |

Army Form C. 2118.

# WAR DIARY
## or
## INTELLIGENCE SUMMARY

(Erase heading not required.)

Instructions regarding War Diaries and Intelligence Summaries are contained in F. S. Regs., Part II. and the Staff Manual respectively. Title Pages will be prepared in manuscript.

| Place | Date | Hour | Summary of Events and Information | Remarks and references to Appendices |
|---|---|---|---|---|
| From line to REIGERSBURG CAMP. | Oct 4 1917 | | 2 Platoons A Coy & 2 Platoons 'D' Coy left in line to act as an outpost Coy during forming up & first phase of attack. Remainder of Bn. left their positions at 6.30 am & moved direct to REIGERSBURG CAMP H6a (sheet 28 NW 1/20000). Outpost Coy left at 9 am. Casualties to then forming: killed – 4, wounded – 2. Zero for 143 Bn. & 73 Bde attack was 6 am on the night to help to help. Attack supported by an intense artillery & MG barrage. 1st objective (TWEED Mo – YORK & WINCHESTER F.ms – ALBATROSS F.M.) was captured by 8.30 am. 2nd objective except for VACHER FARM & BURNS Mo captured by 10.30 am. In country, no men as could be made out, are done now. TERRIER F.M. – COUNTY X rds. – V26d70 – D3a03 – KRONPRINZ F.M. (east). 3 Officers & 320 or passed thro' Divl Cage. These were of 369 IR, 370 IR, 371 IR, 2 ant. Takhyrer & numerous light MG captured. Ration Strength 15 off 652 OR. | Ref Map WIEGENHOEK Edn 3. |

**Army Form C. 2118.**

# WAR DIARY
## or
## INTELLIGENCE SUMMARY

*(Erase heading not required.)*

Instructions regarding War Diaries and Intelligence Summaries are contained in F. S. Regs., Part II. and the Staff Manual respectively. Title Pages will be prepared in manuscript.

| Place | Date | Hour | Summary of Events and Information | Remarks and references to Appendices |
|---|---|---|---|---|
| RETURNBURY CAMP to CANAL BANK | Oct 1917 5. | | Batt'n moved at 9.30 a.m. to encampments in CANAL BANK arriving at 9.45 a.m. Received band instruments. Rained off and on all day. Ground very wet. Ration strength 20 off 529 o.r. | |
| | 6. | | Quiet day. Rain pretty continuous – hardening parts of 1 off. 5.0 ors in afternoon at ST JULIEN. Ration strength 20 off 522 or. | |
| CANAL BANK | 7. | | Batt'n moved by car to DAMBRE CAMP, leaving CANAL BANK at 9 a.m. Very cold & frequent heavy showers. Received notice at 1.30 pm to be ready to go up to line, starting at 3 pm. This was confirmed abt 3.30 pm. Eventually left in busses at 5.30 pm to take over front line from 6th & 7th R. WARWICKS. Busses ran as down to WIELTJE | |

| Place | Date | Hour | Summary of Events and Information | Remarks and references to Appendices |
|---|---|---|---|---|
| THE LINE V 28 & 63 | Oct 1917 | | Whole new platoons at ARTILLERY HO (Northernmost house in ST JULIEN). Relief which was complicated by extreme darkness of night & the very bad ground, completed by abt 1.30 A.M.<br>Dispositions:- Bn HQ at HÜBNER FM<br>C Coy (left front line) - TERRIER FM - COUNTY X rds (well (M1 V 2.6))<br>- CEMETERY (part in wd cut)<br>B Coy. (Right front line) from CEMETERY to D 2 b 4.5<br>D Coy. (left support coy) in front of TWEED HO<br>A Coy (Rt support coy) just behind YORK FM.<br><br>11th Div on left. 1/6 R. BERKS on right.<br>Ration dump 20 yds S of D.o.R. | Ref map<br>TURCO FARMS<br>1/10,000<br><br>Whorwill |
| D2 b 4.5 | 7 | | | |

# Army Form C. 2118.

## WAR DIARY
or
## INTELLIGENCE SUMMARY
*(Erase heading not required.)*

| Place | Date | Hour | Summary of Events and Information | Remarks and references to Appendices |
|---|---|---|---|---|
| The ZING V26a 63 to D2 b 45. | Oct 1917 | 8 | Family quiet day. V met Received orders at 4 p.m. that We should be relieved during evening by 1/4 Gloster's Ref 11 H.Q. on left & 1/6 Gloster's on right, who were to attack BELLEVUE Y/pres in morning. The relief returned by 11 p.m. Great difficulty experienced in getting 4" guns (on left) to their forming up positions owing to extreme darkness, & scarcity of guides. However they were eventually got to landmarks on tracks. They did eventually get there by about 3·30 a.m. Left an outpost coy consisting of 2 platoons B coy & 2 platoons C coy in the true north orders to withdraw at Zero. Owing to left platoon not receiving their orders as to withdrawal they did not get away until dawn | |

Army Form C. 2118.

# WAR DIARY
## or
## INTELLIGENCE SUMMARY

(Erase heading not required.)

Instructions regarding War Diaries and Intelligence Summaries are contained in F. S. Regs., Part II. and the Staff Manual respectively. Title Pages will be prepared in manuscript.

| Place | Date | Hour | Summary of Events and Information | Remarks and references to Appendices |
|---|---|---|---|---|
| Div¹ Reserve | Oct 1917 8 | | Hours after Zero. On actual Batt⁵ (item outfront conforms agreed data) concentrated in civilisation + Kultur forms and a few Batt⁵ moved Dispositions. Bn H.Q. at CHEDDAR VILLA AT Belwong Rd MOUSETRAP FM. C Coy GOLF RESERVE D ALBERTA. Reward went on kept continuous during night. Ration strength 738 officers 540 OR. | Ref Map BELGIUM Sheet 28NW 1/20000 |
| | 9 | | Zero 1m 144 2nd/ Batt⁵ who attacked in Coperation with Division on right + left, at 5:20 p.m. Fine during attack, but recent rain had made ground unfit for rapid progress much in consequence. | |

Army Form C. 2118.

# WAR DIARY
## or
## INTELLIGENCE SUMMARY
(Erase heading not required.)

| Place | Date 1917 | Hour | Summary of Events and Information | Remarks and references to Appendices |
|---|---|---|---|---|
| | Oct. | | VATCHER & BURNS HOUSES CAPTURED. OXFORD HOUSES taken but counter attack drove us in 4/4/5FDRs. 1/4 R. BERKS went up to STRINGFIELD abt 10am - Ration Strength 23 offrs 544 OR. | Ref map Poelcapelle 1/20,000 Appx III |
| Div'l Reserve | 10 | | Stood to from 4am to 6.30am. Movement of enemy importance took place - Kitchen up 6/2pm - Carried in wounded from NIEUWE to DAMBRE CAMP. (B27c) arriving abt 11pm Division relieved by 9th Division in line. Ration Strength 22 offrs 546 OR. | Ref map Beacon Sh 17 & 28 NW 1/20,000 Appx III Appx III |
| DAMBRE CAMP. (B27c) | 11. | | All coy resting. Ration Strength 530 OR 25 offs. | |
| | 12 - | | Road from DAMBRE to ST JEAN TER BIELEN station at 5.20pm - Pouring rain throughout the march. Batt'n reached ROAD CAMP at 8.30pm - Ration Strength 25 offrs 530 OR | Appx III |

# WAR DIARY or INTELLIGENCE SUMMARY

Army Form C. 2118.

| Place | Date 1917 | Hour | Summary of Events and Information | Remarks and references to Appendices |
|---|---|---|---|---|
| ROAD CAMP ST JAN TER BEIZEN | Oct 13 | | All Companies resting. Rain fell continuously throughout the day. The following officers joined the Battn.:— 2nd Lieuts. GRACE, R.W., BUTLER, W.G., CORNISH, O.H. Ration Strength 28 offrs. 855 ors. | Rat full |
| " | 14 | | All Companies resting. Capt. H.E.N.C. WOOLERTON rejoined Battn. from England taking over command of B. Company. The Battn. marched out of Camp at 10.50 p.m. to march to HOPOUTRE for entraining. Ration Strength 29 offrs. 846 ors. | Rat full |
| MAISNIL-BUCHE | 15 | | Battn. entrained at LIGNY ST FLOCHEL about 10 p.m. Breakfasts were eaten, and Battn. marched off at 1.10 p.m. arriving in billets at MAISNIL-BUCHE at 6.15 p.m. Very comfortable billets Battn. came under orders of II Corps. Ration Str. 29 offrs. 844 ors. | Ref LENS 1/100,000 Rat full |
| " | 16 | | Coys. resting in the morning. Brigade Parade near CAMBLIGNEUL in the afternoon for presentation of medal ribbon by G.O.C. 145 Brigade. Ration Str. 32 offrs. 829 ors. | Rat full |
| " | 17 | | Coys. training in the morning. Reinforcement from Mechanical Transport training separately. Reinforcement route marched in afternoon 2.30–4.30. All officers attended lecture by B.O.C. 145 Brigade at CAMBLIGNEUL in the evening. Following officers temporarily attached to 1/5 GLOUCESTERSHIRE REGT. 2nd Lieuts. C.H.G. SANDERS, G.W.E. EAGO, and P.A. MORFEY. | Rat full |

Army Form C. 2118.

# WAR DIARY
or
## INTELLIGENCE SUMMARY
*(Erase heading not required.)*

Instructions regarding War Diaries and Intelligence Summaries are contained in F. S. Regs., Part II. and the Staff Manual respectively. Title Pages will be prepared in manuscript.

| Place | Date 1917 | Hour | Summary of Events and Information | Remarks and references to Appendices |
|---|---|---|---|---|
| VILLERS-AU-BOIS. | Oct. 18 | | All Coys. training in the morning. Bn. marched to billets at VILLERS-AU-BOIS in the afternoon, about 2½ miles. Billeted in Adrian and Nissen Huts. | Posted |
| " | 19 | | 2nd Lieut. E.T.C. COXON, (WEST KENT REGT.) joined the Battn. for duty. Ration Strength 29 off. 816 OR. All Coys. training in the morning. Reinforcement route marched in the afternoon. Ration Strength 31 off. 822 OR. | Posted |
| " | 20 | | All Coys. training in the morning. Revolver practice for Lewis Gunners in the afternoon. Ration Strength 30 off. 875 OR. | Posted |
| " | 21 | | 300 O.R. had baths during the morning. All reinforcements had a grouping practice during the morning. All officers had practice in firing revolvers and Lewis guns in the afternoon. Ration Strength 30 off. 875 OR. | Posted |
| " | 22 | | Heavy rain fell at beginning of the morning. All Coys. training. Half the reinforcement fired on the range. Ration Strength 31 off. 870 OR. | Posted |
| " | 23 | | All Coys. training. All reinforcement fired on the range. Ration Strength 32 off. 873 OR. | Posted |

**Army Form C. 2118.**

# WAR DIARY
## or
## INTELLIGENCE SUMMARY

*(Erase heading not required.)*

| Place | Date 1917 | Hour | Summary of Events and Information | Remarks and references to Appendices |
|---|---|---|---|---|
| VILLERS-AU-BOIS | Oct. 24 | | Coy. training according to programme. Two Companies reinforcements fired on the range. The following officers joined the Battn. for duty:- 2nd Lieuts. WILCOX, F.J., HERBERT, P.T., SHERWIN, G. The following were awarded the Military Medal:- No. 285063 Pte. SMITH, S.       C. Coy. " 265-637 " CATTELL, W.    H.Q. " 265-119 L.Cpl. HOLLYOAKE, A.G.  C. Coy. B. Coy. moved at 7 p.m. to LE PENDU CAMP (W.d. 30.8.0) to occupy it and carry out improvements to the Camp. | Rainfall |
| " | 25 | | Coy. training according to programme. Rain gauge 35°/100 814 OR | Rf. Gauge 36 B.S.E. 1/20,000 |
| " | 26 | | | |
| " | 27 | | 160 O.R. went on night-working party burying cable near VIMY. Rain gauge 35°/100 809 OR | NFell |

# WAR DIARY
or
INTELLIGENCE SUMMARY

Army Form C. 2118.

| Place | Date | Hour | Summary of Events and Information | Remarks and references to Appendices |
|---|---|---|---|---|
| VILLERS-AU-BOIS | 1917 Oct. 28 | | Brigade Parade in the morning for presentation of medal ribbons by G.O.C. 145th Inf. Brigade. This was followed by Church Parade on Bn. Parade ground. 150 O.R. went on night working party burying cable near VIMY. Ration strength 34 Offrs 816 O.R. | |
| " | 29 | | All Companies training. All Lewis Gunners fired on the range. Ration etc 34 Offrs 821 O.R. | |
| " | 30 | | All Reinforcement fired on the range. Companies continued training. CAPT. V.B. HALES rejoined from 145 Inf. Bde. Hqrs. and assumed command of D. Coy. 2nd Lieut. CORFIELD and FISHER rejoined from XIIIth Corps. School. Ration etc. 34 Offrs 832 O.R. | |
| " | 31 | | Reinforcement continued training. Numerous small working parties found by Coy. Ration etc 33 Offrs 806 O.R. | |

V.H.E. Reynolds
Lt. Col.
comg 1/Bucks Bn.

CONFIDENTIAL

Appendix "B"
to
War Diary
of
1st Bucks Bn. Oxf & Bucks L.I.

From 1st Oct. to 31st Oct. 1919

APPENDIX - A and B    Nil.

www.ingramcontent.com/pod-product-compliance
Lightning Source LLC
Chambersburg PA
CBHW080858230426
43663CB00013B/2571